How Americans Make Race

How do people produce and reproduce identities? In *How Americans Make Race*, Clarissa Rile Hayward challenges what is sometimes called the "narrative identity thesis": the idea that people produce and reproduce identities as stories. Identities have greater staying power than one would expect them to have if they were purely and simply narrative constructions, she argues, because people institutionalize identity stories, building them into laws, rules, and other institutions that give social actors incentives to perform their identities well, and because they objectify identity stories, building them into material forms that actors experience with their bodies. Drawing on in-depth historical analyses of the development of racialized identities and spaces in the twentieth-century United States, and also on life narratives collected from people who live in racialized urban and suburban spaces, Hayward shows how the institutionalization and objectification of racial identity stories enable their practical reproduction, lending them resilience in the face of challenge and critique.

Clarissa Rile Hayward teaches political theory at Washington University in St. Louis. The author of *De-Facing Power* (Cambridge, 2000) and of many articles in journals and edited volumes, she writes broadly on the themes of power and identity in the contemporary United States.

How Americans Make Race

Stories, Institutions, Spaces

CLARISSA RILE HAYWARD
Washington University, St. Louis

CAMBRIDGE
UNIVERSITY PRESS

CAMBRIDGE
UNIVERSITY PRESS

32 Avenue of the Americas, New York NY 10013-2473, USA

Cambridge University Press is part of the University of Cambridge.

It furthers the University's mission by disseminating knowledge in the pursuit of
education, learning and research at the highest international levels of excellence.

www.cambridge.org
Information on this title: www.cambridge.org/9781107619586

© Clarissa Rile Hayward 2013

First published 2013

A catalogue record for this publication is available from the British Library

Library of Congress Cataloguing in Publication data
Hayward, Clarissa Rile.
How Americans make race : stories, institutions, spaces / Clarissa Rile Hayward,
Washington University, St. Louis.
pages   cm
Includes bibliographical references and index.
ISBN 978-1-107-04389-3 (hardback) – ISBN 978-1-107-61958-6 (pbk.)
1. United States – Race relations – History.   2. Blacks – Race identity –
United States – History.   3. Whites – Race identity – United States – History.
4. Race awareness – United States – History.   5. Communities –
United States – History.   I. Title.
E184.A1H386   2014
305.800973–dc23   2013017431

ISBN 978-1-107-04389-3 Hardback
ISBN 978-1-107-61958-6 Paperback

For Chris, Ryland, and Isaiah

Contents

Acknowledgments

My first debt is to the men and women I interviewed for this project, who volunteered their time and in some cases welcomed me into their homes to be interviewed. I am grateful to each of them for their insights and for their stories.

I am grateful, as well, to my husband, Chris, and to our children, Aidan, Elias, Ryland, and Isaiah, for their love and support. Chris is not only my closest friend, but also an exceptional reader and interlocutor. The boys are my inspiration. Chris, Ryland, and Isaiah are new since the last book, and so I dedicate this one to them.

One of my interview respondents (cited in Chapter 3) noted, as she told me her story, that "a wonderful babysitter" enabled her to continue to work when her children were born. Like my respondent, I am grateful to the women and men – the babysitters and the many teachers – who helped me care for my sons while I completed this work. Special thanks are due to Nara Cornell, who played countless (and endless) games of Candyland with Eli and Zay during the early phases of this project.

Some of the ideas developed in this book grew out of earlier articles, including "The Difference States Make: Democracy, Identity, and the American City," *American Political Science Review*, vol. 97, no. 4 (November 2003); "Doxa and Deliberation," *Critical Review of International Social and Political Philosophy*, vol. 7, no. 1 (Spring 2004); "Making Interest: On Representation and Democratic Legitimacy," in Ian Shapiro, Susan Stokes, Elizabeth Wood, and Alexander Kirshner, eds., *Political Representation* (Cambridge, UK: Cambridge University Press, 2009); "Black Places," *Theory and Event* vol. 12, no. 4 (2009); and "Bad Stories: Narrative, Identity, and the State's Materialist

Pedagogy," *Citizenship Studies* vol. 14, no. 6 (December, 2010). Although I have drawn on and expanded some of the arguments presented in these articles, I have also changed them in some cases, as my thinking developed.

In addition, I have presented various parts of this book at academic conferences, workshops, and seminars. I am grateful to the participants in the following sessions for their comments and suggestions: the Fall Fellows Forum of the National Academy of Education at Stanford in September 2004; the annual meeting of the American Political Science Association in Boston in September 2008; the Open University Symposium on the Pedagogical State in Milton Keynes, UK, in September 2008; the Washington University Political Theory Workshop in St. Louis in October 2008; the Columbia University Center for Urban Policy Research seminar in New York in March 2009; the annual meeting of the Western Political Science Association in Vancouver in March 2009; the annual meeting of the International Political Science Association in Santiago, Chile, in July 2009; the annual meeting of the American Political Science Association in Toronto in September 2009; the "Race across the Atlantic" workshop at Washington University in St. Louis in April 2011; the annual meeting of the American Political Science Association in Seattle in September 2011; the Washington University Law Faculty Workshop in St. Louis in March 2012; and the Program in Ethics and Public Affairs seminar at Princeton in November 2012.

I am especially grateful to the participants in the two-day workshop on this book held at Washington University in St. Louis in September 2012, including Michael Neblo, Rogers Smith, and Sarah Song, who traveled to St. Louis for that event, and to my colleagues Randy Calvert, Frank Lovett, and Andrew Rehfeld, who, with their usual drive and energy, helped organize the workshop. In addition to Neblo, Smith, and Song, Randy Calvert, Adrienne Davis, Frank Lovett, Cricket Keating, Laura Rosenbury, and Rebecca Wanzo offered invaluable feedback over the course of those two days.

As many will attest, writing a book can be a torturous process. This time around, my torture was greatly alleviated by friends and colleagues who helped shape, support, and sustain the work. For their comments and criticisms, and for their camaraderie, I am grateful to Randy Calvert, Adrienne Davis, Maggie Garb, Courtney Jung, Loren King, Peggy Kohn, Chris Lebron, Ian MacMullen, Linda Nicholson, Tim Pachirat, Ron Watson, and Kit Wellman.

For research assistance, I am grateful to Emma Hine, Rohan Mathur, Ben Noble, and Mindy Wang.

For research support, I am grateful to Washington University in St. Louis, the Ohio State University, the Institute for Advanced Study in Princeton, the National Endowment for the Humanities, the National Academy of Education, and the Spencer Foundation.

Introduction

Comme Il Faut

In *Racial Culture*, the legal scholar Richard Ford asks his readers to imagine what would happen to a female tango dancer who refused her gendered role in the dance.[1] She would be sanctioned by her dance instructor, he suggests, who would "correct" her "mistake." She would be sanctioned by the other female dancers, who would let her know, whether subtly or not so subtly, that she ought to behave more appropriately. She would be sanctioned by the male dancers, as well (the "leads"), who would, in Ford's words, "silently punish her by refusing to ask her to dance."[2] If the dancer wants approval, if she wants acceptance, if she wants the rewards distributed through this particular social practice, she will conform to the gendered expectations of the tango.

I was struck by this example when I first read Ford's book because at that time I was in the middle of what would prove an ill-fated attempt to learn to dance Argentine tango. Ford's characterization of the dance rang true. The tango *is* a strongly gendered dance in which the man leads while the woman follows. His characterization of why the woman follows rang true, as well. I, for one, followed, not because I endorsed an identity story according to which women are graceful, but never strong and assertive, according to which following male leads is "what women do," but instead because the practice of tango dancing incentivized me to follow.

Or at least that is one important part of why I followed. I also followed because of my Comme Il Fauts.

---

[1] Richard Thompson Ford, *Racial Culture: A Critique* (Princeton, NJ: Princeton University Press, 2005), 62–4.
[2] Ibid., 63.

What are Comme Il Fauts? The phrase, of course, means "proper." It means "according to accepted standards or conventions." But Comme Il Faut is also the brand name for top-of-the-line Argentine tango shoes, which are handmade exclusively in Buenos Aires. One online retailer describes Comme Il Fauts as "ultra chic," "outrageously sexy, and superbly crafted with … a very distinctive stiletto heel."[3] My tango shoes conformed to gendered expectations of how a woman's footwear should look.

But that is not all they did. The ad continues: "Don't let the heel scare you – it is designed specifically for walking backwards and is perfectly positioned to provide incredible stability."[4] The shoes did help me walk backward. They helped me pivot on the ball of my foot. They tilted the axis of my body forward toward my (forward-walking, dance-floor-navigating, male) partner, heightening both my capacity and my disposition to read and to respond to the moves that he led. My shoes, in short, together with the rules and the standards that govern the practice of dancing Argentine tango, prompted me to perform my gendered role well.

In this book, the principal question I ask is: "How do people produce and reproduce identities?" My central case is, not gender identity, but racial identity in the late twentieth- and early twenty-first-century United States. My starting point is theories of the narrative construction of identity. Although storytelling is one important part of how people *produce* identities, I argue in the pages that follow, it is not the only, and it is not the most significant way they *reproduce* them. People reproduce identities, not just by telling and retelling the stories from which they were constructed, but also by *institutionalizing* those stories: by building them into norms, laws, and other institutions (such as the rules and the standards that govern Argentine tango dancing) that give social actors incentives to perform their identities well. People reproduce identities, in addition, by *objectifying* identity stories: by quite literally building them into material forms (like Comme Il Faut tango shoes) that social actors experience with their bodies as they engage in practical activity.

I advance this argument through historical analysis of the development of racial identities and racialized spaces in the twentieth-century United States, and also through the interpretation of life narratives that I collected from people who live in racialized American urban and suburban spaces. As is well known, early twentieth-century racial narratives were

---

[3] http://www.malevashoes.com/aboutcommeilfaut.html. Accessed December 27, 2012.
[4] Ibid.

scientifically discredited by the end of the 1940s. After World War II, they were widely regarded to be normatively illegitimate. Yet many, even most, Americans continued to use racial identities, long after repudiating the narratives from which they were constructed.

Why? (Why, for that matter, did I "use" my gender identity as I danced the Argentine tango, even though I reject the narrative from which that identity was constructed?) The institutionalization of identity narratives, my central claim is, along with their objectification, enables their practical reproduction. It lends them resilience in the face of challenge and critique.

My argument begins, in Chapter 1, with what has been called "the narrative identity thesis": the idea that "who we are," both as unique individuals and as members of social collectivities, is largely a function of narrative construction.[5] I am not unsympathetic to this view. Identification, I argue, has at least four key characteristics that render it amenable to construction in specifically narrative form. Identification is unavoidably selective, exegetical, productive, and evaluative. Narrative as a discursive form captures and mirrors these qualities. Nevertheless, people do not *only* learn their identities in narrative form. They learn them practically, as well, as they navigate institutional settings structured by identitarian norms and expectations, and as they experience corporeally the material forms in which those norms and expectations are objectified. The narrative production of identity, I argue, is compatible with the reproduction of identities that, when (or if) spelled out as narratives, take the form of "bad stories": stories that violate people's beliefs about the world as it is and as it ought to be and/or that include important internal inconsistencies.

An example is dominant early twentieth-century American racial stories, to which I turn my attention in Chapter 2. Starting around the time of the "Great Migration" of Southern blacks to Northern and Midwestern cities, narratives of racial identity and difference began to highlight an alleged black/white racial divide, to interpret black racial identity in particular as the cause of unfitness for home ownership and admission to high-status residential neighborhoods, and to advocate and celebrate a strict (and, in most Northern cities, a *newly* strict) segregation of "the races."

[5] The phrase "narrative identity thesis" comes from James Phelan, "Who's Here? Thoughts on Narrative Identity and Narrative Imperialism," *Narrative* 13, 3 (October 2005): 205–10.

As noted earlier, these early twentieth-century stories were largely discredited by mid-century. However, before they were discredited, they were built into the American urban and suburban landscape. They were institutionalized in laws and in rules, such as the rules governing the Federal Housing Administration's mortgage insurance program. They were objectified in spatial forms, such as the new black ghettos that were constructed starting in the early decades of the century. The channeling of public and private investment toward white enclaves incentivized whites to perform their (in some cases, new) racial identities well. Meanwhile, systematic disinvestment from black ghettos localized there a host of collective problems, including joblessness, poverty, and social problems associated with concentrated poverty.

How do the institutionalization and objectification of old stories shape perception and action in the present? In the third chapter, I draw on the life narrative told by one of my interview respondents to make the case that the institutionalization and objectification of collective identity stories encourage the construction of what I call *ordinary* life stories. Ordinary stories of personal identity are stories in which collective identities function as narrative frames: as unthematized background assumptions that people rely on to sort the events of their narratives from nonevents.

Ordinary stories, my claim is, are depoliticizing in the sense in which Wendy Brown uses that term. They "remove ... political phenomen[a] from comprehension of [their] *historical* emergence and from a recognition of the *powers* that produce and contour them."[6] Yet ordinary stories are the stories most social actors tell themselves (and others) most of the time. Hence their political import: these are among the tools most frequently used to translate lived experience into the narratives that shape our perception and direct our action.

Chapters 2 and 3 thus function as a pair: the second chapter traces the institutionalization and objectification of the early twentieth-century racial narrative, while the third considers its effect on ordinary stories. The fourth and fifth chapters have a parallel structure. In Chapter 4, I turn my attention to a second collective identity narrative that was institutionalized and objectified in the twentieth-century American metropolis: a story of white Americans as a home-owning people. This narrative, I argue, was self-consciously fashioned by a relatively small set of political actors – including, importantly, early twentieth-century "community

---

[6] Wendy Brown, *Regulating Aversion: Tolerance in the Age of Identity and Empire* (Princeton, NJ: Princeton University Press, 2006), 15, emphasis in original.

builders" – who stood to gain directly from its acceptance. According to this narrative, (white) Americans value, and they deserve, privately owned single-family detached suburban residences. Such "homes" (and this narrative worked to distinguish "homes" from mere "houses") are a critical component of the American Dream. Americans therefore ought to use their collective power (the power to create and enforce zoning laws, for example) and their collective resources (tax dollars) to support private, profit-driven housing development. Doing so serves the good of the American public.

This narrative of Americans as a home-owning people overlapped substantially with the racial identity narrative that is the focus of Chapter 2. It assumed, very often without explicitly making the case for, a normatively significant divide between "the black and white races," and it relied on that assumption to exclude (again, often implicitly) African Americans from "the public" whose good it claimed home ownership promotes.

It differed from the early racial narrative, however, in that, during the first decades of the last century, it was widely understood to be a bad story. The United States was not, at that time, a nation of home owners. What is more, the dominant view was that the government had *no* proper role in the private market in housing.

But the stock market crash of 1929 and the depression that followed produced a new coalition of actors who favored state intervention in the housing market, which they hoped would help create, not just homes, but also jobs. The Home Owners Loan Corporation and the Federal Housing Administration (agencies treated in Chapter 2 with a focus on their role in institutionalizing the dominant early twentieth-century racial narrative) institutionalized, as well, this narrative of (white) Americans as a home-owning people. Together with other New Deal programs and institutions, they fundamentally restructured the market for private home mortgages, expanding home finance credit to an unprecedented level and directing the capital they helped generate toward racially exclusive suburban developments.

The result was a late twentieth- and early twenty-first-century American metropolis characterized by massive direct and indirect state support for private, profit-oriented residential development, which disproportionately served the wealthy and the racially privileged. In Chapter 5, I turn my attention to New Albany, Ohio, which was, until the late 1980s, a small, rural village on the outskirts of Columbus. When Leslie Wexner, the billionaire founder of The Limited, Inc., redeveloped New Albany into an upscale, Georgian-themed suburban enclave, he was able to leverage considerable public resources to reduce his expenditure, and hence his investment risk. At the same time, Wexner was able to site his development in an incorporated suburban municipality with the power to engage in exclusionary zoning, to raise and spend taxes for services made available to residents only, and to decline to participate in a range of federal and state programs, from affordable housing to cross-jurisdictional school desegregation programs.

Wexner could leverage public resources and public powers to support and subsidize his development in large part because of the efforts of early housing industry elites, who had constructed, and then worked to institutionalize and objectify, a narrative of Americans as a home-owning people. Nevertheless, I argue, using a thought experiment centered on a hypothetical school I call "Exit Academy," even at the start of the twenty-first century, most Americans regard as *illegitimate* state-subsidized "exit" that benefits the wealthy and the racially privileged.

Most nevertheless accept state-subsidized exit to enclaves like Wexner's New Albany, because the institutionalization of the story fashioned by early twentieth-century community builders constructed an interest in home ownership in such enclaves. Most accept state-subsidized exit because the objectification of that narrative helped obscure the political actions and the collective choices that create and maintain such places. The institutionalized and objectified narrative of (white) Americans as a home-owning people serves as a frame to countless ordinary life stories. It enables the privileged to write their own privilege out of the stories of their lives.

In the conclusion to this book, I turn to the question of identitarian change. The telling of new identity stories, I underscore, is never sufficient. Change requires storytelling, to be sure, but storytelling of a particular kind: storytelling that targets both institutional redesign and the reconstruction of material forms.

The story I tell in the pages that follow begins in New Albany, Ohio, in the home of Steven Mullins (a pseudonym), who is telling me the story of his life. Throughout this book, I draw on similar life narratives, which I collected from residents of East Side Columbus and the "new" (post-Wexner) and "old" (pre-Wexner) New Albanies.[7]

---

[7] See the appendix for a detailed description of my interview respondents and a schedule of interview questions.

These narratives do not, of course, provide access to the *internal* narratives that people tell themselves inside their own minds, let alone to an unmediated social reality. Instead, they are versions of the stories that people construct when they present themselves to other people. But such stories, I hope to show, are well worth attending to, because they serve as important windows into the processes whereby people produce and reproduce identities.

Identities and Stories

Steven Mullins characterizes the story of his life as "the American story." He is an American, first and foremost, he tells me. He feels deeply tied to his nation and to its history. Mullins expresses great pride in his country (if he had to rank all the countries in the world, he says, the United States would be at, or at least very near to, the top of his list) and he articulates a ready willingness to sacrifice for it. "I'm proud to be an American," Mullins tells me, "[which] means that I understand why my ancestors came here." He elaborates:

The Egans were Irish, you know. Ireland was terrible. Irish famines ... it was a place where you didn't want to live. The French Huguenots, the Mullins side, we came out of Germany, came to America. Both families fought in the American Revolution... So ... I would like to think that if I was alive then, the beginning of this country, would I be a Tory or a Patriot? I would have definitely been a Patriot. Would I be willing to die for my country? Yes.

As Mullins recalls his life, and as he recounts to me what he has learned about the lives of his ancestors, he gestures toward the barn that stands on the farm where he grew up, and where he now lives. His mother was raised on this same farm. His maternal great-great grandfather, one of the first settlers of what, in 1837, would become the village of New Albany, Ohio, purchased the land for the farm in 1828. "[O]n this farm," Mullins says, "is a beautiful barn, with a thirty-five star [Union] battle flag painted on [it]." "So, I grew up," he tells me, "under the flag."

1. Identity Thinking

As even these brief interview excerpts make clear, for Steven Mullins, American national identity – who "we," as an American people, are – is deeply constitutive of personal identity. The American nation is not, by Mullins's view, merely an association he has elected to join. Nor is being American reducible to juridical citizen status. It is a matter of blood ties, he makes clear over the course of the interview. It is a matter of affective attachment to America's people, to its history, to the land that is the American territory. It is a matter of sharing (both of having internalized through socialization processes that begin in childhood, and also, as an adult, of reflectively endorsing) the values and principles Mullins regards as definitive of American identity.

What does it require for Steven Mullins to have an identity in this sense? More generally, what does it require for an individual to identify with a collectivity, membership in which she regards as constitutive of her personal identity? It requires, first and perhaps most basically, an understanding of the relevant identity category (in Mullins's case, an understanding of the category "American") as both meaningful and significant.

Such a subjective understanding does not necessarily follow from the objective fact of its possibility. Steven Mullins might, in principle, identify as "propertied." He might, in principle, understand who he is as a unique individual to be significantly shaped by "who we property owners are." Similarly, he might identify as "white," "able-bodied," or even "bespectacled." But he does not. He mentions none of these categories during the course of our approximately four-hour-long interview, not even when I prompt him to think about and to name his social identities.[1] Identity thinking – identifying oneself and others with particular delimited collectivities – requires dividing the social world into some conceivable groupings, but not others.

It requires, as well, holding a relatively clear and stable set of beliefs about, not only which actors, but also which actions and attributes fit particular groupings and lend them distinctiveness. Steven Mullins, during the course of our interview, emphasizes as distinctively American traits a strong work ethic, a willingness to contribute to communal life, and a commitment (in his words) to "stand up for what's right ... whatever consequences it means." He stresses a willingness to learn and to use

---

[1] I prompt Mullins to think about and to name his identities as part of a semi-structured interview following his life history interview. In the semi-structured interview, Mullins tells me a number of ways he would complete the statement "My name is Steven Mullins, and I am _____." These include "American," "conservative," "Republican," "New Albany resident," and "Christian." He then answers a series of questions about the identity categories he lists. For a detailed schedule of interview questions, see the appendix.

the English language, singling out as "not American" "Mexicans who will not speak English."[2] Mullins claims, in addition, that a belief in racial equality is a distinctly American belief, and he asserts that Americans endorse and support civil liberties, especially freedom of conscience and freedom of speech.

Just as Steven Mullins might, in principle, identify with a different collectivity from the one with which he identifies, he might, in principle, highlight a different set of dispositions and/or a different set of traits as definitive of that collectivity. He might define acquisitiveness and consumerism as distinctly American traits, for example. He might underscore American individualism or American tolerance of economic inequality. He might stress a different set of constitutional principles from the set he stresses, what is more, or he might define as fundamental to American national identity a different interpretation of the particular principles he names. That it is objectively possible to understand particular actions and particular attributes as constitutive of a given social identity does not mean such an understanding necessarily obtains.

Nor is it necessarily the case that particular actions and attributes can be seen as constitutive of particular identities only if *all* persons assigned to the relevant identity categories perform those actions and exhibit those attributes. A case in point is Mullins's linguistic definition of American national identity. Some Americans, of course, do not speak English. Indeed, during the course of our interview, Mullins reveals he is consciously aware of this fact. Immediately after categorizing non-English speakers as not American (in fact, as "Mexican"), he shifts terms and refers to them as "minorities" within the American population. "I think we need to make sure that everybody realizes," he tells me, repeatedly pounding the table that sits between us with his fist, "English is the number one language in this country. It always has been, and we're going to keep it that way. We should not give in to the minorities to change it."

Mullins claims, in other words, that some American "minorities" do not speak English, asserting that they aim to alter the status of English as "the number one [American] language." Still, he insists that whether a person knows and uses English is an important indicator of whether or not that individual is (the implication being: a *real* or a *good* or a *true*)

---

[2] "For two hundred years," Mullins tells me, "there [have] been immigrants coming to this country … There [were] German newspapers, but the intent of that generation … the first ones over here, was to teach their children English … and I don't see that happening with the Mexican population that's coming to this country."

American. A real or a good or a true X – the logic is – *ought to* perform action x, or ought to have trait x, *because x is a sign of X-ness*. Women ought to follow male leads when dancing Argentine tango because gracefulness (but not assertiveness) is a sign of (real) womanhood. Americans ought to know and speak English because knowing and speaking English is a sign of (real) Americanness. If some Americans (or some women) do not exhibit the traits or do not perform the actions that are the outward signs of their identities, one should take that data as evidence of, not a flaw in the definition of the identities, but a shortcoming of those particular people. Those particular individuals perform their identities poorly.

For an individual to identify with a social collectivity, then, she needs to conceive the world as divided into some possible groupings (but not others); to regard some people (but not others) as members of the relevant identity category; and to view those people as sharing some (but not others) of the traits and dispositions they might reasonably be understood to share. At the same time, for an individual to identify with a collectivity in a constitutive sense (for her to understand her membership in that collectivity as an important part of who she, as a unique individual, is), she needs to cull from her own lived experience (from all of the actions she has performed, and that she remembers performing, from all of the traits and dispositions she has exhibited, and of which she is aware) a set of actions and characterizations that prompts her to understand herself as *like these particular others*, and like them *in these particular ways*.

Such acts of self-understanding often appear, to those who effect them, as obvious, even inevitable. "*Of course* I understand myself to be someone who has trait x, or who performs action x," I might tell myself (and I might tell others), "because on many occasions I, in fact, *have exhibited* trait x, and on many occasions I, in fact, *have performed* action x. In characterizing myself this way, I am doing nothing more than stating a readily apparent truth: an incontrovertible fact about the kind of person I am."

Steven Mullins thus characterizes himself as a person who contributes to the life of his community by recalling the fact that he helped to found, and for many years participated actively in, a local chapter of the Jaycees.[3] He characterizes himself as having a strong work ethic by describing the self-discipline and the effort he brought to his studies when he was in

---

[3] That is, the United States Junior Chamber of Commerce, a community-based civic organization that promotes leadership training and service.

school, and that he later brought to his work in the small business his family ran. Similarly, he characterizes himself as a person who "stand[s] up for what's right" by citing decisions he has made to defend what he regards as important moral principles. On more than one occasion, he says, he prosecuted people who stole from his business. He divorced his first wife, he tells me, when she revealed to him that she had had an extra-marital affair. Commenting on the latter decision, Mullins makes it clear that he sees it as a reaction against what he understands to be an unam-biguous moral wrong. "Maybe I could have said, 'OK. It's ok with me that you slept with that guy, '" he tells me. "'Let's get back together.'" But he adds quickly, "No. That was wrong. That's ... you know, we're done. Period. It's black and white with me."

To be sure, in each of these instances, it is possible that Steven Mullins recalls what happened inaccurately, and/or that he reports the events as he recalls them untruthfully. Perhaps Mullins in fact wavered before deciding to divorce his first wife, for instance, but has since forgotten his original indecision and/or is motivated to neglect to mention it by his desire to present an image of himself as a person who "stands up for what's right." It is worth underscoring, however, that even if this is *not* the case – even if Mullins recalls what happened in a way that is entirely accurate, and even if he reports what he recalls in a way that is entirely truthful – his account is, necessarily, both *selective* and *exegetic*.

Imagine a set comprised of all the things that happen to an individual like Steven Mullins over the course of a day: all the actions he takes, all the decisions he makes, all the traits, the impulses, the dispositions he exhibits. Prior to the date of our interview, Mullins had lived a total of 16,688 days. Even if, on average, only a single memorable thing had happened to Mullins per day, for him to recall any one of these (such as his decision to prosecute his former employee or to divorce his former wife) is to highlight .006 percent, or six ten-thousandths of "what happened."

Mullins's account is selective, then, and necessarily so, in the sense that to recall any particular happening is to pick out from all of what happened an infinitesimally small fraction, or subset. His account is ex-egetical, as well (and again, necessarily so) in that to assign a particular meaning to a particular happening is to pick from what is often a very wide range of plausible interpretations a subset or, more typically, a single interpretation. When Mullins took his employee to court, he says, this was an instance of his standing up for an important moral principle. Other plausible interpretations are that it was an instance of his acting in a self-interested manner, to protect his property; or of his making an example of an errant worker, to shore up the power relation involving himself and his other employees; or of his acting vengefully against an individual who had wronged him, to feel the sense of satisfaction that comes from doing so.

Even if Mullins sometimes behaves in ways one might reasonably interpret as evidence of "standing up for what's right," in other words, even if Mullins sometimes behaves in ways one might reasonably interpret as examples of "contributing to communal life" or of being "hard working," there are likely other plausible interpretations of each of these very same behaviors. In addition, there are likely *other* behaviors in which Mullins engages that might be interpreted as evidence of *different* traits and *different* dispositions. At other times in his life, no doubt, Steven Mullins relaxes. At other times, no doubt, he withdraws into his private life. No doubt there are instances of actions Mullins has taken that might reasonably be interpreted as *failures* to respond to nontrivial moral wrongs. In short, that it is objectively possible for Steven Mullins to understand himself as a person who has the traits he regards to be definitive of American national identity does not mean it is necessary or inevitable that he will do so.

At this point, one might reasonably wonder about the relationship among the various component parts of the sense of having an identity. I want to defer this question for now, except to note that it is likely a complex, rather than a simple, relation. Steven Mullins's perception that he himself exhibits particular traits likely influences how he defines distinctively American attributes, given his strong desire to identify as American. At the same time, the fact that Mullins comes to believe that Americans have particular attributes likely motivates him to develop and/or to perceive himself as having those characteristics, again, given his strong desire to identify as American. Yet Mullins's very desire to identify as American likely follows at least in part from his belief that particular traits, which he has and/or understands himself to have, and which he values, are traits that define this identity group.

There is no reason, in short, to assume a neat and a unidirectional causal chain linking (a) the formation of the desire to understand the self in particular identitarian terms, (b) the conceptualization of some collective identity, and (c) the development of a self-understanding that is compatible with that conceptualization. Nevertheless, the principal claim advanced above holds: neither identity categories, nor beliefs about the actors, actions, and attributes assigned to particular categories – not even beliefs about the actions and the attributes of the self – follow inexorably from the raw data that comprise the social world.

Still, people tend to arrive at answers to the questions "Who am I?" and "Who are we?" that are relatively coherent and consistent. They tend to arrive at answers that overlap with the answers to these questions that (at least some) other people give: answers that attain (at least a minimal level of) social intelligibility. As I listen to Steven Mullins talk about his past and his present, I do not find myself wondering why he identifies as "American." As I listen to his account of what it means to be (a real or a good or a true) American, his claims strike me as, if less than fully persuasive, still far from unintelligible. Mullins has a subjective sense of who he is (an American, a patriot) that links a subset of his actions and attributes (as he recalls and interprets them) to a category, which he defines and delimits in a socially meaningful way.

This feat would be next to impossible to achieve through pure analysis and induction. Were Mullins systematically to examine the totality of his lived experiences, were he then methodically to list those experiences and to observe and plot trends, patterns, and relationships among them, his answers to the questions "who am I?" and "who are we?" would look radically different. If Steven Mullins were to do this, and if I were to confront my lived experience of the social world in a similar fashion, the odds that the two of us, reasoning imperfectly from different sets of experiential data, would converge on the same, or even on substantially overlapping sets of identitarian beliefs (the odds that Mullins would say to me, "I'm proud to be an American," and that I would understand) are exceedingly small.

But that is not how Steven Mullins processes his lived experience, and it is not how I do. He does not *analyze* and *define* "who he is" and "who we are," so much as tell a personal life narrative (to recall his words, an "American *story*") into which he incorporates a social narrative of collective identity. That "American" is a meaningful and significant category, that members of this identity category (Americans) endorse liberal and egalitarian principles, that they work hard and contribute to communal life, and that they "stand up for what's right" – these are beliefs Steven Mullins did not arrive at inductively and analytically, but rather acquired through exposure to narratives of American national identity: through the mass media, through formal education in the various schools he attended, and through the informal education of communal and associational life.

2. Identity Stories

Storytelling is how people make sense of the social world. It is how they make sense of their place in that world: how they take what, in raw form, might seem an undifferentiated mass of experiential input (all of the other persons with whom they come into contact, whether face to face or through mediated interactions, all of the actions each of those persons takes, all of what each does, all of what each says, all of their own reactions to those words and to those actions) and impose upon it a structure that renders it readable, and hence usable. Storytelling is how social actors give to lived experience a shape or a form that enables them to comprehend it and to use it as a guide to future action.

This claim is hardly controversial. It is all but commonplace in contemporary social and political theory to suggest that people construct both their personal and their collective identities, and that they do so in specifically narrative form.[4] Seyla Benhabib, to cite one prominent example, writes, "We are born into webs … of narrative – from the familial and gender narratives to the linguistic one to the macronarrative of one's collective identity. We become who we are by learning to become a conversation partner in these narratives."[5]

---

[4] There is a large and influential literature on narrative identity, on which I draw in the discussion that follows. Key works include Jerome Bruner, *Actual Minds, Possible Worlds* (Cambridge, MA: Harvard University Press, 1986); Bruner, "Life as Narrative," *Social Research* 54, 1 (1987): 11–32; Bruner, "The Narrative Construction of Reality," *Critical Inquiry* 18, 1 (August 1991): 1–21; Mark Freeman, *Re-writing the Self: History, Memory, Narrative* (New York: Routledge, 1993); Anthony Paul Kerby, *Narrative and the Self* (Bloomington: Indiana University Press, 1991); Alasdair MacIntyre, *After Virtue: A Study in Moral Theory*, third edition (Notre Dame, IN: University of Notre Dame Press, 2007); Donald Polkinghorne, *Narrative Knowing and the Human Sciences* (Albany: State University of New York Press, 1988); Paul Ricoeur, *Time and Narrative*, vol. 1, transl. Kathleen McLaughlin and David Pellauer (Chicago, IL: University of Chicago Press, 1984); Ricoeur, *Time and Narrative*, vol. 3, transl. Kathleen Blamey (Chicago, IL: University of Chicago Press, 1988); Margaret Somers, "The Narrative Constitution of Identity: A Relational and Network Approach," *Theory and Society* 23 (1994): 605–49; Charles Taylor, *Sources of the Self: The Making of Modern Identity* (Cambridge, MA: Harvard University Press, 1989); and Hayden White, "The Value of Narrativity in the Representation of Reality," *Critical Inquiry* 7, 1 (Autumn 1980): 5–27. Claims that identity is inherently and inevitably narrative, however, are far from undisputed. See Galen Strawson, "Against Narrativity," *Ratio* XVII, 4 (2004): 428–52, who argues that some people (himself included) do not experience the self as continuous over time and do not construct their identities narratively.
[5] Seyla Benhabib, "Sexual Difference and Collective Identities: The New Global Constellation," *Signs* 24, 2 (1999): 335–61.

But why is it that people create identities *as stories*? In this section, I draw on theories of narrative identity to sketch what I want to suggest are four key characteristics of identification that render it amenable to narrative construction. The first two I have already briefly introduced: *identification is selective* and *identification is exegetical*. I expound on these claims next, explicating the link between these characteristics and the narrative form. I then introduce two additional characteristics – *identification is productive* and *identification is evaluative* – that I want to suggest serve as further links between identities and stories.

Identification Is Selective

Steven Mullins does not catalogue everything that happens to him: everything he does and everything he observes, moment to moment. He does not keep a running tally of "what happens at time t and what happens at time $t + 1$ ... what happens at time $t + n$" and refer to that log as an objective record of experience. He does not say to himself at time t, and looking back to time t he does not recall: "While pushing the button to begin the dishwasher cycle, I was thinking about the errand I was planning to run, and the meteorologist was reading the weather report, and my son was staring at him on the screen, and the gardener was trimming the hedges out back, and my wife was walking into the kitchen, and she began speaking to me the following words..."

He does not process his experiences that way. Nor does he remember them that way. Instead, in the moment, he attends to some of what happens, but not all, making running judgments about significance. (*My wife is telling me she had an affair!*) When the moment has passed, and he reflects back on what he recalls, he makes additional judgments, perhaps assigning to a particular occurrence a significance it did not seem, in the moment, to have: relating that occurrence to a past he now thinks it decisively redefined, for example, and/or to a future he now believes it helped produce. (*That was when my wife revealed she had betrayed me, irremediably damaging the bond we once had.*)[6]

Hayden White's contrast between historical narratives and historical annals can help explain why and how the particular kind of selectivity

---

[6] According to Seymour Chatman, such selectivity is "a logical property of narratives": "[A] narrative, as the product of a fixed number of statements, can never be totally 'complete' the way that a photographic reproduction is, since the number of plausible intermediate actions or properties is virtually infinite." Chatman, *Story and Discourse: Narrative Structure in Fiction and Film* (Ithaca, NY: Cornell University Press, 1978), here 29.

characteristic of narrative as a discursive form renders identification amenable to narrative construction. Consider the following excerpt from the *Annals of Saint Gall*, which, as White notes, is "a list of events that occurred in Gaul during the eighth, ninth, and tenth centuries":

> 709. Hard winter. Duke Gottfried died.
> 710. Hard year and deficient in crops.
> 711.
> 712. Flood everywhere.
> 713.
> 714. Pippin, Mayor of the Palace, died.
> 715. 716. 717.
> 718. Charles devastated the Saxon with great destruction.
> 719.
> 720. Charles fought against the Saxons.
> 721. Theudo drove the Saracens out of Aquitaine.
> 722. Great crops.[7]

Annals are like narratives in that they are selective. Certainly *something* must have happened in 711, and flooding cannot be the *only* thing that happened in 712. But, while the annalist records happenings (in White's words) "as they come to notice," the narrator of a story (whether fictional, historical, or based on lived experience) constructs events from those happenings he or she deems significant for what White calls the "social center."[8] White conceives the social center as necessarily a "political-social order."[9] But for someone like Steven Mullins telling his life narrative, the social center is the self.[10] When Mullins constructs his wife's betrayal as the start of a marital crisis, he narrativizes this event, which he deems significant. Through his narrative's plot, Mullins relates this event to the other life events that he constructs.

Collective identification is selective, no less so than is personal identification: selective not just of actions and experiences, but of persons as

---

[7] White, "The Value of Narrativity in the Representation of Reality," 11.

[8] Ibid., 22, 15.

[9] Ibid., 15.

[10] Not only is it not the case that the focal point of a narrative need be a "political-social order"; it also need not be a human agent or a collectivity. Imagine a narrative about the building of the Panama Canal in which the focal point is the project itself rather than any particular actor or set of actors. Still, I find White's basic insight compelling. Simply relating a set of happenings is insufficient to construct a narrative. Narratives organize events, and they do so with reference to some focal character(s), collectivit(ies), institution(s), practice(s), or project(s).

well. Shared understandings of "who we are" as an American people (or of "who we are" as women) constitute some, but not other, past actors and actions as definitive of "our" history. They identify some, but not other, contemporary people, practices, and values as component parts of "who we are." Just as personal narratives that select and order significant events are the mode through which individuals construct their self-under-standings, so are selective *collective* identity narratives the mode through which shared understandings are made.

Identification Is Exegetical

The language of "selecting" events to construct a narrative might be mis-leading, however. People do not select ready-made events as they tell their life stories, the way they select products at a convenience store or clothing at a mall. To the contrary, the actions and the interactions that comprise the events from which identity narratives are constructed must first, if they are to be meaningful, be interpreted.

If you were to enter my office at this very moment, you would see me pounding with my fingers on the keys of my computer's keyboard, while staring intently at its screen. If you were to do so, you could accu-rately describe my *behavior* simply by reporting what you saw. To give a meaningful account of the *action* I am performing, however, you would need to know something about why I am behaving the way that I am behaving: what it is I think I am doing, what my beliefs are about this behavior that I am performing, what my purposes are, and what I intend to accomplish through these motions.

What is more, because my beliefs and intentions are not freestanding – because they are related to other beliefs and other intentions I hold, and because they are shaped by beliefs I share with others and by practices and institutions in which I participate with others – you could not stop there.

I am pounding the keys of the keyboard, you might say, because I am writing about narrative and identity. You might add: I am writing part of a book I am working on and that I intend to publish. I intend to do so in part because I want to communicate with an audience of readers whom I imagine as I write, in part because publishing books is what people do when they engage in the practice of academic political philosophy, in part because the university that employs me encourages and rewards book publishing, etc., etc. To paraphrase Alasdair MacIntyre (on whom this paragraph and the previous three draw), one cannot interpret actions without reference to beliefs and intentions and to what MacIntyre calls the "settings" that lend beliefs and intentions both their subjective and their intersubjective intelligibility.[11]

Narrative is among the discursive forms that best enable such interpretation. Narratives are comprised, not only of events, but also of characters: human agents, whether individual or collective, or alternatively, agent-like beings such as gods or anthropomorphized animals or even anthropomorphized objects (think of "The Little Engine That Could").[12] Characters hold beliefs. They form thoughts and intentions. They act purposely. And they do so in the context of settings that help shape the meaning of their thoughts, words, and actions. The engine overcomes her limitations through determination and hard work, for example, and succeeds in meeting the challenge others had refused to face. Or: Steven Mullins makes the judgment that his wife's infidelity is morally wrong and acts on that judgment, telling her "we're done."

Jerome Bruner, in *Actual Minds, Possible Worlds*, distinguishes narrative from what he calls "paradigmatic" or "logico-scientific" discourse. The latter, he writes, "deals in general causes" and tests for logical coherence and empirical truth.[13] It includes "formal, logically consistent theories … that can be stated in mathematical or near-mathematical terms," as well as claims that can be tested against objective reality.[14] Narrative, by contrast, creates believable, but not necessarily empirically true, accounts. It "deals in human or human-like intention and action and the vicissitudes and consequences that mark their course."[15] Compare the opening lines of Hans Christian Anderson's "The Princess and the Pea" (*Once upon a time there was a prince who wanted to marry a princess, but she would have to be a real one. He traveled around the whole world looking for her; but every time he met a princess there was always something amiss*) with the claim "x causes y" or the statement "$2 + 2 = 4$."[16]

To this point, I have used the terms *narrative* and *story* interchangeably (and I will continue to do so, following colloquial usage, as my argument progresses). However, in the literature on narrative theory, there is a fairly widely agreed upon distinction between a story (a *fabula* or

---

[11] MacIntyre, *After Virtue: A Study in Moral Theory*, chapter 15.
[12] Watty Piper, *The Little Engine That Could* (New York: Penguin, 1976).
[13] Bruner, *Actual Minds, Possible Worlds*, 13.
[14] Ibid., 48.
[15] Ibid., 13.
[16] From Anderson's "The Princess and the Pea" as quoted in Emma Kafalenos, *Narrative Causalities* (Columbus, OH: Ohio State University Press, 2006), 28.

historie) and the narration of that story (the *discours* or *sjužet*), which interprets and represents it.[17] The fabula is that which is presumed to have happened (or, in the case of a fictional story, that which is imagined to have happened): the characters, the events, and the settings that comprise the content of the narrative. Once upon a time, a prince wanted a "real princess" for his wife; a queen used the pea test to find one; and then the prince and the princess were married. Or: Years ago in New Albany, Ohio, Steven Mullins's wife had an affair; one day she confessed it to him; and soon after he divorced her. Narration, by contrast, is the *representation* of what happened: the discursive form through which the story is interpreted and conveyed to a reader (or to a listener).

For every story, there are multiple possible narratives. I have no access to Steven Mullins's ex-wife's account of the end of their marriage. But my guess is that, even if she agrees with him on the *fabula*, her narration of their story departs substantially from his.

Emma Kafalenos, comparing Hans Christian Anderson's version of "The Princess and the Pea" with the Brothers Grimm's "The Pea Test," underscores that significant differences mark these narrative interpretations of a near-identical story.[18] Anderson's narration presents the prince as an agentive character whose decisions and actions drive key events, including the search for the princess. The Brothers Grimm, by contrast, narrate him as relatively passive, emphasizing instead the agency of the female characters, especially the queen. In the latter version but not the former, for instance, the prince and the king disappear from the narrative relatively early on; the princess's motivations for making her journey to the castle are narrated; and the tale ends before the wedding, with a private meeting between the princess and the queen.

Compare the two endings, Anderson's in which the prince [active / subject] *marries* the princess [passive / object]:

The prince married her. The pea was exhibited in the royal museum; and you can go there and see it if it hasn't been stolen.

and the Brothers Grimm's, in which the queen informs the princess that she will marry the prince (who is absent from the scene):

[17] Structuralist theorists distinguish *historie*, the events, characters, and setting that comprise the story, from *discours*, the discursive expression that represents it. Russian Formalists call the story the *fabula* and distinguish it from the plot or *sjužet*, that is, "the story as told by linking the events together." See Chatman, *Story and Discourse*, 20. For clarity, I will use *fabula* to denote story in this technical sense and either *discourse* or *narration* for the technical sense of narrative discourse.

[18] Kafalenos, *Narrative Causalities*, chapter 2.

"Now I know for sure," said the queen, "that you're a genuine princess. I shall send some royal garments up to you with pearls and jewels. Dress yourself as a bride, for we shall celebrate your wedding on this very day."[19]

The difference is not the fabula. Even the Brothers Grimm's version implies that a wedding eventually took place. Instead, the difference is how the story is narrativized: how the actions the characters take (and their beliefs, motivations, and purposes) are interpreted and presented to the reader. Because narrative as a discursive form necessarily interprets characters' actions and intentions, it is well suited to managing the exegetical dimension of identification.

Collective identification, it is worth noting, is no less exegetical than personal identification. Every shared understanding of "who we are" is but one interpretation of the meaning of the data from which it is comprised. And collective identity narratives, no less than narratives of personal identity, are interpretations: interpretations of shared memories, shared projects, shared meanings and symbols. (Recall Steven Mullins's invocation of the "thirty-five star [Union] battle flag.") Collective identity narratives associate shared meanings with some, but not other, historical and contemporary actors (with "Patriots," for instance, but not "Tories"), whose actions and purposes they interpret and relate to a (contestable) vision of what unites "us" and makes us a group.

Identification Is Productive

Identification – the process of recognizing discrete and bounded identity categories; associating particular actors, actions, and traits with particular categories; and placing the self in some categories but not in others – is a productive process in the sense that it helps engender the very behaviors and characteristics it associates with the relevant categories. Conceiving of myself as like these particular others (Americans, for instance, or women) and as like them in these particular ways does not simply *represent* (some of) my past beliefs and values and (some of) my actions and affinities. It also *shapes* how I act in the present and which characteristics and which habits I form, and hence how I act and how I interact with others in the future.

Narrative aids this process. In *Narratives from the Crib*, a study of fifteen months' worth of the pre-sleep monologues of a two-year-old girl, Katherine Nelson argues that most of the stories the child tells herself

[19] Quoted in ibid., 28, 35.

are "heuristic" stories, which she uses to "sort out how the world is, what categories can be constructed from it, [and] how to explain its phenomena."[20]

Adults, too, use narrative to guide perception and action, since narratives (which select from and then interpret "what happened") invariably shape their understandings of the self and of the social world.[21] When Steven Mullins constructs and relates his life narrative, the telling does not simply reflect so much as (to borrow Mark Freeman's language) it "rewrites" the self it names as its subject.[22]

Recall the episode in which Mullins relates his decision to end his first marriage. But imagine now that the fabula (what actually happened) differs from the narrative as Mullins constructs it. In reality, suppose, Mullins was indecisive: he wavered before divorcing his wife, wondering about the costs and deliberating about whether he should attempt reconciliation. As he tells and retells his story, however, he narrativizes himself as having acted decisively. ("No, that's it. It's black and white with me.") Now, imagine that Mullins's second wife confesses an infidelity. In such a scenario, not only the earlier experience, but also the way Mullins has narrativized that experience, will shape how he thinks about and responds to the later event.

Of course, there are multiple possible ways that, in such a situation, Steven Mullins might respond. His narrative does not *determine* his present or his future. But it shapes it. He might act more decisively the

---

[20] Katherine Nelson, "Monologue as Representation of Real-Life Experience," 27–72 in *Narratives from the Crib*, ed. Katherine Nelson (Cambridge, MA: Harvard University Press, 1989), 16. Interestingly, the child's narratives do not center on what most older children and adults would regard as major life events, such as the birth of her younger brother or the start of her preschool education. Instead, as Jerome Bruner and Joan Lucariello argue, she uses narrative to accomplish the important first step of sorting out what is normal or canonical. Only after arriving at a basic understanding of what is to be expected can the child note and narrativize events that are out of the ordinary. Bruner and Lucariello, "Monologue as Narrative Recreation of the World," 73–97 in Nelson, ed., *Narratives from the Crib*.

[21] Not only life narratives, but also fictional narratives are productive in this sense. Recall the two representations of "The Princess and the Pea" / "The Pea Test" fabula: Hans Christian Anderson's, which prompts me as a reader to see the prince as an agentive character who makes decisions and effects outcomes, and the Brothers Grimm's, which prompts me to see him as a relatively passive character and to understand the queen as agentive and efficacious. As I work my way through the narratives, I develop expectations about the prince and the queen. How each is represented early on shapes what I expect from them as the story progresses, how I interpret (the authors' representations of) their words and actions, and how I make sense of the later parts of the tale.

[22] Freeman, *Rewriting the Self: History, Memory, Narrative*.

second time, for instance, because he has come to understand himself as someone who "stand[s] up for what's right ... whatever consequences it means." Alternatively, he might decide that his "black and white" attitude has been an important contributing factor to his marital problems, and therefore resolve to change, perhaps by seeking relationship counseling with his second wife. If so, Mullins will revise his life narrative, perhaps marking this second marital crisis as a turning point. In either case, the original narrative will have shaped his perception of and his reaction to this life event by prompting him to understand himself as, at least until this point in time, highly intolerant of marital infidelity.

In "Life as Narrative," Jerome Bruner, analyzing life narratives that he and his colleagues had collected, makes a similar point. "You will ask whether the narrative forms and the language that go with them in our ... subjects are not simply expressions of their inner states," he writes (anticipating a view of life narratives as simply reflecting, rather than also always shaping, lived experience). "But ... ways of telling and the ways of conceptualizing that go with them ... become recipes for structuring experience itself, for laying down routes into memory, for not only guiding the life narrative up to the present but directing it into the future."[23]

Collective identity narratives, much like personal identity narratives, are productive in the most basic sense of that word. When people tell stories of "who we are" as an American people (or as women), they do not simply record and represent "what happened." Instead, by constructing shared trials and triumphs (the American Revolutionary War, to cite an example from Mullins's interview), by naming "our" heroes and "our" enemies, they shape how people perceive and evaluate their past. They thereby influence the affective- and the value-orientations of those they interpellate, along with their motivations and their dispositions to act.[24]

Identification Is Evaluative

I would like to think that if I was alive then, the beginning of this country, would I be a Tory or a Patriot? I would have definitely been a Patriot. Would I be willing to die for my country? Yes.

---

[23] Bruner, "Life as Narrative," 31.

[24] Thus, for Margaret Somers, "[E]xperience is constituted through narratives ... people are guided to act in certain ways, and not others, on the basis of the projections, expectations, and memories derived from ... social, public, and cultural narratives." Somers, "The Narrative Constitution of Identity," 614.

I want to draw attention to the first six words of this excerpt from Steven Mullins's interview in order to introduce and to illustrate Charles Taylor's claim that what he calls "strong evaluations" are central to identification. Strong evaluations, for Taylor, are the deep-seated evaluative beliefs that provide the framework people rely on (often unconsciously) when they make normative judgments.[25] If I think I ought to finish writing this paragraph before leaving the office to meet my colleague for an after-work drink, for example, that belief is parasitic on a strong evaluation about the worth of the activity of writing (and of drinking). Similarly, if Steven Mullins would like to think that, had he been alive at the time of the American Revolution, he would have been a Patriot and not a Tory, that desire is predicated on his belief that to be a Tory would have been bad, and to be a Patriot would have been good. To be a Patriot would have been good, Mullins believes, because the traits and the actions of the early American revolutionaries accorded with values to which he finds himself deeply committed: values he uses (whether consciously or not) to judge the worth of, not only historical, but also contemporary, traits, actions, desires, and motivations.

For Taylor, strong evaluations are central to identification. Without them, people would lack a sense of where they stand in relation to "the good" and therefore in relation to particular attributes, principles, collectivities, and traditions. The very act of defining who I am with respect to a particular goal, community, or trait, Taylor argues, depends on a prior evaluative belief:

> [O]ur identity is defined by our fundamental evaluations. The answer to the question "What is my identity?" cannot be given by any list of properties of other ranges, about my physical description, provenance, background, capacities, and so on. All these can figure in my identity, but only as assumed in a certain way. If my being of a certain lineage is to me of central importance, if I am proud of it, and see it as conferring on me membership in a certain class of people whom I see as marked off by certain qualities which I value in myself as an agent and which come to me from this background, then it will be part of my identity.[26]

In other words, a (healthy or positive) personal identity requires an understanding of the self as, not just like these particular others in these

---

[25] See Charles Taylor, "What is Human Agency?" 15–44 in *Human Agency and Language: Philosophical Papers I*, ed. Charles Taylor (Cambridge, UK: Cambridge University Press, 1985).

[26] Ibid., 34.

particular ways, but like these particular others in these particular *good* or valuable ways.[27]

For Taylor, the evaluative dimension of identification is what links personal identity to narrative:

[B]ecause we cannot but orient ourselves to the good, and thus determine our place relative to it and hence determine the direction of our lives, we must inescapably understand our lives in narrative form, as a "quest." But one could perhaps start from another point: because we have to determine our place in relation to the good, therefore we cannot be without an orientation to it, and hence must see our life in story.[28]

This link between identity and narrative, Taylor argues, derives from people's temporal relation to their understandings of the good. Life is not a single moment in which an individual has a static relation to the good as she conceives it. Instead, life is flux. As a person lives her life, she changes. She develops. At any given moment, an individual understands who she is as *who she has become*, in particular (on Taylor's view) as how her life has developed in relation to her understanding of the good. The best way to express such a sense of development, his claim is, is through a narrative – a sequence of chronologically ordered events – that traces where her life has taken her and how she has come to be the person she is today.[29]

On Taylor's view, then, the connection between (evaluative) identity and the narrative form is the temporal structure of people's relation to the good. Some narrative theorists suggest a second possible link. Narrative

---

[27] If I have captured Taylor's view correctly here, he is partly mistaken. People can have personal identities based on membership in "a certain class of people" whom they see as "marked off by certain qualities" that they *de-value*, as when members of Alcoholics Anonymous identify as alcoholics, a group they see as distinguished by pathological qualities. Taylor's larger point stands, however, since such a (negative) self-understanding would be no less evaluative than a positive identity. Both depend on and derive from background evaluative beliefs.

[28] Taylor, *Sources of the Self*, 51–2.

[29] Ibid., 47–8. In elaborating this claim, Taylor cites Heidegger on "the inescapable temporal structure of being in the world." Ibid., 47. His view here is consonant, as well, with that of Paul Ricoeur, for whom people reconstruct their lived experience in a specifically narrative form because it is narrative that best captures what Ricoeur calls the human experience of time (Ricoeur, *Time and Narrative*, vols. 1 and 3). Although we often represent time in a linear fashion, Ricoeur claims, we experience the temporal progression of actions and interactions from the particular perspectives we occupy, relating differently to now than to the past and future. "[N]arratives," according Ricoeur, "are the modes of discourse appropriate to our experience of time." Paul Ricoeur, "The Human Experience of Time and Narrative," *Research in Phenomenology* IX (1979): 17–34, here 25.

itself, many underscore, has an important evaluative dimension.[30] William Labov and Joshua Waletzky, analyzing some 600 narratives of personal experience that they collected from "unsophisticated" subjects, found that most include an "evaluation section," which "reveals the attitude of the narrator toward the narrative," for example, through direct statement ("I said to myself: this is it"), repetition ("And he didn't come back. And he didn't come back"), or reference to culturally particularistic evaluative markers ("I crossed myself").[31] The exceptions, they argue, are incomplete as narratives: at once difficult to understand and seemingly without a point. For example, consider the following excerpt from an interview in which a subject describes a cartoon about a pig he had watched on television:

See he – they threw him out, you know. So he wanted to get back in, 'cause, you know, it was sn-raining hard. So he got on this boat and tried to – go somewhere else. And the boat went over. And he tried to swim.

So this other man was fishing in the rain. So he seen the pig, and went over there and, and picked the pig up and put it in the boat and brought it back to shore, so he would land there.

And that was that.[32]

The excerpt includes a temporal sequence of events, which define what Labov and Waletzky call a "complication" ("they threw him out") and a resolution. But "[a] simple sequence of complication and result does not indicate to the listener the relative importance of these events or help him distinguish complication from *resolution*."[33]

Anyone who has been subjected to a story that caused her to wonder "*What's the point?*" will recognize that normative beliefs structure most narratives, even when those beliefs are not explicitly thematized. As

---

[30] For Charlotte Linde, for instance, evaluation is one of the five constituent parts of a narrative. Linde, *Life Stories: The Creation of Coherence* (New York: Oxford, 1993), chapter 3. For Elinor Ochs and Lisa Capps, moral stance is one of narratives' five key dimensions. Ochs and Capps, *Living Narrative: Creating Lives in Everyday Storytelling* (Cambridge, MA: Harvard University Press), chapter 1.

[31] William Labov and Joshua Waletzky, "Narrative Analysis: Oral Versions of Personal Experience," 3–38 in *Essays on the Verbal and Visual Arts*, ed. June Helm (Seattle: University of Washington Press, 1967), 3, 32–3.

[32] Ibid., 10.

[33] Ibid., 30, emphasis in original. Labov and Waletzky underscore that "there are a great variety of evaluation types, more or less deeply embedded in the narrative." "But," they write, "this variety should not obscure the fact that unevaluated narratives are exceptional as representations of personal experience, and unevaluated narratives lack structural definition." Ibid., 34.

implied by Labov and Waletzky, conventional narratives move from equilibrium to disequilibrium and finally to resolution and the restoration of equilibrium. They thus invoke and depend on an understanding, however tacit, of "how the world works" or "how things ought to be."[34] Hence if identification is evaluative – if the background belief that "*x* is good" strongly informs my sense of who I am and how my life has gone to this point – then narrative as a discursive form is well suited to expressing this self-understanding. I can structure the story of my life around equilibria (moments in which I achieve or come close to achieving *x*) and disequilibria (moments in which I fail to achieve or move away from the aim of achieving *x*).

Not only personal life narratives but also narratives of collective identity capture identity's evaluative dimension. Consider the following possible ways of defining what it means to be a real or a true American:

1. Real or true Americans hold Christian beliefs and values. They are family people: men and women who practice traditional marriage and uphold the sanctity of life.
2. Real or true Americans are "the 99 percent."[35] They are working people: women and men who value and promote fairness, economic justice, and equality.
3. Real or true Americans value individual freedom, first and foremost. They guard their personal liberties jealously, abjuring governmental intrusion, whether in the form of redistributive taxation or the regulation of marriage and other private relationships.

If you were tasked with trying to induce an audience to accept one of these three definitions over the others, how would you proceed? If you are like most political actors, an important part of your strategy would involve telling your audience a story: a story about the "Founding Fathers" having created America as a Christian theocracy, perhaps; or a story about the effect of the economic downturn on one or more "ordinary Americans"; or a story about how the "death tax" prevented a

---

[34] For Jerome Bruner, to be categorized as a narrative, a recounted sequence of events must "warrant telling about" by including a "tellable" disruption of an initial state of equilibrium. Bruner, "The Narrative Construction of Reality," 11. On his view, narrative involves "canonicity and breach": "to be worth telling, a tale must be about how an implicit canonical script has been breached, violated, or deviated from in a matter to do violence to … the 'legitimacy' of the canonical script." Ibid.

[35] "We are the 99 percent" was the slogan of the Occupy movement of 2011–12, a protest movement directed against economic inequality. See http://wearethe99percent.tumblr.com/. Accessed February 22, 2012.

simple farmer from passing his hard-earned money down to his children and his children's children.[36] A collective identity story that resonates with listeners' moral and ethical intuitions – with their general sense of "how the world works" and "how things ought to be" – is often more rhetorically effective than a logical argument or a rational proof, for the simple reason that background evaluative beliefs are often insusceptible to proof or to demonstration.

3. Bad Stories

It is for this reason that what Rogers Smith calls "stories of peoplehood" are so prevalent in political discourse.[37] Particularly significant are "ethically constitutive stories": "accounts that present membership in a particular people as somehow intrinsic to who its members really are, because of traits that are imbued with ethical significance."[38] Would-be leaders of a given political society, Smith argues, want its members to consider themselves part of a particular *kind* of collectivity: a political community that is circumscribed in certain ways and defined by certain constitutive traditions, values, and attributes. Specifically, they want members to consider themselves part of a political community for which they, themselves, are appropriate leaders.[39]

As Smith underscores, the processes through which "ethically constitutive" identity narratives are produced are competitive processes. There is never simply one story on offer: *the* story of "who we Americans are" (or we women). Instead, different actors, with different beliefs, desires, and interests, construct competing versions of "the story" of almost every group: nation, race, caste, class, community.

Taking Smith's insight as a starting point, I want to begin to make the case in this final section that, although the approach to theorizing identity sketched in section two – the approach that stresses identity's *narrative* construction – produces real insights, it also has important limits.

---

[36] See, respectively, John Eidsmoe, *Christianity and the Constitution: The Faith of Our Founding Fathers* (Ada, MI: Baker Academic, 1995) (Eidsmoe was the mentor of evangelical congresswoman and 2012 Republican presidential primary candidate Michelle Bachmann); http://wearethe99percent.tumblr.com/; and Michael Gratz and Ian Shapiro, *Death by a Thousand Cuts: The Fight over Taxing Inherited Wealth* (Princeton, NJ: Princeton University Press, 2005).

[37] Rogers Smith, *Stories of Peoplehood: The Politics and Morals of Political Membership* (Cambridge, UK: Cambridge University Press, 2003).

[38] Ibid., 64.

[39] Ibid., chapter 2.

In the previous section, I highlighted the strengths of the narrative identity approach, suggesting that the selective, exegetical, productive, and evaluative qualities of identification render narrative a discursive form that is well suited to identity construction. I now turn to the shortcomings of the narrative approach. Although storytelling is an important part of how people *produce* identities, my claim is, it is not the only, and it is not the most significant way they *reproduce* them.

Let me begin by considering the relation of mutual constitution between, on one hand, collective identity stories, and on the other hand, stories of personal identity. As K. Anthony Appiah has argued, "By way of my identity I fit my life story ... into larger stories – for example, of a people, a religious tradition, or a race."[40] At the same time, I fit those larger stories into my own life narrative. As Steven Mullins tells his "American story," he weaves into the story of his life a narrative of American national identity: a story, already in circulation at the moment in which he formulates his own life narrative, about the boundaries to the category "American"; about the actors, actions, and attributes that fit that category; about the right or the proper relations among members of that category; and about right relations across its boundaries, between members and nonmembers.

Personal identity narratives attain intelligibility in part by incorporating collective identity narratives. ("I'm proud to be an American," Steven Mullins tells me, and because he cites a story that I know, I know what he means.) At the same time, collective identity stories take root, they survive, in part through incorporation into personal identity stories. (The version of "the American story" that Mullins cites survives in part because he and others cite it.) To the extent that identities are produced and reproduced *as narratives*, in other words, collective identities must work *through* narratives of personal identity. They can succeed only if some substantial number of individuals build them into their stories of "who [they] are."

Hence one might expect only those collective identities to succeed that take the form of *good stories*. By "good" stories, I do not mean *objectively* good stories. Instead, I define "good" relative to dominant beliefs. An identity story according to which "who we are" is a patriarchal

---

[40] K. Anthony Appiah, "The State and the Shaping of Identity," in *Tanner Lectures on Human Values*, ed. Grethe B. Peterson (Salt Lake City: University of Utah Press, 2002): 235–97, here 243.

society can be a good story, if dominant beliefs support patriarchal relations. An identity story according to which "who we are" is a nation of slaveholders can be a good story, if dominant beliefs support the institution of slavery. So, too, can a story be good if it incorporates objectively false claims, such as the claim "the world is flat," just so long as those claims are widely believed to be true. Good stories, in short, are politically powerful stories: stories that resonate with their audiences sufficiently that, in a given context, they can prevail in political contest and become dominant.

More specifically, good stories exhibit the following three traits. First, they are *credible* stories: stories that accord with widely known, or at least knowable facts, and/or with widely held beliefs about the world as it is. Good stories are, second, *legitimate* stories, where *legitimate* is used in its strictly sociological sense to signal stories that accord with widely endorsed moral and/or ethical principles.[41] Good stories are, third, minimally *coherent* stories: stories the basic elements of which (whether empirical claims about the self or the social world, or moral or ethical claims about what is right or what is good) accord with, or at the very least, do not obviously conflict with, one another.

Thus a story of American national identity would be a good story if the elements that comprised it (for example, the definition of "who we Americans are" in terms of our strong valuation of liberty and equality, including racial equality) accorded with widely known or readily knowable facts about the world. When Mullins tells me that "being American [means] ... freedom of speech, freedom of thought ... freedom of actions," he goes on to suggest that this claim accords with knowable facts about the world by backing up his assertion with what he presents as supporting evidence. "The fact that you can come to my house," he tells me, "and even talk to people about this, and I can say anything to you today without being in trouble, is something three-fourths of this world cannot do."

But Mullins's version of the American story is not entirely good along this first dimension. The expropriation of Native Americans by the early colonists, the enslavement of blacks from the colonial era through the

---

[41] Allen Buchanan and Robert Keohane distinguish legitimacy's normative and sociological senses. "To say that an institution is legitimate in the normative sense," they write, "is to assert that it has the *right to rule* ... An institution is legitimate in the sociological sense when it is widely *believed* to have the right to rule." Buchanan and Keohane, "The Legitimacy of Global Governance Institutions," *Ethics and International Affairs* 20, 4 (2006): 405–37, here 405.

time of the Civil War, and the disfranchisement of white women until the passage of the Nineteenth Amendment in 1920 are all readily knowable facts: facts at odds with Mullins's sanitized version of "The Revolution" and of "Patriot" values.[42] Other readily knowable facts at odds with Mullins's narrative of Americans as a people who strongly value racial equality include the disproportionately high rates of African American incarceration and the gross racial inequalities in income and wealth that characterize the contemporary United States.[43] If you are strongly committed to the narrative identity thesis sketched in section two, however, you might assume that Steven Mullins does not know about, or perhaps has repressed his knowledge of, contemporary racial inequality and the racist aspects of his nation's history. Alternatively, you might assume that a strong valuation of racial equality functions for Mullins much as does knowing and using the English language: that is, that it characterizes *real* or *true* Americans, even if many who are nominally American fall short of this ideal.

If you are strongly committed to the narrative identity thesis, you will make some such assumption. Otherwise, you would think, Mullins would reject this particular version of "the American story," since he would find jarring its discord with what he knows to be true.

You will make similar assumptions about the other ways stories can be "good" (or not good). You will assume a story will have to be legitimate (in the sociological sense) to succeed. You might think, for instance, that even if it is not wholly surprising that Mullins defines American identity in linguistic terms, it would be quite surprising were he to define it in

---

[42] Mullins does, at one point in his narrative, make several oblique references to the historical fact of racial inequality in America. Discussing his maternal great-great-great grandfather, he tells me: "Now, the story has it, that he brought with him the first black man to this area ... Probably it was a freed slave, or, you know, we don't really know, but he brought a black man to these parts." (The statement is confusing, perhaps reflecting Mullins's own uncertainty. If the black man was a freed slave, then in what sense did the white ancestor "bring him" to Ohio?) Moments later, Mullins notes that his father's ancestors were "Southern Virginians, you know, that ... were on that political spectrum, totally opposite of [how] I was brought up." His father's great-grandfather, he adds, married into a family "that was at one time the largest slaveholders in the state of Virginia."

[43] Of course, Mullins is hardly unique in citing a national identity story that is less than completely "good" along this first dimension. The unity of every nation is a fiction, and historically, the production of national unity has depended on both internal and external othering. See Clarissa Hayward, "Binding Problems, Boundary Problems: The Trouble with 'Democratic Citizenship,'" 181–205 in *Identities, Affiliations, and Allegiances*, ed. Seyla Benhabib, Ian Shapiro, and Danilo Petranovic (Cambridge, UK: Cambridge University Press, 2007).

explicitly racial terms. Such a definition (you might argue) would violate
the principle – widely endorsed since the second half of the last century –
that American national identity should be open to all without regard to
racial identity. Were Mullins to attempt to incorporate into his life narrative an explicitly racial version of the narrative of American national
identity (you might think), he would be disquieted by its violation of the
widely endorsed principle of racial inclusiveness.

You will assume, finally, that a collective identity story must be minimally coherent to succeed: that the various elements that comprise an
identity narrative must complement, or at the very least that they must
not directly contradict, one another. If Mullins believes and endorses one
element of the national identity narrative that he incorporates into his
narrative of personal identity (if, for example, he endorses a principle of
racial equality), then, you will think, he will not endorse a conflicting element, such as an institution or a practice that promotes racial inequality.
Were Mullins to attempt to weave into his life narrative a narrative of
national identity that was self-contradictory in this way, he would experience cognitive dissonance and revise or even reject the narrative.

These assumptions bring to mind Alasdair MacIntyre's claims about
what he calls "epistemological crises."[44] Not only scientists and philoso-
phers, MacIntyre suggests, but also "ordinary agents" – people like you
or me or Steven Mullins – find themselves thrown into such crises when
faced with the fact that part or all of the narratives they have been telling themselves about the world and about their lived experience cannot
comprehend some experiential datum or data. MacIntyre conceives the
trigger of such crises in terms of a new experience: one that challenges
some extant (and the implication is: some extant *good*) narrative.

Suppose, for example, that Steven Mullins were to be presented with
the opportunity to sacrifice his life for his country but, in a moment
of intense fear, were to run away or to otherwise back down. Suppose
Mullins were to choose to save his own life rather than "die for [his]
nation." By MacIntyre's account, at that point Steven Mullins should
experience "radical interpretive doubt."[45] He should wonder how it is
that he could have been so terribly mistaken about himself and about
his patriotism. Mullins then would face the task, MacIntyre's claim is, of
rewriting the story that he tells himself (and others) about his personal

[44] Alasdair MacIntyre, "Epistemological Crises, Dramatic Narrative, and the Philosophy of
Science," *The Monist* 60, 4 (October 1977): 453–72.
[45] Ibid., 455.

identity: reinterpreting all the experiences he previously had interpreted, but now in a way that accounts for both his failure to die for America when given the chance to do so *and* his previous belief that, faced with such a choice, he would act otherwise. Mullins would face a similar task, on MacIntyre's view, were he to confront some datum or data that challenged his narrative of Americans as deeply committed to racial equality.

MacIntyre's unstated premise is that "ordinary agents," much like good scientists, have a relatively low tolerance for internal inconsistencies in the stories they tell about the world and their experience in it, and for dissonance between those stories and their considered ontological and evaluative beliefs. In practice, however, ordinary agents often exhibit a very high tolerance for such incoherence and such dissonance. Ordinary agents very often are not thrown into epistemological crises when new data contradict old stories. Indeed, they very often do not revise even those identity narratives that seem in desperate need of revision.

I would be willing to bet that Steven Mullins has been exposed, on multiple occasions, to data that contradict his narrative of American identity. But I do not need to make that wager to illustrate my point. Think back to the gender narrative cited in the introduction to this book: a narrative that divides the social world into some, but not other possible categories (man/woman, male/female) and assigns those categories, not only actors, but also actions (leading and following) and attributes (assertiveness, strength / passivity, gracefulness). As noted in the introduction, I personally do not endorse that narrative. In this, I am hardly alone. At least since Simone de Beauvoir's *The Second Sex*, gender identity has been rationally deconstructed.[46] It has been critically interrogated and it has been normatively critiqued. Judith Butler famously extended this critical-deconstructive project to include not only gender, but also biological sex.[47] Still, as Linda Zerilli notes, most people (myself included) continue to perform their sexed and their gendered identities and to perform them well, even though – even *as* – they repudiate the narratives from which those identities were constructed.[48]

[46] Simone de Beauvoir, *The Second Sex*, transl. and ed. H. M. Parshley (New York: Vintage, 1989 [1952]).

[47] See especially Judith Butler, *Gender Trouble: Feminism and the Subversion of Identity*, second edition (New York: Routledge, 1990).

[48] Linda Zerilli, "Doing without Knowing: Feminism's Politics of the Ordinary," *Political Theory* 26, 4 (August 1998): 435–58. See also Amy Allen, *The Politics of Our Selves: Power, Autonomy, and Gender in Contemporary Critical Theory* (New York: Columbia University Press, 2007).

Or consider the principal example on which the remainder of this book focuses: the example of racial identities. In his Tanner Lecture, one of Anthony Appiah's principal claims is that racial identity stories are not good stories. Appiah focuses on the third of the three senses in which I have suggested that narratives of collective identity can be (not) good. He argues that dominant racial identities in this country fail to pass a minimum threshold of internal coherence. The principal reason he cites is that conforming to some of the norms that comprise these identities militates against conforming to others.[49] For example, the so-called one-drop rule, according to which persons with any African American ancestry count as African American, defines as black a substantially large number of people who are widely perceived as and who are routinely treated as if they were white.[50] Combined with the norm of black solidarity, which directs those who understand themselves to be African American to act solidaristically toward other members of their racial identity group (e.g., by supporting policies, such as affirmative action policies, that promote the interests of black Americans, even when and if such policies do not promote individual self-interest), the one-drop rule, if strictly followed, could lead blacks to support policies promoting the interests of nontrivial numbers of people whom they regard as white: people who in fact enjoy the privileges attached in this country to white racial status.[51]

As Appiah notes, dominant racial identity stories are not only internally incoherent. They are also inconsistent with readily knowable facts about the world, most significantly the fact that scientific evidence unequivocally refutes popular understandings of "race" as biological type.[52]

---

[49] Appiah, "The State and the Shaping of Identity," 282.

[50] As many as twenty-eight million by the mid-twentieth century, he suggests, citing a study published in 1958. Ibid., p. 284, note 3.

[51] Ibid., 286.

[52] The notion of "races" as human types analogous to animal species, which first gained credence in the nineteenth century, was discredited in the middle of the twentieth. Michael Banton explains that, "where 'race' suggests that individuals may be classed as belonging in a relatively few discontinuous categories, phenotypical variation more readily implies a continuous variation in which differences of appearance shade into one another with no sharp lines of variation." Banton, *Racial Theories*, second edition (Cambridge, UK: Cambridge University Press, 1998), 13. In the wake of the Human Genome Project in the early 2000s, the debate about biological race was revisited. Several studies found patterned differences between African and non-African population groups in the structure of the DNA sequence: differences that can have important implications for medical treatment. Participants in the scientific debate agreed, however, that there is a nontrivial gap between patterns of human genetic variation and "race" understood as biological type. Summing up the research presented at the inaugural "Human Genome Variation and 'Race'" meeting in 2004, Charmaine Royal and Georgia Dunston write, "[T]here

What is more (and which Appiah, in this particular lecture, does not stress), many racial identities, including the identities of the racially privileged, contain elements that are, and that have been at least since the time of the civil rights movement, widely regarded as illegitimate.[53]

Dominant racial identity stories, in short, are bad stories. Granted, one can imagine a retelling of these narratives (and a reconstruction of the identities to which they correspond) such that they would take the form of good (credible, legitimate, and coherent) stories. Lionel McPherson and Tommie Shelby, responding to Appiah's claims about the incoherence of black American racial identity, underscore that a sense of solidarity among African Americans, along with a sense of shared political interests and collective political will, are in principle compatible with an understanding of race as socially significant, but not biologically grounded.[54] A good racial identity story, on their view, would be one that was credible, legitimate, and coherent: one that put ending racial subjugation at the fore.

But such an understanding of race is not the understanding most contemporary Americans adopt and employ. In Chapters 3 and 5, respectively, I explore the racial understandings of my interview respondents who identify as "African American / black" and "white." Notwithstanding significant differences between the two groups, most understand "race" not only and not principally in social and political terms, but also and significantly, as a marker of shared ancestry and common origin. My

---

seems to be consensus that 'race,' whether imposed or self-identified, is a weak surrogate for various genetic and non-genetic factors in correlations with health status." Royal and Dunston, "Changing the Paradigm from 'Race' to Human Genome Variation," *Nature Genetics Supplement* 36, 11: 5–7.

[53] Examples are some whites' definitions of white and black identity in terms of positive and negative stereotypical traits, such as intelligence / lack of intelligence or responsibility / irresponsibility. Such definitions are less prevalent in the post–civil rights era then they were in the middle decades of the past century, but they are far from extinct. See Eduardo Bonilla-Silva, *Racism without Racists: Color-Blind Racism and the Persistence of Racial Inequality in the United States*, second edition (New York: Rowman and Littlefield, 2006), especially chapter 1. Other examples are the categorization and perceptions that inform what Bonilla-Silva calls "color-blind racism," including the inability or refusal to see white privilege, which perpetuates, by obfuscating, racial hierarchy. Ibid.

[54] Lionel McPherson and Tommie Shelby, "Blackness and Blood: Interpreting African-American Identity," *Philosophy and Public Affairs* 32, 2 (2004): 171–91. McPherson and Shelby perform a thought experiment in which people who identify as black Americans (and whom others thus identify) are compelled to choose between rejecting or accepting *both* the one-drop rule and solidaristic identification with "functional whites." "It is obvious," they assert, "that the African Americans under consideration would overwhelmingly choose the first option."

respondents are (to recall Labov and Waletzky's term) "unsophisticated" in the sense that none is a natural or social scientist, or a social theorist. But even academics who are fully aware of the speciousness of claims about race as biological type very often adopt this commonsensical usage. "Her mother is black, but she looks white," I might remark to you in conversation, even if in my scholarly work I would studiously avoid any suggestion that "black" and "white" racial identities are biological inheritances made plain through phenotypical variation.

In short, people very often reach for, they very often use, as they interpret and negotiate the social world, collective identities that, when spelled out in storied form, are not good stories. People often use such identities even when they know on some level – even when, if pressed, they would readily acknowledge – that the stories that support them are not credible, legitimate, and coherent. People often use identities that are supported by bad stories, not just to characterize the beliefs of others, but also as component parts of the stories they tell about their own lives: as component parts, that is to say, of their personal identities. They often incorporate into their personal identities collective identities (of race, of gender, of nation) that an Alasdair MacIntyre would expect them to find unincorporable.

How can that be?

To answer this question is the principal task of the remainder of this book: a task that requires distinguishing the processes through which people *produce* identity narratives from the processes through which they *reproduce* them. If the telling of identity stories is one way people learn their collective identities, my principal claim is, it is never the only way. People learn identities *practically*, as well. They learn who they are in an identitarian sense as they learn how to "get by" in institutional settings and in other contexts that are structured by identitarian norms and expectations.

Consider a very basic skill that every competent social actor must master: the skill of communicating with others. When a young child forms her first words, when she forms her first sentences, she begins to learn, not just how to communicate effectively the ideas that she forms in her mind (that is, not just how to match the thoughts she has to those sounds that, in her language, represent them), but, more specifically, how to communicate in the ways "we" do.

The child begins to learn how to talk like "one of us": like one of the members of the identity groups of which she herself is a member – even

as she learns that she *is* "one of us." She begins to learn to talk the way
that a girl talks, for example. She begins to learn to talk the way that an
African American girl from the Bronx talks, or the way that an upper-
middle-class white girl from suburban Connecticut talks. She begins to
acquire a set of communicative habits and dispositions, that is to say,
including habits of pronouncing particular sounds in particular ways,
habits of gesturing, of holding the body, of gazing at (or away from) her
interlocutors, habits of interrupting, or of acquiescing when others inter-
rupt. She begins to acquire dispositions to use particular speech patterns,
such as qualifiers or hedges, tag questions, or verbal intensifiers or rein-
forcers.[55] She begins to acquire these habits and dispositions as she interacts with those around her: as she interacts with socializing agents whose
communicative habits are, themselves, shaped by identitarian norms and
expectations.[56]

Such skills are sometimes taught and learned through explicitly thematized identity narratives. Think of highly gendered children's stories
like *Cinderella*, *Rapunzel*, or for that matter, *The Princess and the Pea*.

---

[55] "Sort of" and "I guess" are examples of qualifiers or hedges. Tag questions, such as
"right?" are questions that are "tagged" to the end of declarative sentences. "So" is a
common example of a verbal intensifier, and "mmmm hmmmm" is a common reinforcer.
That these and other communicative dispositions are strongly gendered is a robust finding
in the social psychological literatures on communication. See, for example, Linda Carli,
"Gender, Language, and Influence," *Journal of Personality and Social Psychology*," 59, 5
(1990): 941–51; Mary Anne Fitzpatrick, Anthony Mulac, and Kathryn Dindia, "Gender-
Preferential Language Use in Spouse and Stranger Interaction," *Journal of Language
and Social Psychology* 14, 1–2 (March 1995): 18–39; Howard Giles and Richard Street,
"Communicator Characteristics and Behavior," 103–61 in *Handbook of Interpersonal
Communication*, second edition, ed. Mark Knapp and Gerald Miller (Thousand Oaks,
CA: Sage, 1994); and Catherine Johnson, "Gender, Legitimate Authority, and Leader-
Subordinate Conversations," *American Sociological Review* 59 (February 1994): 122–
35. For a discussion, see Clarissa Hayward, "Doxa and Deliberation," *Critical Review
of International Social and Political Philosophy* 7, 1 (Spring 2004), 1–24, on which this
discussion draws.

[56] In Pierre Bourdieu's terms, the child begins to develop a *habitus*: a complex of relatively
enduring dispositions, which include, but are not limited to, linguistic and other communicative dispositions. *Habitus* encompasses habits of action, perception, and valuation,
which manifest themselves in, for example, tastes and distastes, ways of comprehending
and interpreting and evaluating a wide range of social phenomena, and ways of walking
and holding the body. See Bourdieu, *Outline of a Theory of Practice*, transl. Richard
Nice (Cambridge, MA: Cambridge University Press, 1977), especially chapter 2, and
Bourdieu, *Language and Symbolic Power*, ed. John Thompson, transl. Gino Raymond
and Matthew Adamson (Cambridge, MA: Harvard University Press, 1991). For a thor-
ough overview of the role the concept of habitus plays in Bourdieu's social theory, see
David Swartz, *Culture and Power: The Sociology of Pierre Bourdieu* (Chicago, IL:
University of Chicago Press, 1998), chapter 5.

More commonly, however, they are learned *implicitly*: through subtle rewards (an affirming smile) and sanctions (an almost-stifled laugh), or through everyday contact with the material forms that embody those narratives (gender-segregated spaces, for example, like the girls' and the boys' restrooms).

Recall the claim (from the discussion of Rogers Smith's work) that collective identity construction is a competitive process. As actors create and circulate identity stories, they compete with other actors who offer other stories of who "we" are (as a race, a nation, a people) and of who "they" are ("our" others). When a narrative emerges successful from such competition, the winners do not rest content continuing to tell and retell it. Instead, they institutionalize it. They build it into rules and laws and other institutions that define norms and standards that distribute rewards and sanctions as the narrative dictates. Consider Richard Ford's example (cited in the introduction) of the rewards and sanctions distributed through the practice of dancing tango. Or, if tango seems trivial, consider the economic and social rewards that attend in the contemporary United States to becoming and to remaining a wife. A woman who refuses to perform well her identity as institutionalized in this state-sanctioned role will – *even if she is wholly unconvinced by the narrative that informs that identity* – face significant sanctions.

Winners translate successful narratives into institutional form, then. They also translate them into material form or (to borrow a term from Pierre Bourdieu's lexicon) they "objectify" them. Bourdieu offers the examples of the division between the Kabyle house and the public world (the assembly, the field, the market), and the division of spaces interior to the house itself. In constructing such divisions (in building walls and relegating particular persons and particular activities to one side or the other), people objectify identity categories and also the meanings and expectations they attach to those categories.[57] They make them into objects, in other words. They quite literally build gendered (and other) collective identities into material forms.

To continue with Bourdieu's example, the Kabyle designate specifically "male" spaces, which they make the spaces of politics, production, and exchange. They designate "female spaces," which they make the spaces of domestic work, sex, and reproduction. As people engage in practical activities in such physical spaces, his claim is (as they sow and reap in the fields, as they buy and sell at market, as they cook and care for the sick

[57] Bourdieu, *Outline of a Theory of Practice*, chapter 2.

and the dying in the house), they learn and they relearn *implicitly* the meanings built into these material forms.[58]

Implicit learning differs from explicit learning in that it is corporeal. It happens not only and not principally at the level of the conscious mind, but also, and significantly, in the muscles, in the nerves, in the tendons that make up a human body. Think of how you learned (and how, if you were to stop now and concentrate, you might recall) the rules for factoring quadratic equations. Then try, if you can, to remember how you learned (and think how, daily, as if by instinct, you are re-called) to speak (or to walk or to sit or to eat) like "a civilized woman" (or like "a real man.") The latter differs from the former in that it is an instance of, not rule following – not deliberate conformity to an explicit norm – so much as the practical mastery of a social competence.[59] It shapes your action less through conscious thought and judgment than through (in Bourdieu's words) a "feel for the game."[60]

In drawing attention to these aspects of Pierre Bourdieu's work, I do not mean to endorse his social theory *tout court*. As critics have argued, Bourdieu tends to emphasize the structural determination of practice at the expense of reflective human agency, and to focus on social reproduction at the expense of transformative collective action.[61] Nevertheless, I

[58] Bourdieu treats *habitus* as it applies to gender identity at greater length in Pierre Bourdieu, *Masculine Domination*, transl. Richard Nice (Cambridge, UK: Polity Press, 2001). For an insightful discussion of Bourdieu's treatment of gender identity, see Leslie McCall, "Does Gender Fit? Bourdieu, Feminism, and Conceptions of Social Order," *Theory and Society* 21, 6 (December 1992): 837–67.

[59] See Charles Taylor, "To Follow a Rule ... ," 45–60 in *Bourdieu: Critical Perspectives*, ed. Edward Lipuma, Moishe Postone, and Craig Calhoun (Chicago, IL: University of Chicago Press, 1993).

[60] "Action guided by a 'feel for the game,'" he writes, "has all the appearance of the rational action that an impartial observer, endowed with all the necessary information and capable of mastering it rationally, would deduce." "And yet," he continues, "it is not based on reason. You need only think of the impulsive decision made by the tennis player who runs up to the net, to understand that it has nothing in common with the learned construction that the coach, after analysis, draws up in order to explain it and deduce communicable lessons from it." Pierre Bourdieu, "Fieldwork in Philosophy," 3–33 in *In Other Words: Essays towards a Reflexive Sociology*, transl. Matthew Adamson (Stanford, CA: Stanford University Press, 1990), 11.

[61] See, for example, Paul DiMaggio, "Review Essay: On Pierre Bourdieu," *American Journal of Sociology* 84, 6 (May 1979): 1460–74; Craig Calhoun, "Habitus, Field, and Capital: Historical Specificity in the Theory of Practice," 132–61 in *Critical Social Theory*, ed. Craig Calhoun (Oxford: Blackwell, 1995); James Bohman, "Practical Reason and Cultural Constraint: Agency in Bourdieu's Theory of Practice," 129–52 in *Bourdieu: A Critical Reader*, ed. Richard Shusterman (Oxford: Blackwell, 1999); and Richard Jenkins, *Pierre Bourdieu*, second edition (London and New York: Routledge, 2002).

want to suggest, his work serves as a useful counterweight to theories of narrative identity. An identity, I have argued, is comprised of sets of rules and norms that divide and sort the social world: sets that are very often constructed in narrative form. But if people can be incentivized by institutions that distribute rewards and sanctions, if they can be taught classificatory dispositions implicitly through bodily contact with material forms, then the narrative production of identity is fully compatible with the successful *reproduction* of identities that, when (or if) spelled out as narratives, (would) take the form of bad stories.

Assume you have learned, *practically*, that a particular identity category is meaningful. Assume you have learned practically which social norms and expectations attach to that category, and also that that category names you. If so, you have learned your identity without thematizing – and hence, necessarily, without interrogating – the narratives from which it was constructed. Were you now, in this moment, to find yourself confronted by some experiential datum that the narrative of your identity cannot comprehend, you might very well proceed happily on your way, wholly untroubled by the epistemological crisis into which that datum might, in principle, have thrust you. The practical reproduction of identity lends it a resilience it would not otherwise enjoy.

I learn the feel for the gender game with the help of my Comme Il Fauts. I learn it with the help of the gendered division of the public and nonpublic spaces that I inhabit corporeally. And even if I take my shoes off, I will still dance "properly," because I want the rewards that people distribute through the practice of dancing the tango.

In the remainder of this book, I explore in greater depth the institutionalization and the objectification of one set of collective identities: dominant racial identities in the contemporary United States, identities that are deeply entwined with the American national identity that Steven Mullins cites when he tells his life story. Over the course of the following four chapters, I trace two principal paths by which institutionalization and objectification can occur. In Chapters 2 and 3, I make the case that a story can be institutionalized and objectified *because it is a good story* in the sense (sketched at the start of this section) that it is a politically powerful story. Once such a narrative has been institutionalized and objectified, my claim is, it works as a frame to ordinary stories, influencing people's beliefs and actions, *even if a shift at the level of discourse changes dominant perceptions of the original narrative.*

The second path, which I trace in Chapters 4 and 5, is different. Here the relevant identity story, at the time of its institutionalization and objectification, is *not* a good story. It is a narrative that many people, perhaps even most people, do not find compelling. But a contingency (in the case on which I focus, the dislocations produced by the Great Depression) opens up space for, not a new story, so much as a new set of institutionalizations and objectifications. The result is, again, ordinary stories – everyday stories in which the original narrative, now institutionalized and objectified, functions as a frame – but with the following twist: *the institutionalization and objectification can make the bad story better.* Institutionalization and objectification, in other words, not only can resist, but at times can *effect* change at the level of discourse.

This argument starts, in the next chapter, with an historical account of the production and reproduction of racial identities in the early twentieth-century American polity. Focusing on the years leading up to and encompassing the Great Depression and the New Deal, I consider the racial narratives that were dominant at that time: a period that I want to suggest was a critical juncture. How, my principal question is, were these narratives institutionalized and objectified? Through what processes and through what laws, rules, and material forms were (and are) they practically reproduced?

2

Black Places

It is only a slight exaggeration to say there are as many definitions of *narrative* as there are examples: definitions that range from the relatively narrow to the exceedingly expansive.[1] Those who favor a definition toward the narrow end of the spectrum argue that to engage in what James Phelan calls "narrative imperialism" – to define more and more discursive forms as narratives – is to empty the category of meaning.[2] The point is well taken. My schedule of meetings for today is not a narrative. My course syllabus is not a narrative. My curriculum vitae is not a narrative. Nevertheless, in this chapter, I intend to err on the side of expansiveness in my thinking about racial identity narratives by suggesting that not only novels and films, but also texts as seemingly (to recall Jerome Bruner's term) "paradigmatic" as an early American real estate textbook, have an important narrative logic.

Consider a prototypical narrative, one that would fit even the most restrictive of definitions: D. W. Griffith's notorious 1915 film *The Birth of a Nation*. Based on Thomas Dixon's novel *The Clansmen*, the film is set on the Cameron Plantation in Piedmont, South Carolina, where benevolent masters and happy slaves live together in a "quaintly way that is to be

[1] See, for example, H. Porter Abbott, *The Cambridge Introduction to Narrative*, second edition (Cambridge, UK: Cambridge University Press, 2008), especially chapters two and three; and the articles collected in David Herman, ed. *The Cambridge Companion to Narrative* (Cambridge, UK: Cambridge University Press, 2007), especially chapter two, Marie-Laure Ryan's "Toward a Definition of Narrative."

[2] James Phelan, "Who's Here? Thoughts on Narrative Identity and Narrative Imperialism," *Narrative* 13, 3 (October 2005).

no more."[3] The South's defeat in the Civil War changes everything. Freed former slaves, egged on by carpetbaggers and black Union soldiers, roam the Southern streets, terrorizing innocent whites. They take over the polls and Congress, and they even, as one dramatic title card announces, pass a bill "providing for the intermarriage of blacks and whites."[4] Finally, just when it seems all is lost (the young Cameron daughter jumps off a cliff to escape rape by a black man), the Ku Klux Klan comes to the rescue and conquers the rebels. Order is restored.

The 1923 real estate textbook I cite in the first section of this chapter differs from *Birth of a Nation* in obvious ways. It presents itself as factual and general: not a story about particular characters and particular happenings, but rather an objective explanation of scientific facts, such as the economic laws that govern real estate markets. There is a "natural inclination," the authors inform their readers, for black people "to live together in their own communities."[5] When African Americans moved north starting around the time of the First World War, the text explains, they began to "overrun their old districts," "naturally" causing land values to fall.[6] The best solution to this difficult problem is "rigid segregation."[7]

Here we have what is clearly not a prototypical narrative along the lines of *Birth of a Nation*. Nor, however, is it (as it purports to be) an objective account of empirical reality. It is a *representation* of reality: one that is selective (for example, in that it takes as its starting point segregation, rather than the events that preceded and caused segregation), interpretive (consider its interpretation of segregation as "natural" and of desegregation as causing a decline in property values), and evaluative (for instance, in its not-so-subtle assertion that African Americans "overrunning" segregated neighborhoods is a bad thing). What is more – and much like Griffith's film – it sketches a temporal sequence that includes an equilibrium state (racial segregation) followed by a disruption (blacks move north and beyond the boundaries of black ghettos), which it represents

---

[3] Thomas Dixon, *The Clansmen* (Lexington: University Press of Kentucky, 1970 [1905]). Title card quoted in Donald Bogle, *Toms, Coons, Mulattoes, Mammies, and Bucks: An Interpretive History of Blacks in American Films*, fourth edition (New York: Continuum, 2001), 10.

[4] Quoted in Bogle, *Toms, Coons, Mulattoes, Mammies, and Bucks*, 12.

[5] Robert F. Bingham and Stanley L. McMichael, *City Growth and Values* (Cleveland, OH: The Stanley McMichael Publishing Organization, 1923), 181.

[6] Ibid.

[7] Ibid.

as causing a disequilibrium (land values fall).[8] There is no resolution to this particular story – no happily ever after in which the KKK saves the day – but there is a clear suggestion for how we might arrive at resolution (by imposing "rigid segregation").

David Herman argues compellingly that narrative is characterized by membership gradience. Some members of the category are more obviously members than others, even if those others count as narratives (just as robins are more obviously members of the category "bird" than are emus, even if emus count as birds).[9] "Narrative" is characterized by category gradience, as well. Categories shade into one another, such that it can be difficult to know where exactly to draw the line (Herman illustrates with the example of the categories "tall person" and "person of average height.")[10] Texts that have some narrative qualities, but that are not prototypical narratives, he suggests, might be called "narrativized descriptions": a label I would happily accept for some of the texts I cite in the first part of this chapter.[11] I am sympathetic, as well, with Marie-Laure Ryan's suggestion that "rather than regarding narrativity as a strictly binary feature, that is, as a property that a given text either has or doesn't have," we view it as a "fuzzy set allowing differing degrees of membership."[12]

In short, although I will continue to use the term *narrative* as I turn from personal identity narratives to collective identity narratives, I have no interest in staking out definitional territory. My focus is on dominant racial narratives in the United States in the early decades of the last century, and my principal concern is, not how those narratives were told and

---

[8] Throughout this book, I use the word *ghetto* rather than a more euphemistic term, such as *inner city*, to stress the involuntary quality of American racial segregation. A *ghetto*, according to Loïc Wacquant, is "a bounded, racially and/or culturally uniform sociospatial formation based on the forcible relegation of a negatively typed population … to a reserved territory in which this population develops a set of specific institutions that operate both as a functional substitute for, and as a protective buffer from, the dominant institutions of the encompassing society." Wacquant, "The New Urban Color Line: The State and Fate of the Ghetto in Postfordist America," 231–76 in *Social Theory and the Politics of Identity*, ed. Craig Calhoun (Oxford, UK: Basil Blackwell), here 236.

[9] David Herman, ed., "Introduction," in *The Cambridge Companion to Narrative* (Cambridge, UK: Cambridge University Press, 2007), 8. See also George Lakoff, *Women, Fire, and Dangerous Things* (Chicago, IL: University of Chicago Press, 1987) and Eleanor Rosch, "Principles of Categorization," 91–108 in *Fuzzy Grammar: A Reader*, ed. Bas Aarts, David Denison, Evelien Keizer, and Gergana Popova (Oxford: Oxford University Press, 2004), on which Herman draws.

[10] Ibid. The example comes from Lakoff, *Women, Fire, and Dangerous Things*, 45.

[11] Ibid., 11.

[12] Ryan, "Toward a Definition of Narrative," 28.

retold, but how they were institutionalized and how they were objectified in the physical spaces of America's cities and suburbs.

The chapter's principal claims are three. First, over the course of the early decades of the twentieth century, stories of race as a significant and durable feature of the social world – stories of race as causing different traits and behaviors, and hence warranting the differential treatment of members of "the black and white races" – were institutionalized and objectified through the construction of the black ghetto and the racially exclusive white enclave. Second, the systematic channeling of public and private investment away from black ghettos and toward white suburbs layered material inequalities atop identitarian distinctions, thus helping produce, not just racial identities, but also a (white) racial *interest* in state-subsidized home ownership and residential exclusivity. Third, the concentration in "black places" of joblessness, of poverty, and of a host of social problems that accompany concentrated poverty transformed what were, in a causal sense, *collective* problems into – both in practical effect and in popular consciousness – "black problems."

1. Racial Stories, Racialized Places

Calvin Moore lives near the railroad tracks that mark the border between Columbus, Ohio's Near East Side ghetto and the adjacent affluent and predominantly white suburb of Bexley.[13] The experience of crossing those railroad tracks, Moore says, is "like stepping into a different world." He explains:

One side of the tracks, you know, if I cross the tracks ... into the hood, I'm back into the lower income area. And when I cross back over the tracks, I'm in high society: Bexley area, the more conservative-type area ... It's like ... crossing over into another state.

Moore, who was born and raised in Birmingham, Alabama, self-identifies as African American. This racial identity category, he tells me during an interview in which I prompt him to name and to reflect on his social identities, is "embedded in [his] mind."[14] "[Race] was installed in my mind

---

[13] The Near East Side is an area of Columbus, just east of downtown, bounded, roughly, by Fifth Avenue on the north, by Interstate 71 on the west, by Interstate 70 on the south, and on the east, by Alum Creek and the city's eastern limits, where it abuts Bexley.

[14] See note 1, Chapter 1 for a description of this semi-structured interview that followed a life history interview. For a detailed schedule of interview questions, see the appendix on method.

as a child," Moore explains. "You know, there's certain places you don't
go. There's certain people you don't socialize with." He characterizes the
Birmingham neighborhood in which he grew up as "an all-black neighborhood." He tells me the school he attended was "an all-black school."
He identifies by name what he refers to as "white" neighborhoods in and
around the city of Birmingham: neighborhoods he says he was taught
at an early age to avoid. If Moore's racial identity is "embedded in his
mind," his responses to my questions suggest, this is the case in significant
part because he learned his race through place.

These descriptions of the racialized urban landscapes of Calvin Moore's
childhood will likely strike most readers – most American readers, at any
rate – as anything but incomprehensible. It is colloquial in this country,
even at the start of the twenty-first century, to speak of the "black" sections of particular cities. It is colloquial to describe schools and other
institutions in similarly racial terms. Many of the respondents I interviewed for this book use language strikingly similar to Moore's, whether
to characterize legally segregated places in the pre-civil-rights-movement
South or to describe post-civil-rights-era Columbus, Ohio, where segregation is de facto. Indeed, in several instances, the association between
racialized place names (such as "inner city" or "urban") and racial identity categories (such as "African American" or "black") is so powerful
that respondents conflate the spatial and the racial terms. A case in point
is the following description, offered by one East Side resident who self-
identifies as black, of the experience of switching from a predominantly
black urban public school to a predominantly white Catholic parochial
school: "[W]hen I went to [Catholic school], I actually, I was out my
domain, in the sense that, you know ... I initially was in a completely ...
urban or black community."[15]

Moore's descriptions are not idiosyncratic, then, not even remarkable.
Yet they are significant, since to experience a particular place as a "black
place" is to experience blackness as a social fact. As argued in the previous
chapter, a constructed identity, when institutionalized, and when objectified in material form, can be reproduced especially efficiently, because
extra-discursively. I cited there Pierre Bourdieu's illustration of this claim
using the example of a gendered identity: the opposition between male and
female and the coding of a wide range of actions and attributes as one or
the other. When such identitarian conventions are institutionalized, and

---

[15] Interview with John Carr, a fifty-eight-year-old resident of East Side Columbus, emphasis
added.

when they are objectified – when they are translated from expressly thematized identity stories into objects or into things (high-heeled shoes, for
example, or the domestic spaces of the bourgeois home) – then competent
social actors master them practically. They learn them, and they relearn
them, not principally as stories, or even as rules ("You are a woman, and
women do things differently than men; they take small, careful steps, and
they congregate in kitchens"), but through a kind of know-how, which
supplements more deliberate and conscious learning.[16]

Calvin Moore's account of his understanding of the racial identity category "African American" invokes just such a sense of practical mastery.
To be sure, at times people learn and relearn racial identities through
racial stories: through literature, film, court opinions, newspaper and
other mass media accounts of contemporaneous happenings, and the
stories presented through the curricula of primary, secondary, and post-
secondary schools. At times (as Moore's comments suggest), people are
expressly informed of the racial coding of space: "*This* is your place. *That*
is not, because you are a member of *this* race and not *that*."

But explicit lessons are inherently vulnerable. They invite questions
("What is a black person?" "What is it that makes me black, and how do
you know?" "What is a white place, and how is it that a place becomes
white?"): questions the answers to which can expose the illogic of racial
categorization and the illegitimacy of racial hierarchy.

When racial stories are institutionalized, however, and when they are
built into the very fabric of urban and suburban landscapes, they acquire
a kind of geographic facticity that renders them lived reality. If race is
embedded in our minds, if race is installed in our minds when we are
children, this is the case, not simply because we are *told*, "There's certain
places you don't go." It is because we come to know – as a matter of fact,
as a matter of practical knowledge – that "there's certain places you don't
go. There's certain people you don't socialize with." Learning to function
as competent actors in racialized space means learning the common sense
of racial practice.

That twenty-first-century Americans like Calvin Moore can experience
particular sections of particular cities as "black places" was made possible by the construction, starting in the early decades of the twentieth

---

[16] Pierre Bourdieu, *Outline of a Theory of Practice*, transl. Richard Nice (Cambridge, UK:
Cambridge University Press, 1977). On the reproduction of gendered identity, see also
Bourdieu, *Masculine Domination* (Stanford, CA: Stanford University Press, 2001).

century, of the black American ghetto. Black ghettos did not exist in Birmingham, Alabama; they did not exist in Columbus, Ohio; they did not exist in almost any American city at the turn of the twentieth century. In Columbus, for instance, 1890 census data show that, although just over half of those residents identified as "black" lived in three of the city's fifteen wards, these areas themselves were not predominantly – not even majority – black. To the contrary, the eleventh ward, which housed the greatest share of the city's black population, was only 16 percent black. No ward in turn-of-the-century Columbus was more than a quarter African American.[17]

These relatively low levels of racial segregation can be captured by two commonly used indices. The black isolation index, which measures the extent to which persons identified as "black" are isolated in predominantly "black" areas, was only 6 percent in Columbus in 1890. Typically, an isolation index must reach 30 percent before it is considered high. That same year, the index of dissimilarity, which measures the unevenness of the distribution of persons considered "black" throughout a city, was, in Columbus, a moderate 41 percent. Generally, a dissimilarity index must reach 60 percent to be considered high.[18] In this relatively low level of racial segregation, turn-of-the-century Columbus was fairly typical. An analysis of all American cities with a thousand or more black residents in 1890 shows that, for the nation as a whole, the index of dissimilarity was 46 percent, well below the 60 percent threshold, while the index of isolation was 22 percent.[19] Only a single city in the United States had an index

[17] Computed by the author using ward-level data from the 1890 U.S. Census. Data collected by David Cutler, Edward Glaeser, and Jacob Vigdor and posted at: http://trinity.aas.duke.edu/~jvigdor/segregation/index.html.

[18] Ibid. The isolation index, in other words, reflects the percentage black, on average, of the subsection (in this case, the ward) where the average black person lives. The index of dissimilarity shows the percentage of a subpopulation in a city or another geographical area that would need to move for that population to be evenly distributed throughout the area. An index of 1.00 would reflect complete segregation, while an index of 0.00 would reflect total integration. For more detailed discussions of both measures, see Douglas Massey and Nancy Denton, *American Apartheid: Segregation and the Making of the Underclass* (Cambridge, MA: Harvard University Press, 1993), chapter 2; and David Cutler, Edward Glaeser, and Jacob Vigdor, "The Rise and Decline of the American Ghetto," *Journal of Political Economy* 107, 3 (1999): 455–506. In addition to isolation and dissimilarity, Massey and Denton measure the clustering of ghettoized areas near one another, their concentration in relatively small areas, and their centralization around an urban core. All five indices contribute to what Massey and Denton term "hypersegregation." These authors argue persuasively that African Americans are the group in United States history to have been ghettoized most thoroughly and most systematically.

[19] Cutler, Glaeser, and Vigdor, "Rise and Decline of the American Ghetto," p. 464, table 1. Both measures are weighted for the number of blacks in a given city.

of isolation above 30 percent.[20] In 1890, on average, black American city dwellers lived in wards that were only 27 percent black.[21]

Change came relatively quickly with what historians have dubbed the "Great Migration" of Southern blacks to Northern cities, beginning with the First World War and continuing through the 1920s. The principal causes of this demographic shift are well known: the sudden decline of Southern sharecropping due to the boll weevil infestation of cotton fields in the 1910s; the almost simultaneous explosion of job opportunities in Northern cities with the onset of war; and the belief – widespread among American blacks at that time – that a move north would mean an escape from the Jim Crow South for a "Promised Land" where racial inequalities and racial hierarchies were significantly less severe.[22]

The principal effect of the movement was a massive change in urban demographics. Between 1910 and 1930, Columbus, Ohio's black population increased by more than 150 percent, from less than thirteen thousand to nearly thirty-three thousand people. This change was nontrivial; the number of new black residents during these two decades was more than twice what Columbus's *total* black population had been at the turn of the century.[23] The change was not, however, extraordinary. In absolute terms, growth was much greater in large cities like New York and Chicago, where between 1910 and 1930 the black population increased by two hundred twenty-eight thousand and one hundred ninety thousand, respectively, and the rate of growth was faster in major industrial centers like Cleveland and Detroit, where during these same years the black population increased, respectively, by 850 and 2,000 percent.[24]

[20] Ibid., 462–3. The city was Norfolk, Virginia.

[21] Ibid., 456.

[22] See James Grossman, *Land of Hope: Chicago, Black Southerners, and the Great Migration* (Chicago, IL, University of Chicago Press, 1989), especially chapter 1; and the essays collected in Alferdteen Harrison, ed., *Black Exodus: The Great Migration from the American South* (Jackson and London: University Press of Mississippi, 1991).

[23] Columbus in 1900 had only eighty-two hundred black residents total. They comprised 6 percent of the city's population. By 1930, the black population had grown to nearly thirty-three thousand. Blacks comprised 11 percent of the city's population. *U.S. Census of Population and Housing, 1900: Population of States and Territories: Sex, General Nativity, and Color* (Washington, DC: Government Printing Office, 1900). http://www. census.gov/prod/www/abs/decennial/1900.htm.

[24] New York's black population increased from one hundred thousand in 1910 to three hundred twenty-eight thousand in 1930, while Chicago's increased from forty-four thousand to two hundred thirty-four thousand during those same years. Cleveland's black population increased from eighty-five hundred in 1910 to close to seventy-two thousand in 1930. Detroit's increased from about six thousand in 1910 to more than one hundred twenty thousand in 1930. *U.S. Census of Population and Housing, 1910: General Report and Analysis* (Washington, DC: Government Printing Office, 1913).

Accompanying these demographic shifts were important revisions to dominant narratives of racial identity and difference. In the terms introduced in the previous chapter, the Great Migration effected a shift in the experiential input from which Northern and Midwestern city dwellers constructed their identity stories. Those with whom established residents competed for jobs and for housing now became, disproportionately, and rather suddenly, black Southern migrants. In Columbus, these migrants came principally from North Carolina. Their ways of speaking and dressing, their habits, and their manners would have seemed at least as foreign to early twentieth-century residents of that city as did those of the Germans and the Italians who had arrived and settled in earlier decades. According to contemporaneous accounts, older Columbus residents soon exhibited a "bitter hatred of" these new arrivals, whose "attitude and conduct" they regarded as "unworthy of the respect of decent people."[25]

A second important shift came not long after the start of this Southern influx, when the Immigration Act of 1924 dramatically reduced the number of new arrivals to U.S. cities from Southern and Eastern Europe. Now it was not Italians or other so-called "new immigrants," but African Americans who took the lowest-paying and the least desirable jobs. Now it was not "foreigners" but black Americans who moved into the oldest and the most dilapidated housing. Now it was not mostly Southern or Eastern Europeans, but black migrants from the Southern states whom, in Columbus as in other Northern and Midwestern cities, business owners exploited as scabs when their workers went on strike.

In response, established residents of Columbus, Ohio, as of other Northern and Midwestern cities, began to revise the racial stories they told, and to do so in at least three significant ways. First, they began to deemphasize racial divisions among those whom eventually they would come to regard as "*white* ethnics," and to focus attention on what they increasingly understood as a black/white racial divide. Matthew Jacobson, David Roediger, and others have argued compellingly that, at the turn of the twentieth century, Southern and Eastern European immigrants to the United States, along with American Jews, occupied an "in-between" place

http://www.census.gov/prod/www/abs/decennial/1910.htm; *U.S. Census of Population and Housing, 1930: Reports by States, Showing the Composition and Characteristics of the Population for Counties, Cities, and Townships or Other Minor Civil Divisions* (Washington, DC: Government Printing Office, 1932). http://www.census.gov/prod/www/abs/decennial/1930.htm.
[25] Frank Quillan, *The Color Line in Ohio: A History of Race Prejudice in a Typical Northern State* (Whitefish, MT: Kessinger Publishing, 2007 [1913]), 145.

in the country's racial hierarchy.[26] Although they were not regarded as "black," nor were these "new immigrants" understood to be fully and unambiguously "white." The immigration restrictions of 1924 (quotas for legal immigration to the United States that were based on would-be immigrants' nations of origin) made possible for the first time in the twentieth century a story of pan-European racial identity that would not threaten those who feared the "mongrelization" of the American nation.[27] It was at this point that dominant narratives began to distinguish "race" – understood as permanent and rooted in biology – from what, by mid-century, would be commonly known as "ethnicity" – a form of social difference understood to be based in voluntarily shared practices and in culture.[28]

Roediger and Jacobson provide multiple examples of this shift in dominant racial identity narratives: examples taken from literature, film, court opinions, racialized newspaper accounts of current events, and other sources. Allow me to illustrate by citing just one. In his 1922 *Babbitt*, Sinclair Lewis has a white character comment: "Thank the Lord, we're putting a limit on immigration. These Dagoes and Hunkies have got to learn that this is a white man's country, and they ain't wanted here."[29] Dagoes and Hunkies are not only not wanted in 1922; they are also not *white*. A quarter century later, however, in his *Kingsblood Royal*, Lewis has his protagonist, Neil Kingsblood, criticize what he characterizes as his employer's outdated animosity toward white ethnics: "He thinks only people like us, from British and French and Heine stock, amount to anything," Kingsblood tells his wife. "He's prejudiced against Scandinavians and the Irish and Hunkies and Polacks. He doesn't understand that we have a new America."[30] The "new America" of the postwar years is one

[26] Matthew Frye Jacobson, *Whiteness of a Different Color: European Immigrants and the Alchemy of Race* (Cambridge, MA: Harvard University Press, 1998); and David Roediger, *Working Toward Whiteness: How America's Immigrants Became White* (New York: Basic Books, 2005). See also Karen Brodkin, *How Jews Became White Folks and What That Says about Race in America* (New Brunswick, NJ: Rutgers University Press, 1998).

[27] The Johnson-Reed Immigration Act of 1924 resulted in an immigration quota system based on nation of origin and race, ranking would-be immigrants according to desirability. For an excellent discussion, see Mae Ngai, *Impossible Subjects: Illegal Aliens and the Making of Modern America* (Princeton, NJ: Princeton University Press, 2004), chapter 1.

[28] Roediger, *Working Toward Whiteness*; Brodkin, *How Jews Became White Folks*; Jacobson, *Whiteness of a Different Color*.

[29] Sinclair Lewis, *Babbitt* (Amherst, NY: Prometheus, 2002 [1922]), 145. Quoted in part in Roediger, *Working Toward Whiteness*, 10.

[30] Sinclair Lewis, *Kingsblood Royal* (New York: Modern Library, 2002 [1947]), quoted in Roediger, *Working Toward Whiteness*, 10.

in which intra-European differences ought not to be treated with "prejudice." But tolerance has its limits. Kingsblood continues: "Still and all and even hating prejudice, I do see where the Negroes are inferior and always will be."[31]

Second, during roughly this same period, established residents of Columbus and other older cities revised, in light of the conditions of industrial urbanism, the list of traits and behaviors they claimed biological race caused. Historians of the era have documented a consistent pattern: when Southern blacks moved to Northern cities, entering relations of power that severely constrained what they could do and what they could be, whites racialized the behavioral regularities these relations produced, circulating stories of race as their *cause*. For instance, to cite one widely cited example, because many industrial unions excluded black workers from membership, blacks were uniquely exploitable as strikebreakers. Noticing this pattern, resentful white workers racialized "scabbing" as "turning nigger."[32]

In a similar vein, because many landlords, real estate agents, and home sellers refused to rent or to sell to black migrant families, the latter were constrained to compete in a dual housing market for overcrowded, overpriced, and often physically deteriorated rental units. Black migrants were excluded from relatively high-paying jobs and discriminated against in lending, as well. Hence it was difficult for them to get capital to purchase their own homes and/or to make much-needed repairs. Whites then racialized the failure to maintain one's residence, telling stories of race as the cause of incapacity for home ownership and unfitness for admission to high-status (white) neighborhoods. James Grossman, for example, cites a 1917 *Chicago Tribune* article according to which African Americans suffer from "a childlike helplessness in the matter of sanitation and housing."[33] These patterns continued beyond the early decades of the century. Charles Abrams, in his classic study of racial discrimination in early twentieth-century American cities, cites the following complaints, which were filed by white rioters protesting the Sojourner Truth housing project in Detroit in 1942: "Negroes are filthy and drive white people away"; "How would you like a filthy Negro neighbor?" "Blacks coming in means a 'run-down' community."[34]

[31] Ibid.
[32] Roediger, *Working Toward Whiteness*, 92.
[33] Grossman, *Land of Hope*, 169.
[34] Charles Abrams, *Forbidden Neighbors: A Study of Prejudice in Housing* (New York: Kennikat Press, 1955), 95. See also Thomas Sugrue's account of the racialization of

The third change, although analytically distinct from the first two, was closely related to and more or less coterminous with them. The proper relation between "the races," stories of racial identity and difference now increasingly suggested, was of one strict separation. Even in cities like Columbus, Ohio, where blacks and whites had, for decades, lived side by side, dominant racial narratives began to portray humans as, by nature, congregating only with members of their own race. Because deviations from this pattern threaten both neighborhood stability and property values (the story went) positive steps should be taken to correct them. R. F. Bingham and Stanley McMichael's early and influential real estate text, *City Growth and Values* (cited at the start of the chapter) stated this position unequivocally. "There is a natural inclination of the colored people to live together in their own communities," Bingham and McMichael wrote:

With the increase in colored people coming to many Northern cities, they have overrun their old districts and swept into adjoining ones or passed to other sections and formed new ones. This naturally has had a decidedly detrimental effect on land values, for few white people ... care to live near them.

Bingham and McMichael's suggestion for correcting this problem was straightforward: "Frankly, rigid segregation seems to be the only manner in which the difficulty can be effectively controlled."[35]

This early twentieth-century racial narrative, it is worth underscoring, did not represent a radical break with the past. To the contrary, it built upon and extended a nineteenth-century narrative, which can be traced at least as far back as Georges Cuvier's claim in *Le Regne Animal* that human races are analogous to animal species. Races are permanent biological types (this story went), which cause differences in behaviors, attributes, abilities, and dispositions.[36] A natural hierarchy exists among the races of humankind, with whites, at the top of that hierarchy, by nature dominant, and blacks, at the bottom, subordinate. Josiah Nott and George Gliddon's 1854 *Types of Mankind* neatly summarized this interpretation of race as biological type in a twelve-item list of "conclusions," the first three of which asserted:

1. That the surface of our globe is naturally divided into several zoological provinces, each of which is a distinct centre of creation,

conditions caused by discrimination in *Origins of the Urban Crisis: Race and Inequality in Postwar Detroit* (Princeton, NJ: Princeton University Press, 1996), chapter 2.

[35] Bingham and McMichael, *City Growth and Values*, 181.

[36] See Michael Banton, *Racial Theories*, second edition (Cambridge, UK: Cambridge University Press, 1998), especially chapter 3, on which this paragraph draws.

possessing a peculiar fauna and flora; and that every species of animal and plant was originally assigned to its appropriate province.

2.   That the human family offers no exception to this general law, but
     fully conforms to it: Mankind being divided into several groups of
     Races, each of which constitutes a primitive element in the fauna
     of its peculiar province.

3.   That history affords no evidence of the transformation of one Type
     into another, nor of the origination of a new and *Permanent* Type.

Point twelve of Nott and Gliddon's conclusion reads, "It follows as a
corollary, that there exists a *Genus Homo*, embracing many primordial
Types or 'Species.'"[37]

Through the early decades of the twentieth century, this nineteenth-century understanding of race as permanent, biologically rooted difference
maintained its dominance. Not until the late 1930s and the 1940s, with
the advent of population genetics, would it effectively be challenged, even
at the level of scientific discourse.[38] Meanwhile, the nineteenth-century
racial narrative, amended to highlight the black/white racial divide; to
attribute to blacks a range of undesirable traits that render them bad
neighbors and unfit homeowners; and to prescribe strict separation between blacks and whites in America's cities, was told, and it was retold,
on multiple levels. This racial story was circulated in the discourse of
business elites – among real estate agents, in particular, and real estate
lenders and appraisers. It was circulated among elected officials and
among members of the nascent profession of city planners. It was circulated in popular discourse as well, for example in local newspapers and
in magazines such as *Good Housekeeping*, which wholeheartedly celebrated homes in racially exclusive residential communities.[39]

   Because this racial story was (to recall the argument in Chapter 1) *productive* – because it not only interpreted past experience, but also shaped
and directed future action – it had a dramatic effect on the spatial organization of the American city. It had a dramatic effect, more generally, on
the incorporation (or the lack thereof) of black Americans into urban social, economic, and political life. In Columbus, for instance, where in the

[37]   Cited in ibid., 58.
[38]   Ibid., chapter 4.
[39]   See Abrams's discussion of a series of popular magazine articles in the mid-1930s empha-
       sizing the desirability and the importance of restrictions. Abrams, *Forbidden Neighbors*,
       146–7.

decades leading up to the Great Migration, blacks had achieved a relatively high level of political, economic, and social incorporation, "Negro-white relations" grew tense.[40] There was nearly a race riot in 1919, when the Pennsylvania Railroad used black strikebreakers against white workers. "In 1924," according to J. S. Himes, "by actual count, 55.7 percent of the space given to stories in the three daily papers about Negroes dealt with vice and crime."[41]

During this period, residential segregation in Columbus increased dramatically. As early as 1920, the Chicago School sociologist R. D. McKenzie found that black residents of Columbus were confined to what he characterized as "disintegrated areas" on the perimeter of the central business district and to a few small industrial areas near factories where blacks were employed.[42] On Columbus's Near East Side, along Long Street between Seventeenth Street and Taylor Avenue, there developed in a relatively short time span what McKenzie characterized as "a city of blacks within the larger community."[43] The city's growing racial segregation extended to its commercial facilities, such as theaters, hotels, and restaurants, and also to churches, fraternal organizations, and voluntary associations: institutions that, for the most part, had been racially integrated prior to the Great Migration.[44]

---

[40] Between 1881 and 1912, five black men had been elected to the Columbus City Council, and two to the city's board of education. Blacks had been employed regularly in the city's principal industry at that time, the buggy manufacture. They had worked in its brickyards and lumber mills, and at railroads, hotels, and bars. See J. S. Himes, Jr., "Forty Years of Negro Life in Columbus, Ohio," *Journal of Negro History* 27, 2 (April 1942): 133–54, here 151.

[41] Ibid., 151.

[42] R. D. McKenzie, "The Neighborhood: A Study of Local Life in the City of Columbus, Ohio," *American Journal of Sociology* 27, 2 (September 1921): 145–68, here 150. McKenzie describes the "disintegrated" area this way: "Surrounding the main business section on all sides for a distance of from one to a dozen blocks there is a black and grimy area unfit for human habitation. Here cheap boarding houses and questionable hotels are wedged in between large warehouses and wholesale establishments. This region is very largely given over to colored people and poor whites." Ibid., 150.

[43] Ibid., 155.

[44] William W. Giffin, *African Americans and the Color Line in Ohio, 1915–1930* (Columbus: Ohio State University Press, 2005). African Americans in Columbus responded to this growing racial segregation by creating their own commercial and public institutions. Long Street became home to the Alpha Hospital, the first black-owned hospital in the United States, as well as to black-owned and -operated mortgage and savings and loan companies, theaters, restaurants, printing shops, beauty parlors, tailors, and pharmacies. Himes, "Forty Years of Negro Life in Columbus, Ohio." According to Nimrod Allen, the executive secretary of the Columbus Urban League in 1922, "There [were] nearly one hundred business enterprises on East Long Street and vicinity, embracing haberdasheries,

Columbus's public schools became racially segregated during this period, as well. Although Ohio state law at that time prohibited racial segregation in public education, in 1909, the city school board redrew its boundaries, gerrymandering with a view to making the Champion Avenue School on the Near East Side an all-black institution. Because this gerrymandering produced what, from the district officials' point of view, were less than perfect results, they tinkered at the margins with school assignments. Some black students who lived across the street from a predominantly white school were sent to Champion Avenue, while those white students who lived within the new Champion Avenue boundaries were not sent there, but rather to other (predominantly white) schools. The four black teachers who were employed by the district at that time were assigned to Champion Avenue, and additional black teachers and administrators were hired to staff the school. By 1921, all Champion Avenue students without exception, and all of the school's teachers except one, were African American. It would be seventy years before a court order from U.S. District Judge Robert Duncan would end racial segregation at the Champion Avenue School.[45]

Meanwhile, a distinctly racial geography would take shape in Columbus. By 1940, a single ward out of nineteen – ward seven, in the heart of Columbus's Near East Side – was home to a full third of the city's black residents.[46] Although that year's census identified almost 12 percent of Columbus's residents as "black," in nearly a third of the city's wards *only half of one percent or fewer* of residents were African American.[47] The index of isolation for Columbus had risen more than sixfold in fifty years, from 6 to 37 percent. The index of dissimilarity had grown from 41 to 63 percent.[48]

In this respect, Columbus, Ohio was anything but unique. In the nation's cities overall, black isolation had grown from 22 to 46 percent,

---

photographers, optometrists, music shops, music studios, beauty parlors, printing establishments, corporations, [and] tailors." Cited in Giffin, *African Americans and the Color Line in Ohio*, 97.

[45] See Giffin, *African Americans and the Color Line in Ohio*, chapters 2 and 5, and Bill Bush, "Brown v. Board of Education 50th Anniversary: Embattled Champion," *Columbus Dispatch*, May 16, 2004, p. 2B.

[46] The population of ward seven was a little more than 86 percent black. Computed by the author using ward data posted by Cutler, Glaeser, and Vigdor at http://trinity.aas.duke.edu/~jvigdor/segregation/index.html.

[47] Computed by the author using ward data posted by Cutler, Glaeser, and Vigdor at http://trinity.aas.duke.edu/~jvigdor/segregation/index.html.

[48] Ibid.

while dissimilarity had increased from 46 to 71 percent.[49] By 1940, on average, black American city dwellers lived in neighborhoods that were 43 percent black.[50] A full fifty-five American cities included neighborhoods that, judging by indices of dissimilarity and isolation, could be classified as "black ghettos."[51]

2. Racial Identities, Racial Interests

The year 1940 marked the start of a decade one might reasonably have expected to be a turning point, both in dominant understandings of race in America and in American racial practices. It was in the 1940s that the nineteenth-century understanding of race as biological difference – which had rationalized, by providing an allegedly scientific basis for, the differential treatment of persons based on membership in racial categories – was decisively undermined at the level of scientific discourse. Between 1936 and 1947, scientists in the United States and in Europe achieved consensus on what has since been dubbed the "evolutionary synthesis": an explanation of what previously had been purported to be categorical and permanent racial differences in terms of gradual genetic shifts engendered by evolution within reproductively isolated populations.[52] Phenotypical variation among individuals, which to that point had been widely assumed to be a marker of distinct racial types, was now recognized as continuous, rather than categorical. There is no primordial and biologically rooted difference, scientists came to agree over the course of this decade, that separates human beings into discrete "races." There is no such thing as a biological racial type, analogous to the category "species" and linked to specifically racial traits, qualities, and dispositions.[53]

At the same time, the racial narratives that had legitimized inequality and hierarchy through the nineteenth century and into the early decades of the twentieth came under siege, both in the United States and in the other Allied nations. The strong association of racism with Nazism made American racial beliefs and practices appear to those who opposed Hitler to be, not only empirically misguided, but also morally repugnant. In

---

[49] Cutler, Glaeser, and Vigdor, "Rise and Decline of the American Ghetto," 464, table 1.
[50] Ibid.
[51] That is, they lived in areas with indices of dissimilarity above 60 percent and indices of isolation above 30 percent. Ibid., 465.
[52] Banton, *Racial Theories*, chapter 4.
[53] Biological accounts of race persisted after mid-century in some scientific realms. See Chapter 1, note 52.

1944, the widely circulated Fourth Report of the Commission to Study the International Organization of the Peace underscored that "The cancerous Negro situation in our country gives fodder to enemy propaganda and makes our ideals stick like dry bread in the throat." "Through revulsion against Nazi doctrines," the report continued, "we may ... hope to speed up the process of bringing our own practices ... more in conformity with our professed ideals."[54] Gunnar Myrdal, writing that same year, took a similar stance. Predicting that "The War [would be] crucial for the future of the Negro," Myrdal averred, "There is bound to be a redefinition of the Negro's status in America as a result of this War."[55]

By mid-century, in short, what had at the turn of the century been the dominant racial narrative – a story of race as a primordial difference that produces different traits and dispositions and that justifies people's differential treatment – was well on its way to being discredited. Prior to being fully discredited, however, this narrative was, quite literally, built into the American urban and suburban fabric. It was institutionalized in rules and in laws and eventually objectified in spatial forms, which enabled it to live on as a kind of collective "common sense."

Recall (from the discussion in the introduction) that institutionalizing an identity story creates an incentive for social actors to perform their identities well. The norms that govern the practice of dancing Argentine tango incentivize me to follow, not because I embrace the gender narrative that informed the creation of those rules (I do not), but because I want the rewards that accompany dancing "correctly." In this section, I want to suggest that the institutionalization of early twentieth-century racial narratives (in the form of FHA underwriting guidelines, for example) incentivized whites in a very particular way: by constructing a set of racial interests built around home ownership and property values. First, however, I want to consider two analytically distinct processes through which racial stories were institutionalized and objectified: the construction of (to recall Calvin Moore's language) "black places" and "white places," and the channeling of collective resources toward the latter and away from the former.

[54] Commission to Study the Organization of the Peace, Fourth Report, Part III, "International Safeguard of Human Rights," 163–84 in *Building Peace: Reports of the Commission to Study the Organization of Peace 1939–1972* (Metuchen, NJ: Scarecrow Press, 1973 [1944]), 181.

[55] Gunnar Myrdal, *An American Dilemma: The Negro Problem and Modern Democracy* (New York: Harper and Row, 1944), 997.

The racial segregation of the American city, it is worth underscoring, was not the product of the preferences and the choices of people who lived in the new "black" sections of America's cities. To the contrary, a series of coercive measures that utilized the power of the state and of capital institutionalized what, in the early decades of the twentieth century, was an increasingly widely accepted story about the naturalness and the expediency of the separation of "the races." Among the earliest and most notorious of these measures were racial zoning ordinances: laws that aimed specifically to segregate and to isolate by race.[56] But during this same period, and continuing through the late 1940s, a more significant mechanism of racial segregation was the restrictive covenant.[57] Legally enforced restrictions written into the deeds of private properties, restrictive covenants had been employed prior to the turn of the century to limit what were regarded as "noxious" uses, tanneries being one common instance, and another slaughterhouses.[58] Toward the close of the nineteenth century and into the early years of the twentieth, developers began to realize the value-generating potential of deed restrictions, especially when they were defined relatively extensively and applied relatively broadly within a particular subdivision or urban or suburban neighborhood. By specifying limited uses in a given area (for example, by restricting use to single-family residences) and by requiring of would-be buyers a high level of expenditure (for example, by specifying minimum lot or building sizes, or by limiting construction materials to those that were relatively costly), land speculators and developers could create, and they

[56] In 1910, Baltimore was the first American city to pass a racial zoning law. A host of other cities – including Atlanta, St. Louis, and Dallas – followed suit. The practice spread, but only relatively briefly, until 1917, when the U.S. Supreme Court ruled racial zoning in violation of the Fourteenth Amendment. *Buchanan v. Warley*, 245 U.S. 60.

[57] More significant principally because of scope and duration: although most cities did not enact racial zoning laws, and those that did ceased to do so after 1917, large sections of nearly every major city in the United States were governed by restrictive covenants, which were legally enforceable until 1948. See Robert Fogelson, *Bourgeois Nightmares: Suburbia, 1870–1930* (New Haven, CT: Yale University Press, 2005); Kenneth Fox Gotham, "Urban Space, Restrictive Covenants and the Origins of Racial Residential Segregation in a US City, 1900–50," *International Journal of Urban and Regional Research* 24, 3 (September 2000): 616–33; and Patricia Burgess Stach, "Deed Restrictions and Subdivision Development in Columbus, Ohio, 1900–1970," *Journal of Urban History* 15, 1 (November 1988): 42–68.

[58] According to Robert Fogelson, restrictive covenants were used in England as early as the mid-eighteenth century by nobles who leased lots but wanted to maintain control over how they were used in order to protect their value. Prior to the late 1880s, however, their use was still rare in the United States. Fogelson, *Bourgeois Nightmares*, 43–6.

could market, exclusivity. They thus could boost both property values and profits.[59]

One important type of exclusivity developers produced and marketed during this era was specifically racial in character. Through the first half of the past century, legal prohibitions on the purchase, lease, rental, and/ or occupancy by blacks (and often by other racialized groups, especially Jews) were written into the deeds of countless properties in American cities and in their growing suburbs. In Columbus, for example, the deed for every property in the upscale development of Beechwold explicitly excluded "persons of African descent" as owners, lessees, or occupants.[60] Deeds in Worthington and Upper Arlington – suburbs that remain, to this day, among the city's most affluent and among its most segregated – similarly excluded along racial lines.[61] Patricia Burgess, examining deeds for 335 subdivisions in six major growth corridors of Columbus, found that, from the turn of the century to 1920, roughly a quarter of subdivisions platted included race restrictions.[62] During the city's building boom in the 1920s, that proportion grew to roughly two-thirds.[63] Between 1930 and 1945, almost three-fourths of subdivisions platted were governed by racial restrictions.[64]

In this regard, Columbus was not atypical. In 1928, when the Institute for Research in Land Economics and Public Utilities conducted the first large-scale study of deed restrictions, it found that about half of the deeds analyzed included some form of racial restriction.[65] By mid-century, some

[59] This practice is discussed in greater depth in Chapter 4.
[60] Stach, "Deed Restrictions."
[61] Ibid. In 2000, whites comprised 93 percent of the population of Worthington and 94 percent in Upper Arlington, compared with only 68 percent in the city of Columbus. Only 2 percent of Worthington residents and less than 1 percent of Upper Arlington residents were categorized "black," compared with 24 percent in Columbus. Worthington and Upper Arlington were also considerably more affluent than the city, with median household incomes (MHI) of $68,500 and $72,000, respectively, and median family incomes (MFI) of $83,000 and $90,000, respectively, compared with Columbus's MHI of less than $38,000 and MFI of $47,000. U.S. Census Bureau, Census of Population and Housing 2000: Summary File http://factfinder. census.gov/servlet/ DatasetMainPageServlet?_program=DEC&_submenuId=datasets_2&_lang=en&_ts=.
[62] Patricia Burgess, Planning for the Private Interest: Land Use Controls and Residential Patterns in Columbus, Ohio, 1900–1970 (Columbus: Ohio State University Press, 1994), 42.
[63] Fifty-two of seventy-nine subdivisions platted from 1921 to 1929 were governed by race restrictions. Burgess, Planning for the Private Interest, 48, table 2.6.
[64] Between 1930 and 1945, fewer were platted, but out of twenty-two subdivisions platted, sixteen were governed by restrictions. Ibid.
[65] The study examined deeds for eighty-two subdivisions throughout the United States and two in Canada. Helen Monchow, The Use of Deed Restrictions in Subdivision

80 percent of vacant land in Chicago, Los Angeles, and suburban New York was governed by racial covenants. In St. Louis, 559 city blocks were, by 1944, with covenants particularly prevalent in areas near the boundaries of majority-black neighborhoods.[66]

Turn-of-the century Columbus was what Sam Bass Warner has called a "walking city."[67] Outside its three-mile radius lay largely undeveloped and, for the most part, unincorporated land. The extensive use of restrictive covenants during the first half of the twentieth century – that is, during just those years when the city grew and expanded to include its first genuinely suburban residential neighborhoods – ensured that most of Columbus's African American residents did not move to the newly annexed sections of the city or to its newly incorporated suburbs. Those black Americans who could have afforded to purchase or to build homes in these new areas were largely prevented from doing so by explicitly racial restrictions. Burgess estimates that, by mid-century, African Americans were legally excluded from a little over 77 percent of Columbus's suburban subdivisions. The only residential options for black residents were the racially unrestricted areas of the city: places that were, increasingly, recognizable as "black places."

During this same period, state actors reinforced and perpetuated the residential patterns that private covenants produced. They did so principally through zoning laws that, even though not explicitly racially targeted, had predictable racially segregating effects. In 1923 – just six years after the *Buchanan v. Warley* decision ruling racial zoning unconstitutional – the U.S. Department of Commerce published the Standard Zoning Enabling Act. Three years later, the Supreme Court legitimized the practice of zoning in its landmark *Village of Euclid v. Ambler Reality Company* decision.[68] Columbus was only one city among many to adopt its first zoning code in this era.[69]

Columbus's zoning code was fairly standard. It divided the city into three sets of districts, which governed land use, building height, and lot area, assigning every parcel of land within city limits to one of

---

[66] *Development* (Chicago, IL: Institute for Research in Land Economics and Public Utilities, 1928).

[66] Roediger, *Working Toward Whiteness*, 176.

[67] Sam Bass Warner, *Streetcar Suburbs: The Process of Growth in Boston, 1870–1900*, second edition (Cambridge, MA: Harvard University Press, 2004).

[68] 272 U.S. 365.

[69] In 1916, New York City adopted the nation's first comprehensive zoning law. By the mid-1920s, half of American states had enacted zoning legislation modeled on the Standard Zoning Enabling Act.

each type of district. An A-1 residential district, for instance, prohibited all uses except single-family homes and mandated both a maximum height (fifty feet) and a minimum lot size (4,800 square feet).[70] Burgess, examining all zoning regulations and all zoning actions in her study area over a fifty-year period, found that, from its inception, zoning in Columbus and its suburbs reinforced and perpetuated the residential patterns initially forged by private deed restrictions. Older sections of Columbus were zoned to allow multifamily dwellings and mixed uses, while, with very few exceptions, areas newly annexed to the city, as well as incorporated suburbs, were zoned for single-family homes. Zoning changes, Burgess found, were granted most often in the city's older residential areas. In newer sections, by contrast, zoning tightly controlled both density and land use. The result was an income-based residential stratification that, although not the unique *cause* of urban racial apartheid, played a nontrivial role in reinforcing it, and in extending it, even after 1948, when the Court declared racial covenants legally unenforceable.

Practices of restrictive covenanting and of zoning point to the critical role in the racialization of the American city played by the construction of what I will call *racial interests*. The production of racial interests is analytically distinct from racial segregation. Even if the creation of "black places" and "white places" encourages people to experience racial identities as durable features of the social world, this geographic mapping of race does not, by itself, produce racial interests. Imagine a political society in which people are assigned to physical spaces according to ascribed "race," and yet – in terms of capital investment, in terms of the distribution of collective resources and opportunities – racially coded places are treated more or less equivalently. In such a society, residents of a particular city might come to understand some of its neighborhoods as the proper home to people they perceive as "black," and others as the proper home to people they perceive as "white." But still, collective assets would be invested evenly among these places. The benefits of development (new commercial facilities and jobs, new housing and infrastructural improvements), as well as the burdens (environmental degradation, economic dislocation, the displacement of homes and businesses to make room for new buildings and roads) would be distributed equally, or at least randomly, across space.

[70] Burgess, *Planning for the Private Interest*.

One can imagine a "separate but equal" city where racial identity narratives are lent material reality, but where racial distinctions are *not* overlaid with material interests. Such is not, however, Calvin Moore's experience of his city. As his description of crossing the railroad tracks makes clear, those places Moore perceives as "black places" he also recognizes as "low income," while those places he sees as "white places" he identifies as "high society."

This characterization of "the two sides of the tracks" reflects an important reality about the modern American metropolis. Almost from its inception, the black ghetto has been subjected to systematic disinvestment, while collective investments in new residential and commercial structures, in infrastructural improvements such as new sewer and water systems, and in "public" amenities, such as parks and athletic facilities and well-built and well-equipped schools, disproportionately have been channeled to places that were, first legally, then practically, restricted to those constructed as white.

The mapping of racial identitarian differences, then, is analytically distinct from the inscription in racialized space of place-based economic differences. Historically, however, these two processes were closely intertwined: bound together both by coincidences and by narratives. The principal coincidences were those of the two major postwar migrations of Southern blacks to Northern cities with the century's two major periods of urban geographic expansion. It was in the years just after the First World War, as blacks arrived in Northern cities en masse, that the automobile opened the urban fringe and the surrounding suburbs to extensive residential development. Again in the years following World War II – just in time for the second major northward migration of Southern blacks – the advent of mass-produced tract housing, along with the construction of an extensive network of state and interstate highways, enabled the suburban housing boom. New suburbanites left America's central cities, and blacks moved into the older, often dilapidated housing they had abandoned.

The narratives were narratives of racial identity and difference (as told by realtors, by developers, and by mortgage lenders and appraisers), which linked the physical deterioration of the central city, not to the age of its housing stock, or to overcrowding, or to the dearth of resources for renovation and repair, but rather to the race of its new inhabitants. Some groups, the story went, have undesirable traits and customs. Some racial (as opposed to ethnic) groups are all but unassimilable: their ways of life so deeply rooted that they are impossible, or nearly impossible, to change. These groups destroy whichever neighborhoods they inhabit. They thus pose a grave threat to property values. Because their racially rooted attributes and their deeply ingrained collective habits *cause* the deterioration of the places in which they live, it is risky to invest in those areas of a city to which they have access, or to which they likely will in the future.

In the early decades of the century, this story was told, and it was re-told, at the conferences, in the journal articles, and in the textbooks of the increasingly professionalized real estate industry. According to one early industry text, for instance:

Among the traits and characteristics of people which influence land values, racial heritage and tendencies seem to be of paramount importance. The aspirations, energies, and abilities of various groups in the composition of the population will largely determine the extent to which they develop the potential value of land.[71]

The same text went on to underscore that *racial* differences have a particularly powerful impact on real estate values:

Most of the variations and differences between people are slight and value declines are, as a result, gradual. But there is one difference in people, namely race, which can result in a very rapid decline. Usually such declines can be partially avoided by segregation and this device has always been in common usage in the South where white and negro populations have been segregated.[72]

In 1946 – just as stories of immutable, because biologically rooted, racial difference were being stripped of their scientific credibility and their normative validity – the National Association of Real Estate Boards (NAREB) underscored in a textbook that it published: "The tendency of certain racial and cultural groups to stick together, making it almost impossible to assimilate them in the normal social organism, is too well known to need much comment." Appealing to the reader's commonsense understanding of "the negative influence on neighborhood growth exerted by the presence of undesirable groups, races, and individuals," the authors wrote:

Probably you can quickly name in your own city the areas which have been handicapped beyond recovery by the dance halls, taverns, houses of ill fame, gambling resorts, cheap hotels, and the haunts of notorious gangsters. Just as the stockyards or a tannery may pollute the air and give a good neighborhood a bad name, so do these undesirable human elements work against property values and ruin communities which might otherwise prosper.[73]

[71] Frederick Babcock, *The Valuation of Real Estate* (New York: McGraw, 1932), 86.
[72] Ibid., 91.
[73] Harry Grant Atkinson and L. E. Frailey, *Fundamentals of Real Estate Practice* (New York: Prentice-Hall, 1946), 34.

Mid-century studies surveying real estate textbooks, appraising manuals, and NAREB publications from this era find that almost all endorsed this account of the relation between race and property values.[74] Indeed, the moral of this racial story was written into the NAREB Code of Ethics, according to which, "A Realtor should never be instrumental in introducing into a neighborhood a character of property or occupancy, members of any race or nationality, or any individuals whose presence will clearly be detrimental to property values in that neighborhood."[75]

To the extent that the early twentieth-century racial narrative shaped individual realtors' decisions (as well as those of mortgage lenders and appraisers and of individual home buyers and sellers), it not only reinforced racial segregation (which it prescribed as the best way to protect property values in "white places") but further channeled mortgages and other forms of private investment toward racially restricted neighborhoods and away from black ghettos. This narrative thus heightened the very problem for which it purported to account by promoting the further deterioration of "black places." But narratives are inherently vulnerable to challenge. By the 1940s, the early twentieth-century racial narrative was increasingly vulnerable to the scientific and the normative challenges mounting at that time.

What is more, even prior to those challenges, through roughly the first third of the past century, racial biases in housing and mortgage lending markets were incomplete because of differences in relevant actors' exposure to and/or confidence in the dominant narrative. On Columbus's East Side, for example, the Long Street commercial district included several black-owned financial institutions. There, lenders no doubt found dominant accounts of race and investment risk less than fully compelling. Even those lenders who believed and endorsed the dominant narrative were left to interpret for themselves the soundness of a potential investment in a particular neighborhood. How permeable, in 1920, was the eastern boundary of the black ghetto that was forming on the city's Near East Side? Would Columbus's African American population remain clustered around the Long Street corridor (a racist mortgage lender might have wondered), or would the ghetto expand and extend to the Bexley municipal boundary? To believe the widely circulating narrative

---

[74] Rose Helper, *Racial Policies and Practices of Real Estate Brokers* (Minneapolis: University of Minnesota Press, 1969).

[75] Appendix I: "Code of Ethics of the National Association of Real Estate Boards," 203–9 in *The Administration of Real Estate Boards*, ed. Herbert U. Nelson (New York: MacMillan, 1925), here 207–8.

that linked investment risk to the racial identity ascribed an urban neighborhood was *not* to arrive at any determinate answer to questions such as these.

In the wake of the Great Depression, however, the growing federal involvement in American cities put an end to such indeterminacy. Heavily influenced by private sector actors, in particular by their narratives of race and risk, New Deal agencies including the Home Owners Loan Corporation (HOLC) and the Federal Housing Administration (FHA) systematized and institutionalized these racist stories. The HOLC has been widely criticized for its role in this process, in particular for the classificatory system featured in its City Survey Reports and utilized in its comprehensive Residential Security Maps.[76] This now infamous four-grade system assigned every section of every large and mid-sized city to a category ranging from "A," or first-grade, to "D," or fourth-grade. The Residential Security Maps, by matching a different color to each of the four grades, graphically depicted these ratings. Because an important criterion for earning a first- or a second-grade rating was a stable, predominantly white population, and because "expiring restrictions or a lack of them" and "infiltration of a lower-grade population" were criteria that invariably earned urban neighborhoods either third- or fourth-grade ratings, the HOLC neighborhood rating system effectively codified stories linking racial type to investment risk. The agency consistently rated "D" those neighborhoods with substantial African American populations, outlining them on its Residential Security Maps in the color red, which signaled the highest possible investment risk rating. It is for this reason

---

[76] Established in 1933, the HOLC's mission was to lower the staggering rate of mortgage foreclosure in the United States at that time by granting low-interest, long-term, self-amortizing mortgages to home owners who were in default on their mortgages or who had lost their properties because of foreclosure. Between 1933 and 1936, the HOLC financed roughly 20 percent of U.S. home mortgages. One year before the end of its mortgage program in 1935, the agency conducted its City Survey Program: a study – at that time unprecedented in scale – that aimed to determine the level of financial risk associated with its many investments. Analyzing residential patterns in every American city with a population of forty thousand or more (239 cities total), the HOLC, in consultation with an extensive network of local realtors and lenders, constructed detailed written reports about the age and the condition of housing stock; about population density and the amount of space, if any, left open for development; and about the racial and ethnic composition of every residential section of every city. See Kenneth Jackson, *Crabgrass Frontier: The Suburbanization of the United States* (New York: Oxford University Press, 1985), chapter 11, on which this paragraph and the two that follow draw. See also Mark Gelfand, *A Nation of Cities: The Federal Government and Urban America, 1933–1965* (New York: Oxford University Press, 1975).

that the HOLC is widely credited with nationalizing the practice known as "redlining."[77]

It was the Federal Housing Administration (FHA), however, that ensured that this racist system for categorizing and mapping investment risk would be put to use in ways that shaped urban investment patterns for decades.[78] Together with the Veterans Administration (VA), the FHA helped racialize investment patterns throughout the United States by refusing to insure home mortgages in those urban neighborhoods it identified as high risk: in the very neighborhoods, that is, into which black Americans had been ghettoized.[79] From the start of the program, a prerequisite for a federal loan guarantee was what the FHA termed an "unbiased professional estimate" of the value of the property to be mortgaged. This estimate focused, not only on the would-be borrower and her property, but also on the neighborhood in which that property was located. The FHA gave its underwriters detailed instructions about the criteria they should employ to produce these estimates and about how to weight those criteria. The two most heavily weighted were the "relative economic stability" of the neighborhood and its "protection from adverse influences": criteria that, as Kenneth Jackson has demonstrated, the agency "interpreted in ways that were prejudicial against heterogenous environments."[80]

---

[77] Recent statistical analyses demonstrate that race significantly affected HOLC ratings, even when the age and the condition of housing stock, population density, rate of home ownership, and other factors the agency cited as relevant in its city surveys are held constant. See Amy Hillier, "Residential Security Maps and Neighborhood Appraisals." *Social Science History* 29, 2 (Summer 2005): 207–33. The Lincoln Terrace neighborhood of St. Louis, for example, the HOLC rated in the lowest (red) category, even though the area was comprised of relatively new buildings in good condition. According to HOLC reasoning, property in Lincoln Terrace had "little or no value [in 1937], having suffered a tremendous decline in values due to the colored element now controlling the district." Quoted in Jackson, *Crabgrass Frontier*, 200.

[78] Established by the National Housing Act of 1934, the FHA, like the HOLC, was created in response to the Depression-era housing crisis. Its mission was not to grant loans, however, but to insure loans made by private lenders.

[79] The VA mortgage program was established by the Serviceman's Readjustment Act of 1944 (also known as the GI Bill). It was similar to the FHA in that it guaranteed loans, although in its case exclusively for veterans. Here I follow Kenneth Jackson in treating the two programs simultaneously. "Because the VA very largely followed FHA procedures and attitudes," Jackson writes, "the two programs can be considered in a single effort." *Crabgrass Frontier*, 204.

[80] If a property was "older," for instance, if the surrounding neighborhood was "crowded," or if it included "inferior and non-productive characteristics," its rating went down. "Relative economic stability" was weighted to account for 40 percent of the appraisal score and "protection from adverse influences" was weighted to account for 20 percent. Jackson, *Crabgrass Frontier*, 207.

Racial heterogeneity, in particular, was worrisome to the FHA. In its 1938 *Underwriting Manual*, the agency clearly advised that neighborhood ratings should reflect the presence of what it termed "Adverse Influences." These, it explained, include "incompatible racial and social groups." According to the manual:

Areas surrounding a location are investigated to determine whether incompatible racial and social groups are present, for the purpose of making a prediction regarding the probability of the location being invaded by such groups. If a neighborhood is to retain stability, it is necessary that properties shall continue to be occupied by the same social and racial classes. A change in social or racial occupancy generally contributes to instability and a decline in values.[81]

What is more, the *Underwriting Manual* specifically recommended the use of racially restrictive covenants to promote residential segregation.

From the start of the FHA program in the mid-1930s, and for nearly thirty years after, through the early 1960s – a period during which the agency insured mortgages on close to a third of new housing in the United States – it awarded African Americans less than 2 percent of state-insured mortgages.[82] Even these it allotted disproportionately to segregated areas in the American South.[83] In addition, the FHA's influence during these years extended beyond the market for government-backed mortgages, since, unlike the HOLC (which was highly secretive about its research), it publicized and widely disseminated its rating methods. In 1939, for instance, the agency published *The Structure and Growth of Residential Neighborhoods in American Cities*, in which it singled out the race of the residents of an area as among the most important factors determining economic value and stability, and demonstrated in some detail the methods of risk assessment it employed.[84]

---

[81] Federal Housing Administration, *Underwriting Manual: Underwriting and Valuation Procedure under Title II of the National Housing Act* (Washington, DC: U.S. Government Printing Office, 1938), par. 937.

[82] Gregory Squires, "Community Reinvestment: The Privatization of Fair Lending Law Enforcement," 257–86 in *Residential Apartheid: The American Legacy*, ed. Robert Bullard, J. Eugene Grigsby III, and Charles Lee (Los Angeles, CA: CAAS, 1994).

[83] Arnold Hirsch, *Making the Second Ghetto: Race and Housing in Chicago, 1940–1960* (Chicago, IL: University of Chicago Press, 1998), ix.

[84] The study offered a step-by-step guide to gathering, analyzing, and mapping what it argued were the data relevant to assessing investment risk: data that, it underscored, were readily available to private lenders and appraisers. See Homer Hoyt, *The Structure and Growth of Residential Neighborhoods in American Cities* (Washington, DC: Federal Housing Administration, 1939).

The FHA, the VA, and the HOLC thus helped institutionalize narratives of racial identity and difference, promoting segregation in America's cities and suburbs. In doing so, they helped create new race-based material interests. Clearly the FHA and VA mortgage programs *affected* people's interests profoundly. They significantly lowered down payments and interest rates for those they assisted (and refused to do so for those to whom they denied help). They extended amortization periods, as well, making it possible for many middle-income and working white Americans to purchase and to own private homes for the very first time. They created this new possibility, however, on the condition that the homes whites purchased be sited in racially exclusive neighborhoods. They thus not only affected interests, but further helped to *create* a new constellation of racialized interests, which in "white places" centered principally on home ownership and on property values.

"Politics," as Joseph Lowndes has argued, "is not merely the realm where pre-existing interests, grievances, and passions are given expression. Rather, it is in and through politics that interests, grievances, and passions are forged and new collective identities created."[85] Lowndes's insight applies to the phenomenon commonly known as "white flight," which was not (as it is often portrayed) the simple product of the prejudices of individual home buyers, who irrationally believed what, by mid-century, they should have recognized as false and illegitimate racial narratives. Nor did white flight follow inexorably from the fixed interests of property owners. Instead, it was an instrumentally rational response to a *contingent* set of interests: interests themselves constructed by powerful private actors, such as NAREB, and enabled and supported by democratic state actors, such as the HOLC and the FHA, which helped institutionalize, and then objectify, a story linking the value of residential property to racial exclusivity.

3. Black Problems

Think of interests such as these as interests in what legal theorist Cheryl Harris calls "whiteness as property."[86] Whiteness in this country, Harris claims, accords people legally protected privileges they would not enjoy

---

[85] Joseph Lowndes, *From the New Deal to the New Right: Race and the Southern Origins of Modern Conservatism* (New Haven, CT: Yale University Press, 2008).

[86] Cheryl Harris, "Whiteness as Property," *Harvard Law Review* 106, 8 (June 1993): 1707–91.

if not for their racial status. Harris offers the examples of access to the very best schools and the very best jobs. To continue with the example on which the previous section focused, whiteness as property, through much of the past century, enabled the racially privileged to reap the material benefits of state-subsidized home ownership in a dual housing market.

It is worth underscoring, however, that prior to their construction, the making of "white places" was not obviously in the interests of all to whom white racial status eventually would be ascribed. Racial segregation and urban disinvestment in the early and the middle decades of the past century constrained, not only the housing choices of African Americans, but also those of so-called white ethnics. In many instances, the fear of racialized others that racist narratives incited prompted Italian Americans, Irish Americans, Polish Americans, and others to abandon neighborhoods in which they had invested substantial resources and had established important social networks.[87]

Indeed, through the early decades of the century, new immigrants had good reason to forge alliances, *not* with the unambiguously white, but with African American migrants from the Southern states. They had good reason, that is, to ally themselves against the privileged and with those who, like them, had much to gain from challenging race- and class-based social hierarchies. Roediger cites multiple examples of cross-racial labor organization in the early decades of the century. He emphasizes, as well, that it was a nontrivial challenge, for those who would promote racial exclusivity as a marker of value, to induce home owners to agree to sign away their rights to sell to a large class of potential buyers.

But in urban neighborhoods that bordered nascent ghettos (neighborhoods where covenants typically were very heavily employed), many property owners were recent Southern and Eastern European immigrants, and winning their cooperation was not compatible with "[f]ine distinctions as to which European groups were most desirable."[88] Hence, although some covenants excluded long lists of groups, many followed what, from the point of view of those aiming to market racial exclusivity relatively widely, would have been the dominant strategy: they excluded only people on the bottom of the American racial hierarchy.

From the point of view of new immigrants, one might think about the strategic context they faced at that point as exhibiting the logic of a

---

[87] Sugrue, *Origins of the Urban Crisis*.
[88] Ibid., 172.

stag hunt.[89] They stood to gain the most from a radical challenge to the racial hierarchy. But a leveling of, even any substantial change to, that hierarchy, which would have required relatively enduring inter-group coordination and cooperation, would have been difficult to effect. Hence when these bearers of "in-between" racial status received overtures to join whites – overtures accompanied by the promise of the benefits of whiteness as property – they defected.

Thus, beginning in the interwar years, and continuing after World War II, NAREB, the FHA, and other private and public actors marshaled the power of capital and of the state to create and to reinforce, not an irrational belief in a "bad story," so much as a white interest in racial exclusivity. At the same time, disinvestment in America's black ghettos exacerbated nontrivial collective problems and it effectively localized those problems in "black places."

By "collective problems," I mean problems that were collective in a causal sense–joblessness in older cities, to cite one important example – cities that, with private and public disinvestment, began to bleed not just their wealthy and middle-class residents, but also the manufacturing firms that had been so crucial to their economic well-being. Other examples are the poverty that accompanied joblessness, and the crime, victimization, and other social problems that accompanied concentrated poverty and that taxed city school, police, and health systems, along with other public services. That these problems were collective problems in a causal sense is clear. The loss of manufacturing jobs was caused, not by the decisions and actions of city officials and residents alone, but by a range of decisions made and actions taken well beyond municipal boundaries.[90] Similarly, the deterioration of the physical infrastructure of the ghetto, and the shortage there of affordable, open housing was caused not by ghetto

---

[89] First discussed by Rousseau in the *Discourse on Inequality*, the stag hunt game features two or more players who decide independently whether to hunt a stag or a hare. Each prefers the stag, but hunting it requires cooperation, while each player can successfully hunt the hare alone. The game shows that strategic uncertainty can prevent the realization of an optimal outcome, since players will defect if they are sufficiently uncertain how others will act. Jean-Jacques Rousseau, "Discourse on the Origin and the Foundations of Inequality among Men," 117–230 in *The First and Second Discourses and Essay on the Origin of Languages*, ed. Victor Gourevitch (New York: Harper and Row, 1990), here Part II, par. 9, pp. 172–3. For a discussion, see Joel Watson, *Strategy: An Introduction to Game Theory* (New York: W. W. Norton and Company, 2002), 62.

[90] Barry Bluestone and Bennet Harrison, *The Deindustrialization of America: Plant Closings, Community Abandonment, and the Dismantling of Basic Industry* (New York: Basic Books, 1984).

residents, but by the public and private actions described in this chapter that produced "black places" and subjected them to disinvestment.

In their *effects*, however, these problems were made the problems of "black places." Consider the principal collective problem on which this chapter has focused: the inadequate stock of affordable, open housing in the twentieth-century American city. If a political society makes collective decisions that render it difficult for some portion of its population to obtain housing (if it passes racial zoning laws and enforces restrictive covenants, if it enacts racially discriminatory housing policies), then it will generate a series of collective "bads." It will create the kinds of sanitation problems that accompany overcrowding, for instance. It will create the public health problems that accompany poor sanitation.

If that society sites these collective problems – if it locates the overcrowded residences in which the subjugated population is housed – roughly evenly (or even randomly) throughout its territory, then, even though overcrowding will affect some people more so than others, it will be, in a very real sense, experienced *as a problem* by all. Even the privileged (that is, those advantaged by the dual housing market) will have to pay higher taxes to address sanitation and health issues, or alternatively, they will have to confront those problems in the street and in other shared and public spaces.

But if that society geographically and/or politically isolates collective problems in those places where it isolates its subjugated population – if it not only discriminates, that is to say, but discriminates *and segregates* – then it transforms those problems into the problems *of that population*. This result may seem obvious, even inevitable, in the case of the American dual housing market. After all, the stated aim of racial discrimination was to further racial segregation. But if we consider a different example, if we look at the postwar example of the urban redevelopment/renewal program, we can see that localizing collective problems in "black places," although it necessarily *depends on* segregation, is an analytically distinct process that can constitute a separate step.

Recall the preamble to the landmark Housing Act of 1949, which famously announced a national commitment to the "remedy [of] the serious housing shortage, the elimination of substandard and other inadequate housing ... and the realization as soon as feasible of the goal of a decent home and a suitable living environment for every American family."[91] This legislation did not explicitly aim to further racial segregation. To

---

[91] *Housing Act of 1949*, chapter 338, Public Law 171, 81st Congress, Session 1 (1949).

the contrary, it was inclusive in its language and progressive in its stated distributive ends. The means it adopted to advance those ends included federal aid for "slum clearance," with an emphasis on assisting urban districts that were "predominantly residential" and/or that would be redeveloped as predominantly residential.[92] The act required that relocation assistance be provided to those whom urban redevelopment displaced, and it authorized federal funding for eight hundred ten thousand new low-rent public housing units over a six-year period.[93]

However, because it left much of the implementation to the discretion of local officials, and hence to the business interests that dominated local redevelopment authorities – and because it did so in the aftermath of ghettoization and systematic disinvestment from "black places" – the Housing Act of 1949 enabled a racialized distribution of the collective benefits and burdens that it produced. Consider what was urban redevelopment's most obvious benefit: the many new structures it subsidized with public funds. These could, in principle, have been sited in those places where need was the greatest. They could, in principle, have been planned with a view to meeting the urgent needs of the residents of America's older cities. Urban redevelopment agencies could have built well-designed affordable housing units for those who could not obtain decent market-rate housing, that is to say. They could have built schools and other public facilities in communities reeling from public and private disinvestment. But typically they did not. Most agencies selected project sites based on their potential commercial value, focusing on neighborhoods in or very close to the central business district (CBD). Most developed these sites less with a view to improving living conditions for "slum dwellers" than to boosting economic productivity in so-called blighted neighborhoods.[94] A similar pattern obtained with respect to the distribution of the burdens of urban redevelopment. Critics like Jane Jacobs and Herbert Gans, and more recently Mindy Thompson Fullilove, have

---

[92] Ibid. Title I authorized one billion dollars in federal loans to cities for land acquisition and five hundred million dollars in federal grants over five years to subsidize up to two-thirds the cost of reselling land to private developers at below-market prices.

[93] Ibid., Title III. This authorization represented the greatest commitment to public housing the nation had shown to that point. However, as Charles Orlebeke notes, "'Authorization' means little unless it is followed by appropriations – actual commitment of money – and local implementation." Ten years after the passage of the 1949 act, only a quarter of the authorized units had been built. Charles Orlebeke, "The Evolution of Low-Income Housing Policy, 1949–1999," *Housing Policy Debate* 11, 2 (2000): 489–520, here 493.

[94] For a discussion of the political uses of the term *blight* during this period, see Margaret Farrar, *Building the Body Politic* (Chicago, IL: University of Illinois Press, 2008), 80–5.

argued compellingly that the social, economic, and psychological costs of displacement from this program were borne disproportionately by residents of "black places."[95]

The Columbus case, although again far from extraordinary, is illustrative. Relatively early on in the urban redevelopment/renewal years, the city's redevelopment authority selected two sites as the focus for major projects. The first was the Goodale neighborhood, known locally as "Flytown," which was just north and west of the CBD. The second was the Market-Mohawk district, southwest of the state capitol building, in the heart of downtown. In each case, it was the potential economic value of the site that made it attractive to the city's Metropolitan Committee, the business group that dominated decision making about capital improvement in Columbus in the postwar years.[96]

City officials had difficulty attracting capital to these projects, however. By the time they did, they succeeded only on the condition that they discard the plans they had drawn up and allow the developers to implement their own. Hence what was built in Columbus, as elsewhere, was what developers were willing to build: new commercial and residential structures that commanded rents well above what the neighborhood's original residents could pay.[97]

In dealing with those whom these projects displaced, the city hardly realized the lofty ideals of the preamble to the Housing Act of 1949. The

---

[95] Jane Jacobs, *The Death and Life of Great American Cities* (New York: Vintage Books, 1991 [1961]); Herbert Gans, "The Failure of Urban Renewal: A Critique and Some Proposals," *Commentary* 39, 4 (1965): 29–37; Mindy Thompson Fullilove, *Root Shock: How Tearing Up City Neighborhoods Hurts America, and What We Can Do About It* (New York: One World / Ballantine Books, 2004).

[96] The group was organized in 1945. Its twelve-member executive committee was led by Edgar Wolfe (and after he died, by his son Preston), whose family businesses included the *Columbus Dispatch* and the *Ohio State Journal*, the WBNS radio and television stations, and Ohio National Bank. Because of its ties to the local media, the Metropolitan Committee generated, not only financial backing for proposed projects, but also press access and public relations support. See Robert Wilson Adams, *Urban Renewal Politics: A Case Study of Columbus, Ohio, 1952–1961*, PhD dissertation, Ohio State University, 1970, on which this paragraph and the four that follow draw. My discussion of urban renewal in Columbus also draws on Donald Jean Kreitzer, *Urban Redevelopment and Rehabilitation in Columbus, Ohio*, (PhD dissertation, Ohio State University, 1955; Ed Lentz, *Columbus: The Story of a City* (Charleston, SC: Arcadia Press, 2003); and various newspaper articles from the *Columbus Dispatch* during and after the urban redevelopment/renewal years.

[97] Even when developers adopted plans drawn up by public redevelopment agencies, they did so only *because* they found them attractive. *Any* redevelopment authority that hoped to attract developers to its projects was constrained to anticipate developers' preferences and to incorporate them into its plans.

Columbus Urban Redevelopment Authority (CURA) rejected out of hand proposals by the Columbus Metropolitan Housing Authority (CMHA) to build public housing projects on the Goodale and the Market-Mohawk sites. These places, CURA officials argued, were too centrally located, and hence too valuable to be used for public housing. After a series of conflicts in which local builders, realtors, and property owners opposed projects that might have disrupted the city's racially segregated residential patterns, the CMHA constructed the Bonham Street Project (later renamed Windsor Terrace), which it sited just north of the Near East Side, buffered from white neighborhoods by railroad tracks, a hospital, and the Alum Creek. It followed not long after with the Leonard St. Clair project (later renamed Bolivar Arms) and the Mount Vernon Plaza (later renamed Mid-Town East), both of which it sited in the Near East Side ghetto.[98]

Meanwhile, Flytown was razed entirely. Part of the area where this neighborhood had once stood became home to the northern leg of the city's inner belt, while the rest was rebuilt for high-rent commercial uses and for middle- and upper-income, race-restricted apartments. Market-Mohawk, similarly, was redeveloped for high-end commercial and residential uses. The area's former tenants, who could not afford rents in the district once it had been rebuilt, were displaced. In the years to come, the northern leg of the inner belt would continue east from what had been Flytown and slice through the Long Street-Mount Vernon Avenue corridor: that is, through what, since the 1920s, had been Columbus's principal black commercial and cultural district. When completed, the east-west Interstate 70 and the north-south Interstate 71 would intersect in the Near East Side, dividing Columbus's black ghetto while separating it from the city's downtown.

According to the Arthur D. Little consulting firm, which the city of Columbus retained during the urban redevelopment/renewal period, in the decade from 1960 to 1970, a total of nine thousand housing units were demolished in the city for urban renewal, highway construction, and other public projects. Only twenty-five hundred were constructed. By 1970, the city's low-income housing gap was eight thousand units.[99] Of those displaced as a result of these efforts, black households comprised about 40 percent, or more than twice the percentage of blacks

[98] Adams, "Urban Renewal Politics," chapter 3.
[99] *Columbus Dispatch*, "Low Income Housing Gap is Reported," June 24, 1970, p. 12A.

in Columbus at that time.[100] Generally, blacks who were displaced paid significantly higher rents for relocation housing than they had paid for the housing they had lost, and blacks' rents increased significantly more than did the rents of displaced whites.[101] Because of continued disinvestment in the East Side ghetto, the number of housing units that were open to blacks, but that were designated substandard, *increased* during the urban renewal years, notwithstanding the massive clearance of "blighted" areas.[102]

Figures such as these, although they illustrate the fact that collective burdens were sited disproportionately in "black places," hardly capture the impact of those burdens on the people who were made to bear them. In March 1966, the *Columbus Dispatch* interviewed seventy-four-year-old Sarah Runckles, who, two months prior, had been forced to move from the house her parents had built and in which she had lived since she was one. Runckles's house was razed to make room for an urban renewal project. She told the *Dispatch* that her house was worth more than city appraisers claimed it was. She added that, in addition to losing the house itself, she had lost the small income she made by renting out its garage. And she said she felt isolated in her new neighborhood. "It's like living in the country here," she told the *Dispatch* reporter. "It's so quiet. There was so much more going on on Livingston Avenue."

Runckles shared with the reporter a verse she had written on the Christmas card she had sent to her family members and friends the previous December:

> *As the old year draws to a close*
> *It leaves me with bitterness, anger and woes,*
> *For the City says, "Out I must go."*
> *Having this good old home for 3 and 70 years,*
> *Which has had its Joy, Laughter, very few tears,*
> *NEVER will there be another place like this.*[103]

---

[100] Adams, *Urban Renewal Politics*, 296. Blacks were 16.4 percent of the city's population in 1960, and 18.5 percent in 1970.

[101] Black former residents of Goodale and Market-Mohawk paid on average 40 percent more in rent after displacement, compared with 20 and 15 percent increases, respectively, for whites displaced from the two project sites. Adams, *Urban Renewal Politics*, 305. The difference was the product of the dual housing market. Almost all new housing built in Columbus during these years was sited in the city's "white places," the principal exception being the low-income public housing projects constructed in the Near East Side.

[102] Ibid., 296.

[103] Katherine Warner, "'It Leaves Me With Bitterness, Anger, and Woes': 6000 Local Families Uprooted in Ten Years," *Columbus Dispatch*, March 13, 1966, 34A.

In the second half of the twentieth century, redevelopment in Columbus, Ohio brought the central business district – and those who used it, including suburbanites and visitors from out of town – new high rise office buildings and new hotels. It brought the downtown a state-of-the-art convention center and a three-story indoor shopping mall. In its investment priorities, the city was typical of older American cities. In 1968, when the President's Commission on Urban Problems examined urban renewal projects at the national level, it found that, over the previous two years, 65 percent of federally funded projects had been located in or adjacent to CBDs.[104] A later study of urban renewal in nine cities over the entire course of the program found that 52 percent of federal funds supported projects within a mile of the CBD, while a full 82 percent supported projects within two miles.[105]

To be sure, postwar redevelopment efforts did not leave America's "black places" untouched. In Columbus, they brought the Near East Side an expansion of the Children's Hospital campus, as well as renovation and redevelopment, especially along Long Street and Mount Vernon Avenue. But they also brought the disruption of a long-established commercial and cultural district on that corridor. They brought overcrowding, accompanied by a severe shortage of affordable housing, and they brought thousands of publicly subsidized rental units, which were restricted to the very poorest of tenants.

During this period, state actors devoted relatively little attention and relatively few resources to addressing the structural economic problems at the heart of the so-called urban crisis.[106] Rather than invest in remedying

[104] Cited in Bernard Frieden and Lynne Sagalyn, *Downtown, Inc.: How America Rebuilds Cities* (Cambridge, MA: MIT Press, 1989), 25.

[105] Ibid. Nor was this pattern disrupted by the end of the federal Urban Renewal program in the mid-1970s. Under the aegis of the "New Federalism," Community Development Block Grants combined redevelopment with other funds granted to localities, while continuing to allow discretion at the municipal level over how and where to invest. Together with Urban Development Action Grants, which aimed specifically to stimulate public-private redevelopment partnerships, these had the effect of reinforcing the tendency to channel public investment in cities away from black ghettos and toward the CBD. Between 1960 and the mid-1980s, in America's thirty largest metropolitan areas, so many new office buildings were constructed that the office space available more than doubled. Between 1970 and 1988, more than 100 new downtown retail centers were opened, and in 1970 alone, 100 new convention centers were under construction. Public subsidies enabled the vast majority of these projects. Ibid., chapters 3, 4, and 13.

[106] The "War on Poverty" launched by the Economic Opportunity Act of 1964 was notoriously short-lived and underfunded. In Columbus, the principal agency supported by the Office of Economic Opportunity (OEO), the Columbus Metropolitan Community Action Organization (CMACAO), had an annual budget of just $500,000. Ned Stout,

"the serious housing shortage," "eliminat[ing] ... substandard and other inadequate housing," and realizing "the goal of a decent home and a suitable living environment for every American family," they effectively localized these housing problems, along with related collective problems, in black ghettos like Columbus's Near East Side.

They thus rendered what were, in a causal sense, collective problems, in their *effects*, the problems of "black places." In turn-of-the-twenty-first-century Columbus, Ohio, as Calvin Moore contemplated the two sides of the railroad tracks that divide suburban Bexley from the Near East Side ghetto, more than 9 percent of adult residents on the urban side of those tracks were unemployed. This rate was more than three times that of the Columbus Metropolitan Statistical Area (MSA) as a whole, and it was more than twice what most macroeconomists argued was the frictional unemployment rate of about 3 to 4 percent.[107] Labor force participation rates in East Side Columbus were significantly lower at century's end than those in the Columbus MSA.[108] More than a third of East Side families lived below the poverty line: a rate almost five times that of the MSA as a whole.[109] Home ownership was about half that in the

"CMACAO to Control City's Youth Corps," *Columbus Dispatch*, December 7, 1967, 1B. Founded in 1965, CMACAO had been in operation for less than a decade when Nixon cut OEO funding in 1973.

[107] MSAs are defined by the United States Office of Management and Budget to include core urban and surrounding areas characterized by social and economic interdependence. Unemployment was 2.8 percent in the Columbus MSA in 2000, compared with 9.1 percent in the Near East Side. United States Census Bureau, Summary File 4, DP-3, "Profile of Selected Economic Characteristics: 2000." (The unemployment rate for the Near East Side was computed by the author using tract-level data.) Most macroeconomists argue that some minimum level of unemployment is desirable, because below it inflation will rise to unacceptable levels. Milton Friedman first termed this threshold the "natural" rate of unemployment, and others subsequently called it the "non-accelerating inflation rate of employment" (NAIRU). The NAIRU is thought by most economists to vary over time and across market contexts, responding to changes in labor relations and workers' wages. Through much of the 1990s, economists estimated it at about 5 to 6 percent for the United States, although in the early 2000s most agreed that much lower rates of unemployment were compatible with relatively low rates of inflation. To my knowledge, no mainstream economist believes an unemployment rate of 9 or 10 percent is desirable. For an overview, see the symposium, "The Natural Rate of Unemployment" in the *Journal of Economic Perspectives*, 11, 1 (Winter 1997).

[108] Forty-five point one percent of East Side residents age sixteen and over were not in the labor force in 2000, compared with 30.4 percent of residents of the Columbus MSA. United States Census Bureau, Summary File 4, DP-3, "Profile of Selected Economic Characteristics: 2000." (The labor force participation rate for the East Side was computed by the author using tract-level data.)

[109] Thirty-four point one percent of East Side families were poor in 2000, compared with 7.1 percent in the Columbus MSA. United States Census Bureau, Summary File 4, DP-3,

MSA.[110] East Side homes were significantly older, and they were valued at a significantly lower level, than were homes throughout the metropolitan area.[111] Educational achievement was significantly lower in the Near East Side than in the Columbus metropolitan area as a whole.[112]

These patterns will be all too familiar to most American readers of this text. They are mirrored in older cities throughout the Northern and Midwestern states of this country. Indeed, they are even more pronounced in what were once major industrial centers, such as Detroit, than in Columbus, which benefited through much of the twentieth century from a relatively diversified economy.

That these place-based inequalities are layered atop racial segregation not only influences who feels the *effects* of collective problems. It also influences the phenomenology of their causation. Analysis of discourse on the so-called urban crisis shows that, by the time of the riots of the mid-1960s, that crisis was interpreted and debated across the ideological spectrum in largely racial terms.[113] By 1967, Nathan Glazer could confidently assert that "the Negro Problem" was the "most decisive of the social problems that we think of when we consider the urban crisis."[114] That same year, Irving Kristol declared that "what we call the 'urban crisis' is mostly just a euphemism for problems *created by* the steady influx of Southern Negroes into Northern and Western cities."[115]

"Profile of Selected Economic Characteristics: 2000." (The family poverty rate for the East Side was computed by the author using tract-level data.)

[110] In the East Side, 32.4 percent of occupied units were occupied by their owners, compared with 62.3 percent in the Columbus MSA overall. United States Census Bureau, Summary File 1, QT-H1, "General Housing Characteristics: 2000." (The home owner rate for the East Side was computed by the author using tract-level data.)

[111] Forty-three point eight percent of East Side housing units had been built in 1939 or earlier, compared with just 14.2 percent for the MSA as a whole, while in the East Side, 74.6 percent of owner-occupied units were valued at less than $100,000, compared with only 37.2 percent for the MSA as a whole. United States Census Bureau, Summary File 4, DP-4, "Profile of Selected Housing Characteristics: 2000." (The percentage of older and lower-valued units for the East Side was computed by the author using tract-level data.)

[112] In the East Side, only 14.1 percent of persons age twenty-five and older have a bachelor's degree or higher, less than half the rate for the MSA as whole, which is 29.1 percent.

[113] Robert Beauregard, *Voices of Decline: The Postwar Fate of U.S. Cities*, second edition (New York: Routledge, 2003).

[114] Nathan Glazer, *Cities in Trouble* (Chicago, IL: Quadrangle Books, 1970), 24. Quoted in Beauregard, *Voices of Decline*, 130.

[115] Kristol, "Common Sense about the 'Urban Crisis,'" *Fortune* 76 (October 1967): 234, emphasis added. Quoted in Beauregard, *Voices of Decline*, 172.

If there is a narrative logic to statements such as Glazer's and Kristol's – if Kristol's, in particular, echoes the "bad (racial) story" of the early decades of the twentieth century – that logic can be readily challenged by critics on the left. "The influx of Southern Negroes into Northern and Western cities," such critics can argue, was neither a sufficient nor the principal cause of problems like "white flight," the decline of urban public education, or widespread joblessness and concentrated poverty in central cities. To the contrary (and as argued in detail in this chapter), these and related problems were largely the product of aggressive state-led policies of ghettoization and urban disinvestment: policies initiated long before the "urban crisis" became a topic of public debate.

But assertions such as Kristol's – and, more generally, understandings of racial categorizations as *reflecting* human differences, which themselves *cause* social and political inequalities – survive the attack of scientific and of moral/practical reason, because they are not only, and they are not principally, circulated and transmitted as narratives. Over the course of the last century, racial stories were institutionalized and objectified in America's cities and in their suburbs, effectively ensuring that most Americans would (as did Calvin Moore) learn their race through place. It is the racialization of urban and suburban space that makes possible Calvin Moore's experience of one side of the proverbial railroad tracks as "black" and "low income" and the other as "white" and "high society." It is the racialization of space that helps keep alive, even into the twenty-first century, a widely shared sense of "black" and "white" as socially meaningful categories, and also a complex of what I have called racial interests.

In the next chapter, I shift my focus from the level of the collective, back to that of the personal identity narrative, engaging the life story that Calvin Moore related to me. Taking as my starting point the narrative that Moore constructs from his day-to-day experience, I ask how, as he negotiates life in racialized space, Moore *uses* stories of racial identity.

More generally, how do institutionalized and objectified racial narratives about "who we are" shape stories about "who I am" as a unique individual? How do institutionalized and objectified collective identity narratives shape the life stories people construct as they recall and interpret their experience?

3

Ordinary Stories

The bridge collapses just as you cross over.

At the last possible moment, the life guard rescues your drowning son.

You leave your spouse after nearly twenty years of marriage.

You purchase the winning lottery ticket and retire early from your dead-end job.

When you translate the sensory input of your lived experience into narrative form, it is happenings such as these that you mark as events. At the moment of experience – at the moment when the lifeguard's body breaks the surface of the water – the data that eventually will comprise your narrative are only a fraction of the sensory data to which you are exposed. The smell of chlorine, the rough touch of concrete on bare feet, the slight shift in the sunlight as the clouds move overhead: your conscious mind attends only to a subset of such impressions. It is drawn to the novel, to the variable, to the unexpected.

Even that subset of data on which, in the moment, you focus, far exceeds what you will recall when you narrativize your story. The lottery tickets that did not win, although they may have captured your attention momentarily, are, no less than the movements of the clouds, nonevents in the story of your life.

The present chapter concerns itself with nonevents. Its origin was my own surprise when I first sat down to read Calvin Moore's life narrative. Near the start of the last chapter, I introduced brief excerpts from a semi-structured interview I conducted with Moore shortly after recording his life story. In that interview, I asked Moore to think of a number of ways he might complete the statement "My name is Calvin Moore, and I am _____" and followed with questions designed to probe his understanding of the identity categories he invoked in his responses.[1] In the semi-structured interview, in other words, I prompted Calvin Moore to thematize his identities.

When I did, Moore's responses focused principally on racial, gendered, and place-based identities. His first answer to the "Who am I?" question was "I am an Africa[n] American male." His second answer emphasized his identification with the East Side Columbus neighborhood to which he referred as "the hood" ("I am from the hood"). It was during this interview – and thus only after I had prompted him to name and to reflect on his identities – that Calvin Moore recalled the forcible policing of racial and spatial boundaries cited in the previous chapter (*"there's certain places you don't go"*). During this interview, he thematized, as well, place-based socioeconomic inequalities and the adverse effect of ghetto poverty on East Side residents. For example, he told me:

The community I originally associate in is a [high] poverty, low income … infested with drugs and gangs. And I see those guys out there … and … out of ten of those guys out there, two of them, if they're lucky, will live to be my age.

In the semi-structured interview, in short, Moore explicitly addressed the outcomes of the processes of racialization and urban disinvestment traced in Chapter 2.

Prior to the semi-structured interview, however, when he told me his life story, Moore remained entirely silent on these themes.[2] Hence my surprise. If coercive actions create and maintain black ghettos, if decisions made by powerful public and private actors channel collective resources away from "black places," and if they concentrate collective problems in those places, then such processes and their outcomes (I thought) should play at least some role in the life story of a man like Calvin Moore. They should play some role, that is, in the story of a man they profoundly affect in ways that, when prompted, he readily identifies.

But they do not. Nor do these processes or their outcomes play a role in the life stories of the other East Side residents I interviewed, all of whom, without exception, when presented with the "Who am I?" question, thematize black racial identity.

In the present chapter, I ask "What role do stories of collective identity play in narratives of personal identity?" In Chapter 1, recall, I suggested that the former can function as building blocks of the latter. Personal

---

[1] For a schedule of interview questions, see the appendix.
[2] The prompt for the life history interview was: "Tell me the story of your life: how you came to be who and where you are today." See the appendix.

identity narratives can cite collective identity narratives, that is, incorporating into stories of "who I am" shared or public stories of "who we are" (as Americans, for instance).

In the present chapter, however, I argue that this is not the only role collective identity stories play. Drawing on Calvin Moore's narrative, I suggest that, in what I call *ordinary* life stories, stories of collective identity function less as building blocks than as narrative frames: unthematized background assumptions that shape the translation of experience into narrative by defining some sets of actions as events and others as nonevents.

It is precisely this quality I mean to signal with the adjective *ordinary*. *Extraordinary* narratives are narratives that take collective identity stories as their subject matter, working to explain or to evaluate them, or to motivate efforts to maintain or change shared understandings of "who we are." Many historians and social scientists, many novelists, and most social critics and political activists tell stories that are extraordinary in this sense of the word.

But most of the time, most social actors' life stories are ordinary stories. Hence ordinary stories' political significance. These are the tools people use most often when they translate their lived experience into narrative form: into the form, that is, in which it shapes their beliefs, values, and preferences and directs their future actions.

The principal claim I advance in this chapter is that the institutionalization and the objectification of collective identity stories encourages the construction of ordinary life stories. I introduce this claim with what I regard as a relatively difficult case. As I argue in Chapter 5, people whose identities are *unmarked* – the norms against which identitarian differences are defined – are less likely than those socially defined as "different" to see, and hence to thematize, collective identities. Sexual and gender identities, for instance, are less salient to those who occupy privileged subject positions (to straight people, to men) than to those marked as "other" (gay men and lesbians, women). Racial identity is less salient to the racially privileged (whites) than to racially marked subjects like Calvin Moore.

Even so, Moore's narrative, much like the other life narratives I recorded, is an ordinary story: one that centers on its protagonist's decisions and actions, on his interactions with a circumscribed set of individuals, and on his responses to select nonhuman and intrasubjective forces. Why? Institutionalized and objectified collective identity stories frame this narrative of personal identity. They work to define both ghettoization and the racialization of political interests and collective problems, not as events that comprise the story's action, but as nonevents: mere background to "what happened."

1. "I Become Rage"

I went to Job Corps in Kentucky. I'm from Alabama, and all these guys from all over this country was going to Job Corps here. It was like a big campus, a military base.

And Bleak was one of my sergeants. I was a lieutenant, a first lieutenant, in this military dorm. And these guys came in, first on campus, and they were from Miami. Okay, the biggest was up there at this time, was this guy from New York, and guys from California.

And Bleak came up there and told me these guys jumped on him. You know, cause every time something happened these guys would come and see me. So I found out, well, who are they, and where are they. So we went looking for these guys, just me and Bleak. And ... we found these guys across campus, at a pool hall. So when we went into the pool hall ... I tried to talk to the guy, to be honest with you. And he attacked me. They jumped me.

Okay: big mistake. I got control of half this dorm, this campus, and you jump me?

So, I go back to my dorm, call out every guy at my dorm. I call 'em out: "Let's go!" So that's when the weapons start to come out. You know, we were not supposed to have any weapons of any sort. I found a pipe laying in the field, and I put a bicycle whip on this pipe. And what I did was, it was a handle.

I went looking for this guy on Friday night. He wasn't at the movie theater. He wasn't at the recreation center. He wasn't – well, he was at the gym. The first time we went by the gym, I had about fifty guys with me, looking for four guys. And we found them, they're in the gym. So I had all these guys surround the gym, going to every exit. And: "Block every exit. If you see someone running, you stop him!" So we went in the gym, we found the guy.

And this is just my rage, which I'm trying to have control over now.

This is my rage that there, when we went into the gym, these guys were playing ball. And I walked up to the guy. And Bleak was like, "There you go." And I was like, "Yeah, M.F., you're right, there M.F. go."

And I pull this pipe out of my pants, out of my sweat pants. I pull this pipe out of my pants, and I punched this guy. And I swung at him, but I missed. He ducked. When he ducked, and start running, I immediately screamed out to all these guys who were with me, "If anyone moves, you stomp the hell out of them! Anybody!"

And these guys were standing up there, scared, frozen. They can't move.

He was running out of the gym, and I got five guys outside waiting on him. So he runs out, they grab him, they start stomping him, kicking him in his face, beating him down to the ground.

I take this metal pipe that I got in my hand, get a firm grip like I'm swinging a golf club. And I'm hitting this guy: nothing but in his face and in his head. And I darn near killed that guy. I must have hit him at least eight times. Straight in his face. In his nose, in his mouth, in his eye. I was trying to literally have to make this guy get plastic surgery. I wanted to rearrange his face.

Calvin Moore begins the story of his life with his birth in Birmingham, Alabama. The youngest of five children, he says he was only eight years old when his father died of lung cancer, leaving him to grow up with "no real role models." "[G]rowing up in the neighborhood," Moore recalls, "I hung around a lot of guys. Mostly got involved in gang activities. And I found a way that I could – you know, I got in with the wrong crowd at an early age."

Moore explains to me that he wanted to have the clothes that were in style at that time and that were worn by the older boys, whom he admired. He wanted the cars that they had, the money, the girlfriends, "the lifestyle." "I wanted to be that type of person. I wanted to be the type of person that everybody knows, that everyone respects. Always had money in my pocket. And, you know … it's more like a power thing with me. As long as I had control and power, I'd feel like I was king."

Moore recalls his teen years and his early adulthood in the form of a succession of violent physical confrontations through which he attempted to achieve this control, this power that he craved. The first took place early in adolescence, when he proved himself to high-ranking members of a neighborhood gang, gaining their admiration and acceptance with an unprovoked attack on the gang's leader.

This first recalled act of violence, Moore tells me, was incited by twin brothers, older boys in the neighborhood whom he respected and whose respect he wanted. He describes the pair as "the most ruthless guys I ever met in my life" and explains:

I've seen them shoot people, rob people, and they earned my respect. And how I earned this one twin's respect, who was the leader of a gang: they got me drunk and high one night, and they called me "Young Blood." And it was like, "If you want to hang out with us, you got to do this." So, you know, we were starting out [laughs] – I'll never forget this, it's like yesterday – we were starting out, on the corner. And, you know, I snuck out of the house. My mother was at work. And I got drunk and high with these guys. And this guy tells me, "All I want you to do: drink this, smoke this, and you see this guy with a red hat on? Walk up behind him, and slap the hell out of him." And I did it, because I wanted to be accepted … Lo and behold, it was the president of the gang. This guy beat me like I stole something, you know, and started to shoot me, until the other guys stopped him. And he says, "Well, you know what? Since you got so much heart, we'll let you in the gang."

If Moore's first confrontation won him induction into gang life, later fights earned him expulsion from a series of mainstream institutions: first from public high school, then from an alternative school for boys, and finally, following the incident described in the interview excerpt that opens this section, from the United States Job Corps. In each case, Moore's "rage" was, by his telling, the driving force.

His recounting of an incident in which he assaulted his school's principal is typical in this regard. Here Moore emphasizes the role played by rage, which he describes as taking over his conscious or reflective self so that, momentarily, he tells me, he "*become[s] rage*":

Now when I'm involved in a confrontation, *I become rage*. So, regardless of who touched me, I'm thinking you're out to hurt me. And that was just a violent tendency I had. So … the principal [who had intervened to break up a fight between Moore and another boy] caught me. So I picked the principal up off the floor, threw him on the floor, and stomped him. You know … with my foot, in his face. And, like I said, the rage just hit me, and everything just went black.

Not long after Moore's expulsion from the Job Corps, a series of tragic events prompted him, he recalls, to decide to change the course of his life. His six-year-old stepdaughter and nine-year-old nephew, whom he and his then-wife had been raising together, died in a house fire during an overnight visit with their grandmother. His marriage ended, and he moved, alone, to Columbus, Ohio, to "start a new life." Shortly after, his grandmother died. His best friend was shot and killed while attempting to burglarize a house occupied by drug dealers: in Moore's words, "shot in the head at point blank range for some stuff *I* taught him to do." Finally, Moore's brother, with whom he had had an especially close relationship, died of complications from diabetes at the age of twenty-nine.

The last of these events Moore characterizes as a personal "turning point." He used to have a motto, he tells me: "'I'll stop when someone kills me,' 'cause I was refusing to be taken alive." At the time of his brother's death, he notes, he had a criminal record that included eight counts of assault against the Columbus police. But in the years since, he says, he has returned to and "picked up" values that had been instilled in him as a child, but which he subsequently had "put down."

Calvin Moore tells me he currently is working toward his GED.[3] He attends church regularly, he adds, and he plans to enroll in college. He aspires to become a social worker who will counsel young men who are starting down the dangerous life path that he himself went down. Given his physical appearance and his demeanor, Moore speculates that if he were to return to his former lifestyle, someone would kill him. But today, he says, he wants to live. He "cherish[es] life."

He tells me he often thinks about the people he has harmed, including himself. The reason he changed, he adds, is that he believed the deaths of his loved ones were punishments from God for the things he had done:

I wanted to change, because I felt that, I felt that God was punishing me, because everything in my life that I ever loved or cared about, he took from me. I can remember, vaguely, asking God, " … [L]et them guys kill me. Let me die." Because I felt like my life was worthless. You know, all the things I've done, all the shootouts I've been in, why does my brother have to die? Why do these kids have to die? Why couldn't a stray bullet have hit me? You know, killed me.

He emphasizes that God's sparing of his life, despite his guilt, indicates that God has some purpose he intends for Moore to serve:

Of all the things I've done, I deserve to die. You know, but, but all these battle scars on my body, and with my health, be spared. So, I feel like today I'm here for a purpose. I don't know what it is, I'm not concerned with what it is, but when it happens, I just hope I can fulfill it.

Moore stresses, as well, that he is ready to change. He is ready to grow up, to accept his responsibilities, to take the necessary steps to become "a productive member of society":

I feel like [sighs] the line I need to walk, thirty-six this year, and I should mature. And I should grow up and accept my responsibilities as a human being. Let alone as being a man, but a human being. And … be a productive member of society. I don't want people looking at me for the rest of my life in fear, thinking, "Well, he's crazy, stay away from him," you know … And I just want to change. It's time for a change. It really is. And I know in my heart I'm the only one who can do this.

The event that Calvin Moore recounts in the passage at the start of this section is thematically central to his life as he narrativizes it. The motif

---

[3] The GED (General Educational Development) is a high school equivalency certificate.

of his life story – the overarching theme that unifies the events that comprise it – is Moore's struggle to overcome what he characterizes as an inner rage that rises up from within him periodically, taking control over both his body and his conscious mind. Moore's physical confrontations with other men are key episodes in this larger, intrasubjective struggle to transform himself from a person who is driven by rage – a person who is at once a source of injury and an object of fear – into a responsible man and human being, "a productive member of society" who stands ready to fulfill the purposes for which God intends him.

The event is prototypical, what is more, in its structure. The actions that drive and define this event, not unlike the actions that drive and define the other events that comprise Moore's narrative, are but a small subset of "what happened." At the moment of experience, they captured Moore's attention. At the moment of narrativization, they appeared to him to be both *tellable* – that is, sufficiently novel to warrant reporting – and *causally significant* – that is, exerting some nontrivial effect on his story's outcome.

These actions consist, first and foremost, in decisions that are made and deeds that are performed by the story's protagonist (the self) and by a small cast of characters with whom that protagonist interacts. Here the relevant characters are Bleak, the men who attack Bleak, and the men who live in Moore's dorm, whom Moore "calls out" for his counterattack. More generally, the characters who people Moore's narrative – indeed, the characters who people each of the thirty life narratives I collected – are individuals with whom the protagonist comes into contact in everyday life: family members, friends and significant others, neighbors, bosses and coworkers, teachers, and fellow students.

Not every event that drives Moore's narrative is the product of human action. A second type of force the effects of which Moore posits as causally significant and reportable can be captured by the notion of chance or luck. For Moore, one important example is the early death of his father, which, by his telling, deprives him of a "real" role model, leaving him vulnerable to the influence of "the wrong crowd." When luck enters the various life narratives I collected, it does so both as a force for bad and as a force for good. For one respondent, the sudden collapse of the company for which he worked, and which helped to fund his education, meant the end of his formal schooling.[4] For another, the fact that, when he was born, his mother shared a hospital room with a devout Catholic, whom

4 Interview with Theo Richardson, a fifty-four-year-old resident of East Side Columbus.

she then befriended, meant he was sent to Catholic school, where he acquired the work habits that enabled him to complete college.[5] Whatever its form – tragedy or windfall – the force of luck, when narrated, is narrated as both novel and significant: a chance happening that substantially affects the course of a life.

A third and final set of forces that produce the action of an event consists in nonhuman powers, such as God, and human drives and impulses, such as Calvin Moore's rage. Much like human choices, and much like luck, these are posited as significant in shaping the direction a life story takes. What is more, although these powers themselves often are narrated as constants (God's will is unchanging; Moore's rage is always present just beneath the surface), their role in the narrative is posited as sufficiently novel to warrant telling, both because they are only manifest on select occasions (Moore is not in a constant state of rage, after all, and God's will is often obscure), and because actors are represented as capable of responding to these forces in multiple ways. (Moore can respond to the fact of his rage by declining to engage it, passively allowing it to overcome him, or, alternatively, he can work actively to resist it: to "[try] to have control over" this force that rises up from within. Similarly, God's will is a command Moore can defy, earning retribution, or to which he can conform, "accept[ing his] responsibilities as a human being" who stands ready to fulfill his purpose).

As Calvin Moore narrativizes his lived experience, in short, he molds it in a way that every storyteller must. From the happenings that, in the moment of experience, captured his attention, he selects those he posits to be both tellable and causally significant. Such events he distinguishes from circumstances that he represents as having had little effect on his story's outcome, and also from those conditions that he regards as constant, as unexceptional. These Moore represents as just background to his narrative or, alternatively, excludes from it altogether.

At least three analytically distinct processes of selection are at work as Calvin Moore constructs his life story. The first can be captured by the notion of "tellability" or "reportability," which I gestured toward in the first chapter: an idea I borrow from linguist William Labov. The typical narrative, Labov argues, is not just *any* sequence of events, as in "*x* happened, and then *y*, and then *z*," ("I went to work, and then I wrote this paragraph about reportability, and then I ate lunch at my desk.")

---

[5] Interview with John Carr, a fifty-eight-year-old resident of East Side Columbus.

Instead, it is a *novel* or *surprising* or otherwise *unexpected* – and hence tellable – series of events.[6] Happenings worth reporting, Labov writes, are "terrifying, dangerous, weird, wild, crazy; or amusing, hilarious, wonderful; more generally ... strange, uncommon, or unusual ... not ordinary, plain, humdrum, everyday, or run-of-the-mill."[7] Competent narrators know this to be the case, and so they construct their stories accordingly, preemptively warding off what Labov calls "the withering rejoinder: 'So what?'"[8]

Mark Turner, following Labov, underscores that our judgments of narrative reportability can depart from our scientific judgments of significance. One might well know that, at a given time and in a given place, *something* happened and yet, if that something seems unreportable, remark quite sincerely that "nothing happened." In Turner's words:

It is impossible for us to look at the world and not to see reportable stories distinguished from background, even though distinguishing in this fashion is hard to justify from the point of view of physics and biology. If we look out of the window and someone asks us what is out there, we can reply "Nothing" and mean it, so long as what we are looking at seems like background: a tree and a lawn on a quiet day. But if a lightning bolt strikes the tree, it looks very different, and becomes reportable. We believe that the same laws of physics and biology hold for both scenes and that in a scientific sense a great deal is going on in both scenes. Yet the lightning strike looks like a little story and the other scene looks like background, nothing remarkable.[9]

The second selection process at work in Moore's narrative is also highlighted by Turner, who argues that storytellers have a strong tendency, in his words, to project "action stories" – that is, narratives in which outcomes are caused by clearly identifiable agents – onto events in which there is no agent who causes a particular outcome (Turner gives the example of a wall collapsing), or in which there are many agents who, acting in an uncoordinated fashion, together cause an outcome (a bridge wears away after years of use).[10]

A case in point is Calvin Moore's narration of an apparently unrelated series of deaths (the deaths of the two children, the grandmother, the brother, and the friend) as *God punishing him* for his wrongdoings.

---

[6] See William Labov, *Language in the Inner City: Studies in the Black English Vernacular* (Philadelphia: University of Pennsylvania Press, 1972), especially chapter 9.
[7] Ibid., 371.
[8] Ibid., 366.
[9] Mark Turner, *The Literary Mind* (New York: Oxford University Press, 1996), 145–6.
[10] Ibid., 26.

Here reportable events clearly occurred. The children died in a house fire; the friend was murdered; the grandmother passed away; and the brother died because of medical complications from diabetes. With the exception of the murder, however, no identifiable agent caused these outcomes. Still, Moore narrates them as agent-driven (or as driven by an agent-like supernatural force: God). Indeed, even when he narrates a non-agentive force as causally significant (his rage), he narrates it as agent-like. (Rage "hits me," and "I become rage"). Relatively few events in this narrative, or in the other life narratives that I collected, present causally significant outcomes in non-agent-centric terms.

The third selection process to which I want to point takes place, not in the course of constructing a narrative from recalled events, but rather at the moment of perception. Even before Calvin Moore constructs his version of "what happened" – even back on the Job Corps campus, for example, while he was living what eventually would become an important episode in his life narrative – Moore was attentive to some of the visual, auditory, and somatosensory stimuli to which he was exposed, but not to all.

According to cognitive scientists Christof Koch and Naotsugu Tsuchiya, people cope with the torrent of data to which they are exposed in their day-to-day lives by "select[ing] a small fraction and process[ing] this reduced input in real time, while ... process[ing the remainder] at a reduced bandwidth ... [A]ttention 'selects' information of current relevance ... while [neglecting] the non-attended data."[11]

Selection at this perceptual stage can be "top-down" (controlled), or it can be "bottom-up" (automatic).[12] Top-down selection is at work when Moore, whose goal is to locate particular people, focuses on the men in the gym, rather than on other aspects of his environment, which may have been relevant had his goal been different. (He may have focused on particular pieces of equipment in the gym, for example, had his goal been to exercise). Bottom-up selection, by contrast, is independent of the task at hand. Regardless of one's goal, the novelty of some aspect of the environment, or the suddenness or the intensity of some change, may draw attention. (Had the floor of the gym begun to shift and to move when

---

[11] Christof Koch and Naotsugu Tsuchiya, "Attention and Consciousness: Two Distinct Brain Processes," *Trends in Cognitive Sciences* 11, 1 (2006): 16–22, here 16.

[12] The seminal text is William James, *Principles of Psychology* (New York: Dover, 1950 [1890]). For an overview of theoretical and empirical work on selective attention, see William Johnston and Veronica Dark, "Selective Attention," *Annual Review of Psychology* 37 (1986): 43–75.

Calvin Moore entered, his attention likely would have been drawn to that movement, regardless of his goal.)

Imagine two scenarios in which a human action affects Calvin Moore. Imagine, first, a direct encounter with another person or persons, such as the physical confrontation at the Job Corp gym. Imagine, however, that in the moment of the attack, one of the other men in the gym were to move forward and to reach out a hand, grabbing hold of Moore's makeshift weapon. In that moment, Moore's attention most likely would focus on the other man's movement. Other aspects of his environment – the smell of the gym, the sound of his own breathing, the feel of cold metal in his hands – would be more or less as Calvin Moore expects. This action, by contrast, would be unexpected. It would be unpredicted, unusual, other than routine.

Now imagine a long-standing rule such as "No weapons on the U.S. Job Corps campus." This rule, not unlike the face-to-face action, affects Calvin Moore. If he obeys it, it affects the means he can use to engage another person in combat, or, if attacked, to defend himself. If he disregards it, it affects him through the penalties attached to rule violation. The rule is a form of human action that shapes Calvin Moore's action. But, unlike the violent encounter in the gym, it has been codified. It has been regularized, that is to say. It has been systematized. It has been converted from a novel happening, which in the moment of experience demands attention, and in the moment of narrativization seems tellable and reportable, to a familiar rule that rarely needs stating.

The action has also been institutionalized. The rule "No weapons on the U.S. Job Corps campus" has been integrated, that is to say, into a larger, established order of rules and relations. Because this order (the U.S. Job Corps) structures practices in which Calvin Moore engages, Moore develops, through repeated performances of his roles in those practices, a set of relatively enduring expectations about its norms. He develops a set of background beliefs and assumptions that frame how he processes, and how he narrativizes, his experience.

To be sure, one can imagine instances in which the "no weapons" rule becomes a datum on which Moore focuses attention. One can imagine points in time when the rule becomes salient: points when it seems novel, such as the first time Calvin Moore is apprised of it.

But most of the time, his attention will be elsewhere. Perhaps Moore ate breakfast in the dining hall the morning of the attack. Perhaps he attended class. Perhaps he worked out at the gym. If so, in each instance,

Moore was governed by the "no weapons" rule. He may have been fully capable, during each of these experiences, of articulating that rule. And yet he may not once have attended to it with his conscious mind. If so, as Moore narrativizes those experiences (breakfast, class, gym), he likely will not narrativize them as governed by the "no weapons" rule.

Again, one can imagine exceptions. There may be times when Moore incorporates the "no weapons" rule into the story he tells about his lived experience. Indeed, he does just this in the life history excerpt cited earlier. He explicitly cites the rule as he recalls the event in the Job Corps gym because he understands it to be relevant to his story. (Soon after this event, recall, Moore was expelled from the Job Corps because he had violated the "no weapons" rule).

Even still, when Calvin Moore cites the rule, he cites it as background to the action of his story. He cites it, *not* as an event that drives the narrative, but as a circumstance that helps explain the significance of an event. For the "no weapons" rule to enter Moore's narrative as an event – as a happening that is both causally significant and reportable – it would need to be de-routinized.

Imagine, now, a third scenario: the "no weapons" rule is publicly challenged, perhaps by a Job Corps staff member or by a participant in the program who questions its legitimacy or its efficacy. If this questioning prompts a debate about the advantages and the disadvantages of the rule, if that debate leads to the rule's unmaking (or to its remaking), and if Calvin Moore directs his conscious attention to these processes, then Moore may well narrativize the processes and their outcomes as events. If he does, it will be because he comes to understand rule construction as an action that affects his action, and as one worth reporting: a happening that is both causally significant and tellable.

Collective identities, I argued in Chapter 1, are often constituted in narrative form. But identity thinking has a classificatory logic. A racial identity story can be converted from a narrative, which people actively tell (through literature, for example, through news reports, or through storytelling in the classroom) to a classificatory system on the order of black/white.[13] As I argued in Chapter 2, racial identities can be institutionalized. They can be integrated into a larger system of rules and relations: into a

---

[13] Or: White/Black or African American /American Indian and Alaska Native/Native Hawaiian and Other Pacific Islander/some other race). These are the 2000 U.S. census categories. The fact that the census now offers multiple categories and allows people to check multiple boxes does not mean the relevant identities have not been codified.

legal order, for example. They can be built into the material environment, as well: objectified in racialized space. When identity stories are codified and institutionalized, when they are objectified in material form, then people learn them practically. They develop, through repeated performances of their ascribed identities, a set of relatively stable expectations about those identities and about the social norms that govern them.

Hence people can perform their identities without attending to these expectations with their conscious minds, and without narrating them in their ordinary stories. When they do narrate them, what is more, they can tell them as, not events, but simply background to "what happened."

When identity narratives are institutionalized and objectified, they gain resistance to de-routinization. Institutionalized identity stories – much like the "no weapons" rule at the Job Corps campus – can govern day-to-day action without drawing one's conscious attention. Objectified identity stories – stories that are, quite literally, made into things – appear to be "just background" to the events that comprise life narratives.

I experience the brick exterior of this housing project, the winding road through that subdivision, the railroad tracks that divide this ghetto from that suburb, in much the same way that you experience the concrete at your feet, pool side. I experience each, that is to say, without contemplating the (eminently reportable and causally significant) human decisions and human actions that brought them into being.

2. Frames

Institutionalization and objectification lend identity narratives a life of their own. They help to explain why collective identity stories so very often function in our stories of personal identity, *not* as narrative building blocks, but as narrative frames. By *frames*, I mean those sets of beliefs, valuations, and unthematized background assumptions that order the stories people tell, by helping distinguish events (the causally significant and the tellable) from nonevents.

Consider the following excerpts from the life history interviews of three of my respondents:

And when he took the kids home with him, when the kids came back, they're telling me, "Oh, um, the lady was cooking pancakes," and this and that. And I said, "What lady?" You know, "What are you talking about?" So right then, I knew. Oh, ok, he's staying with a female. So that was the point of no return.
Charlene Johnston-Lewis, East Side Columbus, Ohio

So I go to private school, and almost everyone's parents there are professional. Either they own their own businesses, they're ... doctors, lawyers, dentists. And you get to see how people live, which is different. You get to see country clubs. You get to see big houses. You get to see wait staff: servants and stuff. You're like, "This is really real. This is not something that's on TV that doesn't ... really happen."

Walter Barrett, New Albany, Ohio

[M]y junior year I interviewed at Yale and was accepted to [nursing] school and went for an interview and watched a girl being mugged. And, me being from the country, I'm thinking, and it's in the middle of the ghetto.

Cynthia Arnold, New Albany, Ohio

In each of these life history interview excerpts, the narrator constructs an event. She constructs, that is to say, a happening, which she judges to be reportable and which she presents as significant in shaping the course of her life. The event Charlene Johnston-Lewis narrates, for instance, accounts for an important change in a relationship that is central to her life story. Shortly after realizing that the father of her young children was "staying with a female," she ended her physical relationship with him, and she married another man. Walter Barrett narrates the switch from urban public to private school because of the impact he says it had on his aspirations. The realization that the lifestyles of the affluent are "really real," he tells me, motivated him to pursue a professional career. He goes on to add that it made him "want to make a lot of money." Finally, Cynthia Arnold relies on her account of a witnessed mugging to explain her decision to attend nursing school in Utah, where eventually she met her husband and began her career.

In each instance, the elaboration of the event depends on a set of prior beliefs and assumptions, which help the narrator sort the causally significant and the tellable from those aspects of "what happened" that she backgrounds in the narrative, or that she excludes from it altogether. These framing assumptions include assumptions about the identity categories into which the social world divides, as well as assumptions about what constitutes normal or proper relations among members of those categories. Thus the event Johnston-Lewis relates is framed by the belief that the world divides into male and female and by the expectation that intimate relations will exist between males and females and will be monogamous ("Oh, ok, he's staying with a female. So that was the point of no return").

Framing assumptions include assumptions about shared purposes and about widely agreed upon values and ends. Walter Barrett's event, for instance, is framed by the belief that a nontrivial aspect of "how people live" is what goods they possess and what services they use ("country clubs ... big houses ... servants and stuff").

Framing beliefs can include, not only beliefs about particular persons and categories of persons, but also beliefs about particular places and categories of places. Cynthia Arnold's event, for instance, is framed by the assumption that some aspect(s) or characteristic(s) of a type of place called "the ghetto" render it unsuitable for people who are from (at least some) other places ("And, me being from the country").

Unthematized frames support Calvin Moore's life narrative as well. Some are ontological. Moore's narrative assumes, for instance, that there exists a God, and that it judges people and punishes them for what it views as wrongdoings. It relies on ontological framing assumptions about humans as well, for example the assumption that people can elect to "pick up" and to "put down" the values they have been socialized to accept.

Some frames to Moore's narrative are (to recall the discussion of Charles Taylor from the first chapter) evaluative frames. The narrative assumes, implicitly, the validity of a series of normative judgments, among these the judgment that human life is of value and that it is morally wrong to harm oneself or others.

What is more – and notwithstanding the fact that Moore's life story is an ordinary story, one that does not take collective identities as its subject matter – Calvin Moore's narrative is supported by identitarian framing assumptions. At several points, these become evident. Consider the following excerpt from Moore's life story, in which he explains why his father's early death left him with no "real" role model:

[B]asically, you know, I had no real role models in my family. And in my neighborhood, I couldn't really attach to them and bond with them, because I really didn't get that they was my flesh and blood, so I couldn't really open up to them. And besides, they were older men. You know, I'm eight years old, and these guys were like sixty and seventy years old. So basically what I done was, I grown up in a house with three sisters and one brother. And my brother was only a year older than myself, so we kind of raised each other. We basically hung around in the streets or just anywhere, you know. It's not like we were poverty stricken or anything like that. My mother did the best she could. But a mother can't raise boys.

Here Moore assumes that the social world divides into categories based on age, sex, and "flesh and blood." He assumes that membership in these categories is significant for purposes of social learning. And he assumes that sex and "blood" are more significant for such learning than is age (an assumption revealed both by the use of the phrase "and besides" to introduce the clause "they were older men," and also by the claim that brothers who are separated from one another by only a year can serve as proxies for each other's "real" role model, in a way that their mother, and adult men whom they fail to recognize as "flesh and blood," cannot).

But there are major obstacles to any attempt to tease out of this excerpt, or out of others like it, the precise content of the identitarian assumptions that frame it. It is not possible to deduce, for instance, in what sense (if any) Moore believes the men in his neighborhood to have been, in fact, his "flesh and blood." Is the (implicit) claim that they *were* his flesh and blood, but that, at the time, he failed to recognize that? If so, is this belief a specifically racial identitarian belief, and if it is, in what sense does Moore assume race constitutes a "blood" relation? Similarly, it is not possible to infer the reason(s) Moore believes his neighbors' ages to have been an added barrier to their serving as his role models ("these guys were like sixty and seventy years old"). Nor is it possible to infer the reason(s) he believes "a mother can't raise boys."

The identitarian assumptions that frame an ordinary story are always only partly legible (or at the limit case, they are illegible) from within its text. Not *what* people see, so much as *how* they see, they order the stories people tell, while remaining almost completely (or, at the limit, entirely) outside their purview.

It is for this reason that I followed the life history interviews I conducted with semi-structured interviews in which I prompted respondents to thematize specifically identitarian assumptions. Such framing assumptions, although by definition unthematized, are not unthematizable. The aim of the semi-structured interview was, by posing questions that ordinary stories do not answer, to gain (partial) access to respondents' narrative frames.

Recall that, at the start of these interviews, I asked respondents to think of several ways they might complete the statement "My name is [Name], and I am _____." I then followed with questions centered on their understandings of the identity categories they had named. I asked, for instance, "What is a real or a true [identity category]?"; "Thinking back over your life, are there times that stand out in your memory when you recall thinking about yourself *as* [identity category]; and "Are there people who, when you think about them, you think about them mostly as [identity category]?"[14]

[14] For a complete schedule of interview questions, see the appendix.

A number of pronounced patterns emerged from this semi-structured portion of the interviews, perhaps the most striking of which was a racial pattern. Without exception, each of the thirteen respondents who self-identified as black, African American, or Negro invoked a racial identity during this portion of the interview. By contrast, not a single white respondent did. As the interviews progressed, and as this pattern became evident, I began to ask respondents who had not volunteered racial answers whether they might use a racial identity category to complete the statement. All answered in the negative, explaining that, although they were white, they would not complete the statement with the identity category "white" because it did not name an important part of their self-understanding. In the words of Patrick Webber, a thirty-three-year-old businessman from New Albany, "I wouldn't describe myself as white ... I just don't think it's ... I mean, it doesn't matter."

The respondents who identified as African American, by contrast, were united in their judgment that race matters.[15] In this respect, Calvin Moore was typical. His first response when asked to complete the statement "My name is Calvin Moore, and I am _____," was "a thirty-five-year-old Africa[n] American male." In answering the follow-up questions, Moore underscored the salience of the racial dimension of his identity. It was at this point in the interview that he cited what he characterized as formative experiences with racially segregated places and institutions, as described in Chapter 2 (his "all-black neighborhood" and the "all-black schools" he attended). It was at this point that he told me that race was "embedded in [his] mind."

Following my interview protocol, I then pressed Moore to explicate the meaning of this racial identity. I asked him to imagine that he was talking with an intelligent child who did not know the meaning of the identity category "African American." If that child were to ask him, "What does that mean, to be 'African American,'" I asked, how would he explain?

Race is "a color difference ... in skin tone," Moore responded, elaborating:

There are different types of people in the world. And some people's skins are lighter, and some people's skins are darker, you know. And the darker-skinned people, we're originated in a country called Africa.

[15] For all thirteen, "African American," "Negro," or "Black" is a significant ascribed identity: an important part of how other people perceive and regard them. Twelve of the thirteen claim, in addition, that race is an important part of both their self-understanding and their social identification, while one explicitly dis-identifies racially, characterizing herself as "an American who just happens to be Negro."

Moore responded, in other words, with a version of the nineteenth- and early twentieth-century story of race as biological type, discussed in the previous chapter. Race is rooted in origin, by this view. It is manifest in phenotypical traits (such as skin tone), from which one objectively can read a person's race. Layered atop this originary sameness, Moore suggested as he continued to elaborate his response, and lending race its social and political significance, are a shared African American history and a shared African American culture.

He claimed that members of the African American race share important historical experiences, emphasizing in particular the experience of slavery. He asserted that African Americans share a deep-rooted set of cultural traits and dispositions, underscoring that this is the case despite the fact that some people whom phenotype reveals to *be* African American don't *act* African American. Some people, in other words, get their culture wrong. Calvin Moore has met people, he told me, whose "skin color didn't match their tone of voice, the way they talked, the way they act ... You know, I have met some people ... with the same ... racial background as I have, but their, their character and their voice didn't fit that person."

The racial identitarian beliefs Calvin Moore thematized are anything but idiosyncratic. A widely held view of the meaning of "African American," even at the turn of the twenty-first century, Moore's response was echoed in the answers given by my other respondents. Multiple respondents cited African origin as an important component of black racial identity. Several cited phenotypical markers of blackness, including skin color and hair texture. Several respondents cited the historical experience of slavery, and several identified so-called cultural markers of blackness, such as black speech patterns.

Yet as noted in Chapter 2, beliefs about categorical, biologically rooted "race" were scientifically discredited more than half a century ago. What is more (as others have noted), they suffer from well-documented incoherences.[16] With respect to each component part of the definition, what is alleged to distinguish those persons who are members of the racial identity category from those persons who are not, in fact fails to do so, because many whom convention would *not* assign to the category share the relevant trait(s), and/or because many whom convention *does* assign

---

[16] See, for example, K. Anthony Appiah, "The State and the Shaping of Identity," in *Tanner Lectures on Human Values*, ed. Grethe B. Peterson (Salt Lake City: University of Utah Press, 2002), and the discussion in Chapter 1.

to the category do not. With respect to origin, for instance, although there is some controversy among scientists over the regional origin(s) of human beings, the dominant view – a view largely supported by fossil and DNA evidence – is that the entire species' origin lies somewhere on the African continent.[17] Hence persons who typically would be identified as "white" share with those who typically are identified as "black" the allegedly definitive origin.

Other components of the definition are similarly flawed. As far as the alleged phenotypical markers of blackness are concerned, the practice known as "passing" illustrates that people conventionally defined as black do not necessarily exhibit the physiological traits associated with blackness. And of course, the wide variance in both historical and contemporary experience among those persons typically identified as members of *any* racial category belies the possibility of determinative experiential markers of race. As far as "culture" is concerned, some "whites" engage in cultural practices conventionally defined as "black" (a widely cited example being hip-hop performer Eminem), while many "blacks" (such as the unnamed person Calvin Moore describes in the interview excerpt cited previously) do not. To quote Michelle Wright, "Blacks ... possess an intimidating array of different historical, cultural, national, ethnic, religious, and ancestral origins and influences. At the same time, despite this range of differences, they are most often identified ... as simply 'Black.'"[18]

As suggested in Chapter 1, the story of race as biological type is not a *good* story. It is a story that, when confronted with readily accessible evidence, appears to be full of holes. It is a story that, when translated into a categorical definition, becomes tautological ("Black people are people who exhibit the traits associated with blackness, except for those black people who do not.")

Calvin Moore, when he confronts a hole in this racial story, reacts in much the same way many others do. He props up the failing (in the instance cited previously, the cultural) component of his understanding of "black" with the other component parts of that same definition. If a

---

[17] See Robert Wenke, "The Origin of Home sapiens sapiens," in *Patterns in Prehistory: Humankind's First Three Million Years*, ed. Robert Wenke (New York: Oxford, 2006), chapter 4.

[18] Michelle Wright, *Becoming Black: Creating Identity in the African Diaspora* (Durham, NC: Duke University Press, 2004), 2. As Wright's title suggests, the comment is about blacks in the African diaspora, not simply in the United States. But it applies well to the American context.

person who exhibits the physiological traits associated with blackness nonetheless fails to "act black" (this strategy dictates), do not question the validity of the racial categorization. Instead, assume that the person shares the African American origin and/or the African American historical background and question the authenticity of her conduct.

The racial identity narrative that was discredited in the middle decades of the past century is like a table with four bad legs. When one leg starts to give, we rush around, and we try to prop it up with the others. But the obvious question this strategy begs is: "Why hang on to such a table at all?"

We hang on to racial identity stories – and other bad identity stories, as well – because, more often than not, we do not confront them *as stories*. When racial identities have been codified and institutionalized, when they have been objectified in the built environment, people learn them and relearn them, less discursively than practically. When people build racial narratives into social and political institutions and into urban and suburban landscapes, then (like old furniture that is often used, but rarely examined) race becomes, to borrow the words of Mae James, another of my interview respondents, an "everyday thing."

James, a fifty-seven-year-old East Side resident who, during the semistructured interview, self-identified as "Negro," expressed genuine surprise when I first asked her to explain to me her understanding of that term. "I know I am of the Negro race," James told me, "So why should I think about it?" She continued:

[Y]ou know, [race is] a everyday thing. When I go to sleep, I mean, when I go to sleep, I'm going to wake up the same color. You know, ... I can't change it ... And everybody else, when they see me, they *know* I'm not Caucasian. They *know* I'm not Chinese.

James does not "think about [race]" and thinks she should not think about it because of race's "everyday" quality. Her race is a social fact that Mae James knows, and that she knows *everyone knows*, by virtue of their participation in the routines of a racialized society. Race is *everyday*. It is an everyday *thing*. It appears to those who "know ... [their] race," not as a tellable event, but as a nonevent: a background fact about the social world, one hardly worth reporting.

3. An "Everyday Thing"

Mae James's surprise at my request that she "think about [race]" illustrates just how rare it is for people to consciously tell and retell racial identity stories. Calvin Moore is hardly unique in his failure to do so as he tells me the (ordinary) story of his life. Indeed, not a single one of the thirty respondents I interviewed – not even those who strongly identify as "Negro," "black," or "African American" – explicitly incorporates in his or her narrative of personal identity a racial identity narrative. Several respondents who self-identify as "black" thematize experiences with *racism*. For these respondents, having been being treated unjustly because of their racial identity is an important part of their personal life story. Yet even for such race-conscious individuals, the belief in race itself – a belief in racial categories as significant and as sorting actors, actions, and attributes in meaningful ways – functions as a frame to, more than as a building block of, the personal life narrative. Race (as opposed to racism) remains untellable: a background fact about the social world.

For most respondents, beliefs about sex and gender, and about the relation between the two, function similarly. For Calvin Moore, for instance, the (biological) fact of male sex maps onto gendered attitudinal and behavioral dispositions that, because posited as ingenerate in men, function as normative for males. Sex, Moore explains during his semi-structured interview, not unlike race, is legible through physiological characteristics. One can tell if a person is a man by looking at his reproductive organs, his facial hair, or the size of his frame, even by listening to his voice ("A man's voice is much lower and deeper than a female's," Moore tells me).

People who are biologically men, he insists, should conduct themselves in ways that are appropriately male: a gendered identity he associates with control, with dominance, and with "be[ing] the provider." To be male, Moore explains, is a matter of "being the head," regardless of one's situation or circumstances. He elaborates:

To be male … [is] to be in control, to be the dominant species … I feel like a man should be a man no matter what … You know, we … have to be the provider … We have to be the trainer and … take control of situations. Powerful: we have to be powerful.

A man who fails to act male, by this view, is a man who exhibits signs of weakness or dependency, a man who fails to "be the provider":

Someone who doesn't accept his responsibilities, you know, that runs from problems, that depends on other people to provide for him, you know, that neglects his family … Someone that won't work … won't provide … won't try to better his self, you know, by doing anything for his self.

Moore's understanding of maleness differs from his understanding of blackness in that the former he sees as rooted in sex, and ultimately, in reproductive function, rather than in place of origin. Nonetheless, he views "male" and "man" as categories that, much like "African American," merely reflect what is an obvious, indeed a natural sameness.

If sex and gender are categories that merely reflect enduring truths about men, however, then the action of a man's life story – the reportable events that comprise the narrative of his life – must be how he chooses and how he acts (and how others choose and how others act), given the facts of sex and gender. Who controls whom in the Job Corps hierarchy? Who attacks whom at the pool hall? What form does the ensuing struggle take, and who wins? More generally, how does the narrator (the self) satisfy his desire for power, and how does he respond to the imperative "to be in control"?

Answers to questions like these are the tellable and causally significant happenings that drive Moore's narrative. As frames to that narrative, sex and gender render constants – and hence (to recall Labov's argument) ordinary, plain, humdrum, everyday, and run-of-the-mill – the imperative to be strong, to be the provider, to remain in control regardless of one's circumstances: to "be a man no matter what."

The specific events framed by background beliefs in sex and gender vary significantly across the life narratives I collected. For many of the male respondents, for instance, the struggles on which their life stories focus are not physical confrontations with other men, but rather efforts to achieve success in the workplace. Still, strong gendered patterns emerge. For each of the fifteen women I interviewed, the life narrative centers on intimate and family relationships and on caring work: on pregnancies, mothering, and attending to sick or disabled relatives. Schooling and paid work are also a focus for many of these respondents. Yet, when the demands of caring conflict with the demands of school or career, there is often a taken-for-granted quality to the assumption that the former will and/or should prevail. Erica Jones, for instance, a forty-three-year-old woman from East Side Columbus, offers the following account of why, when she was young, she did not complete her nursing degree:

[T]he reason I didn't finish ... was cause we've always had a family emergency ... First it was my father, who died from diabetes and Alzheimer's and other problems. And next it was my mother, who died from cancer and diabetes. And ... each time I signed up to go to nursing school, somebody got seriously sick.

For those women who balance paid work with caring for family, the balance is, typically, thematized. Tricia Barrett, for instance, a highly paid
professional who lives in New Albany, comments that after her twin sons
were born, she found "a wonderful babysitter ... which really allowed
[her] to go back to work." By contrast, not a single male respondent
thematizes his ability to remain in the paid workforce after the birth of
his children because of the care-giving provided by his wife or by another
person.

Of the fifteen narratives by male respondents, fourteen are strikingly
less centered on intimate and family relationships than are those of the
female respondents. The men's narratives focus, instead, on academic and
professional careers (especially for the middle class and the affluent), on
military service in some cases, and (especially for the poor and the working class) on the struggle to get and to keep jobs. In several instances, male
respondents' life narratives focus almost exclusively on such themes.

In one extreme case, a male respondent, at the end of an approximately sixty-minute narrative that centered on his schooling, his professional internships, and his career, mentioned his family for the very first
time. "You know," he told me, "during that time I've had two wives, and
... four children." He proceeded to explain briefly which schools each of
his (now adult) children had attended and how many children each of his
daughters had had. With that, he concluded his life narrative. Another
male respondent, whose life story focused almost exclusively on work,
did not mention his wife of twenty-two years even once during the course
of his narrative. After he had completed telling his story, I asked about
her. (I interviewed him in his living room, where a family photo was in
plain sight). Only then did I learn that he had been married twice and
once divorced.

Identitarian framing beliefs order narratives by making events of some
happenings (my parents' illnesses at the time when I enrolled in nursing
school), while backgrounding other causally significant happenings that
could, in principle, be narrativized (the construction of the heterosexual
nuclear family and the inegalitarian allocation, within that unit, of caring
work). Identitarian frames do not, however, work discretely on ordinary
narratives. Instead, they interact with one another, and with other frames,
such as evaluative framing beliefs about what it means to be (to recall
Calvin Moore's words) a "responsible" human being or "a productive
member of society."

In Moore's narrative, beliefs about sex and gender intersect with evaluative beliefs to define a set of distinctively masculine virtues. The good man is strong, Moore's narrative assumes. He is powerful. He is "the provider" (but, recall: never in ways that harm others or that incite fear in others or that strike others as "crazy"). He is always in control, but always peaceably, and within the bounds of law.

Framing beliefs about sex and gender also intersect with framing beliefs about race. The latter effectively background in Moore's narrative the place-based inequalities that form the context within which he heeds this imperative to be a good man. Chapter 2 sketched processes of urban spatial racialization, which, over the course of the twentieth century, marked East Side Columbus as (not unlike the Birmingham neighborhood in which Moore was raised) a "black place" troubled by "black problems." Calvin Moore struggles to be "in control," to be "powerful," to be "the provider" in a black ghetto where decades of public and private disinvestment have ensured that unemployment, underemployment, and poverty are at the highest levels in the Columbus MSA, while educational attainment, home ownership, and property values are at the lowest.

Moore is far from unaware of such place-based inequalities. "The community that I originally associate in," he tells me during our semi-structured interview, "is a [high] poverty, low income [place] ... infested with drugs and gangs." He is far from unaware of the forcible policing of racial boundaries ("there's certain places you don't go"). Still, the racial identitarian frame to his narrative helps define the racialization of space as a nonevent.

Imagine, if you can, a political society with no particularistic collective identities whatsoever. Imagine, in addition, that the members of this society strongly value productive labor. It is good, they believe, to build the things that people use and consume. Good people are productive people. Imagine that productive labor is *the* mostly highly valued activity in this society, and that those who perform it are rewarded with material benefits, social respect, and other goods.

Now imagine that some members of this society construct a new particularistic identity story. "We are the *A*s," they say to the others, "and you are the *B*s." "*A*s and *B*s are radically different from one another in constitution and in culture," they add, "and it is important for members of each group to live and to work only with their own kind."

Those who call themselves the *A*s propose to cordon off a section of the political society's territory, which they designate "*A*-land," and to use collective resources to construct and maintain in A-land state-of-the-art productive facilities, which, they propose, will be open only to the As. In the remaining territory, which they designate "B-land," the As propose to house nonproductive functions, as well as the negative externalities that productive activities create.

This new identity story, along with the proposal that accompanies it, will no doubt strike those dubbed the Bs as novel, as surprising, as unexpected (perhaps even "terrifying, dangerous, weird, wild, [and] crazy"). Just as Calvin Moore would be all but certain to notice a man who reached out and grabbed for his weapon during face-to-face combat, the people the As designate Bs are all but certain to notice this new story and the proposal that accompanies it.

Even if this identity story were to become firmly established, what is more – even if it were to become widely accepted, to the point where most designated As incorporated stories of A-ness into their life stories, and most designated Bs incorporated stories of B-ness into theirs – one would still expect most Bs to narrativize the As' proposal as an event: that is, as a reportable and casually significant happening. If the proposal were successful, in particular, and the plans for A-land and B-land were realized, then most Bs likely would thematize these happenings. "It was when the As devised their scheme," they might say, "that (given our B-ness) our capacity to produce, and hence to reap the rewards society confers on the productive, was decisively undermined."

Assume, further, that stories of A-ness and B-ness are not good stories. Assume, in particular, that there is no story that holds up in the face of evidence and reason about why As and Bs must not live or work together, or about why As, but not Bs, should have access to facilities for production. If so, then it is only if A and B identities are *not* taught and learned principally in storied form – it is only if they are taught and learned practically, for example, through participation in the society's major social and economic institutions, and through bodily contact with the landscapes the As have constructed – that Bs will exclude from their life narratives the actions the As took when they made and realized their proposal.

Under such circumstances, the collective identities the As have constructed will confront even the Bs as "everyday things." They will confront them in the form of rules and routines, in the form of the landscapes and the built environment of A-land and B-land: all of which will appear as "just background" to human action. The ordinary stories the Bs tell will focus on the decisions they make and the actions they take. They will focus on interactions with friends and family members and coworkers, perhaps on luck (good or bad), perhaps even on God. *A*-land and *B*-land will serve principally as the setting to these stories.

On those occasions when the *B*s do turn their attention to the backdrop to their narratives, what is more – when they attend, even briefly, to the institutional structure and the landscape the *A*s have constructed – they will see it *through* the identitarian frames they have learned practically. Recall the interview excerpt cited near the start of Chapter 2, in which Calvin Moore describes the experience of crossing the railroad tracks that divide East Side Columbus from suburban Bexley:

> One side of the tracks, you know, if I cross the tracks … into the hood, I'm back into the lower income area. And when I cross back over the tracks, I'm in high society: Bexley area, the more conservative type area … It's like … crossing over into another state.

Immediately following this comment, Moore tells me, "You know, it's different, *because there's a different character of people*" (emphasis added).

Here Moore accounts for the difference between East Side Columbus and suburban Bexley in much the same way that the hypothetical *B*s might account for the difference between *B*-land and *A*-land. These are places that differ dramatically, Moore suggests – in material resources and also in dominant political ideology – at least in part because of the characters of the people who inhabit them.

This (familiar) logic, which reads race back onto (racialized) space, is captured by Charles Mills's characterization of what he calls "the racing of space": that is, "the depiction of space as dominated by persons of a certain race."[19] Even as space is normed by "racing" it, Mills writes, "the norming of the individual is partially achieved by *spacing* it, that is representing it as imprinted with the characteristics of a certain kind of space."[20] Mills continues:

> [T]his is a mutually supporting characterization that … becomes a circular indictment: "You are what you are in part because you originate from a certain kind of space, and that space has its properties in part because it is inhabited by creatures like yourself."[21]

Thus, Mills argues, "savages" inhabit places that need taming: places that aren't even "discovered," let alone civilized, until whites arrive, and

---

[19] Charles Mills, *The Racial Contract* (Ithaca, NY: Cornell University Press, 1997), 41–2.
[20] Ibid., 42.
[21] Ibid.

the "inner city" is "intrinsically doomed to welfare dependency, high street crime, [and] underclass status, because of the characteristics of its inhabitants."[22]

Mills's focus is people who are disadvantaged by place-based racial hierarchies. But for people who are privileged by racial hierarchies, as I argue at greater length in Chapters 4 and 5, this same logic makes possible the belief that race "doesn't matter." "If 'we' live here and 'they' live there" (the logic suggests) "that pattern simply *reflects* our different dispositions and preferences. We are the kind of people who live in places like these, and these places are the way they are, in part, because we live here."

Even those who acknowledge that "race matters" can read race onto place, just so long as they first write race out of their ordinary stories. Calvin Moore, for example, tells me his preference for "activity" and for "loud music" attracts him to what, at one point in our interview, he calls "the inner city life":

I'm not saying that I'm rough or rugged or something ... but I like ... a little activity every now and then. I like ... to see kids playing and wrestling, having fun. I like to listen to loud music sometimes, you know. And I like, just, the inner city life, cause that's what I'm accustomed to.

By contrast, Moore's former girlfriend, who is white, he says, "didn't like the fact that, sitting around ... a bunch of thugs listening to rap music and drinking beer, she felt like was a little bit too intense for her. And she's [the] more settled back, *suburban type*" (emphasis added).

Racialized place (these comments suggest) merely *reflects* racial identity. Hence the names for racialized places can serve as adjectives describing racialized persons. I noted this phenomenon near the start of the previous chapter, citing the East Side respondent who claims he "initially was in a completely ... *urban or black* community." Moore, similarly, uses place to stand for race, not only in the interview excerpt just cited, but at multiple points throughout our conversation. For example, he names as the principal reason his (white) girlfriend eventually left him the fact that he was "too ghetto." He recalls asking her, rhetorically, "Well, you didn't mind me being ... ghetto when we were in the bedroom ... [W]hy do you ... try to judge *my character* now?" (emphasis added). Much as the name of a nation-state can signal those personal qualities imputed to national identity ("He's *very* French"), the name of a racialized place can signal those aspects of a person's "character" imputed to race.

22 Ibid., 51.

At the limit, it can do so independently of any actual connection between the person so described and the place. Immediately after Moore identifies his former girlfriend as the "suburban type," for instance, I attempt to clarify by asking if she lives in the suburbs. He replies that she does not. "Matter of fact," he adds, "the neighborhood that she resides in is a little bit rougher than the neighborhood I took her in." He explains that his former girlfriend lives in what he refers to as a "project," and that, aside from the racial composition and the population density of the neighborhood, he sees no significant difference between where she lives and the "inner city":

Well, yes, we do have a police, yes we do have helicopters, yes SWAT do run up and down the street, you know. But what's the difference? They sell crack over here. They sell crack out there. They have guns over here. They have guns out there. I don't see a difference.

A racialized place can be understood in some nontrivial sense as equivalent to "who I am" (a racialized place can be seen as merely reflecting those aspects of my character that are caused by the fact of my race) only if the racialization of place is not an event in my life story. In Calvin Moore's life narrative, race intersects with other identitarian frames, and race intersects with evaluative beliefs about what is good and what is right, in ways that background the differential distribution of the social capacity to be in control, to be "the provider." Race interacts with other identities, in other words, and with moral and ethical frames, to center the action of Moore's story on interpersonal conflicts for power, especially on intrasubjective struggles against rage. Race centers the action on Moore's struggle to be a good man, *no matter what*.

In this chapter, my principal claim has been that the institutionalization and the objectification of collective identity stories encourage the construction of ordinary life stories: narratives of personal identity in which collective identity narratives work as frames. In Calvin Moore's narrative, institutionalized and objectified racial stories serve as one important such frame, ordering his story's action by helping to sort events from nonevents. Racial stories interact with other frames (including other identitarian frames and moral/ethical frames) to define as an event Moore's struggle to be a good man ("no matter what"), and as nonevents the construction and maintenance of the place-based racial inequalities that form the context within which he wages that struggle.

For Wendy Brown, recall, "[d]epoliticization involves removing a political phenomenon from comprehension of its *historical* emergence and
from a recognition of the *powers* that produce and contour it."[23] The
institutionalization and objectification of racial stories, I have argued,
depoliticize both racial distinctions and racial hierarchy. If, as Brown suggests, "[d]epoliticization involves construing inequality, subordination,
marginalization, and social conflict ... as personal and individual, on the
one hand, or as natural, religious, or cultural on the other," the institutionalization and objectification of racial stories depoliticize along both
dimensions.[24] For Moore, they personalize his failure to achieve his stated
goals: a failure that becomes, in his narrative, the product of his choices
and actions (and of God's retribution), without reference to the processes
of racialization that shape and condition his field of action. At the same
time, the institutionalization and objectification of racial stories work to
naturalize and to "culturalize" race- and place-based inequalities, to the
point where racialized urban and suburban space is seen merely to reflect
(natural, because biological and/or cultural) race.[25]

The racialization of place, in short, writes racial inequality and racial
hierarchy out of the ordinary stories of even those "marked" subjects
who, like Calvin Moore, are conscious of and critical of racial inequality.
It thus militates against the construction of personal life narratives that –
unlike ordinary stories – help motivate a contentious politics oriented
toward change.

What of racially privileged subjects? What of those who were raced
"white" in the twentieth-century United States, whose racial interest in
home ownership I have suggested was first constructed and then promoted by bad racial stories? In the two chapters that follow, I turn my
attention to them, making the case that collective identity stories of
Americans as a home-owning people, stories that were institutionalized
and objectified over the course of the twentieth century in America's new
"white places," also depoliticize, although, in this case, by writing racial
privilege out of ordinary stories.

---

[23] Wendy Brown, *Regulating Aversion: Tolerance in the Age of Identity and Empire*
   (Princeton, NJ: Princeton University Press, 2006), 15, emphasis in original.
[24] Ibid.
[25] *Culturalize* is Brown's construction. Ibid.

4

Home, Sweet Home

In 1868, Emery Childs, an East Coast business entrepreneur and land speculator, founded the Riverside Improvement Company and purchased a sixteen-hundred-acre tract of undeveloped land nine miles west of Chicago. The tract was well situated: it ran along the Des Plaines River and encompassed the first suburban stop on the Chicago, Burlington, and Quincy Railroad. Childs commissioned Frederick Law Olmsted and Calvert Vaux – by then known and celebrated for their design of New York's Central Park – to plan what would become the most influential American suburb of the nineteenth century.[1]

It was Olmsted and Vaux's innovative design that won Riverside, Illinois renown. Unlike almost all other late nineteenth-century suburbs, which were laid out in the familiar grid patterns of the cities they surrounded, Riverside was characterized, in its planners' words, by "gracefully curved lines, generous spaces, and the absence of sharp corners, the idea being to suggest and imply leisure, contemplativeness, and happy tranquility."[2] The plan for Riverside included 700 acres of public parks and greens, among these a 160-acre reserve along the river; multiple playgrounds and croquet grounds; and a lake, which itself was to be surrounded by public

---

[1] See Walter Creese, *The Crowning of the American Landscape: Eight Great Spaces and their Buildings* (Princeton, NJ: Princeton University Press, 1985), 219–40 and David Schuyler, *The New Urban Landscape: The Redefinition of City Form in Nineteenth-Century America* (Baltimore, MD and London: Johns Hopkins University Press, 1986), chapter 8, on which this paragraph and the two that follow draw.

[2] Olmsted, Vaux, and Co., "Preliminary Report upon the Proposed Suburban Village at Riverside, near Chicago" reprinted in Frederick Law Olmsted, *Civilizing American Cities: Writings on City Landscapes* (New York: Da Capo Press, 1997), 292–305, here 300.

walks. It included a wide and richly landscaped parkway to Chicago, which was divided into four separate tracks for pedestrians, equestrians, pleasure drivers, and commercial drivers: a promenade Olmsted imagined would draw a fashionable crowd, as did the Parisian Champs Elysées. It set large houses on large lots (most 100 by 225 feet), specified for these a minimum thirty-foot setback from the road, and required that their generous front yards be fence free and planted with trees. According to Robert Fishman, writing more than 100 years after Olmsted and Vaux designed Riverside, Illinois, "If there is a single plan that expresses the idea of the bourgeois utopia, it is Olmsted's Riverside."[3]

But the best-laid plans, as they say, oft go awry. Early on, the Riverside Improvement Company ran into difficulty obtaining investment capital. The improvements to the rural landscape that Olmsted and Vaux's plan required were expensive: the gravel streets, the stone and asphalt walkways, the sewer pipes and gas lamps, the storage tower for water distribution. Childs defaulted on payments he owed Olmsted and Vaux, and in the spring of 1870 the planners ended their relationship with the Riverside Improvement Company. The Great Chicago Fire of 1871 diverted funds and manpower toward reconstruction efforts in the city. Through the early years of the decade, to make matters worse, Riverside lots sold only slowly, and land values fell. Cost overruns on the development were nontrivial: half a million dollars just five years into the venture. The Panic of 1873 and the depression that followed proved ruinous for the Riverside Improvement Company, which went bankrupt in 1874. Riverside itself survived the demise of the company that took its name. Yet, as the suburb developed, Olmsted and Vaux's original plan, including much of their ambitious design for Riverside's public spaces, fell short of being realized.

It was more than a half century later when Jesse Clyde Nichols, together with his business partner, John Taylor, and several members of the staff of the J. C. Nichols Company, conducted a survey of (in Nichols's words) "the history and record of ... high-class [American] subdivisions."[4] At the time when Olmsted and Vaux had designed Riverside, in the late 1860s, to build, to plan, and to develop a high-end residential district

[3] Robert Fishman, *Bourgeois Utopias: The Rise and Fall of Suburbia* (New York: Basic Books, 1987), 129.
[4] Jesse Clyde Nichols, "Memoir," *Planning for Permanence: The Speeches of J. C. Nichols*, Western Historical Manuscript Collection – Kansas City, 2007, 21. http://www.umkc.edu/whmckc/publications/JCN/JCNPDF/JCN087.pdf (accessed January 1, 2013).

was to engage in an experiment. By the early 1920s, it was to participate in a fairly well-established practice: Roland Park in Baltimore, St. Francis Wood in San Francisco, and Palo Verdes Estates near Los Angeles were just a few of the more prominent examples of planned, exclusive suburban developments. Still, as Nichols recalls in his memoir, he and his colleagues were troubled by the fact that a relatively large percentage of such projects were "financial failures." "It was obvious to us," he wrote, "that it was wise to look ahead and study carefully the many influences which would maintain permanency of good neighborhoods, all of which led to the study of self-perpetuating restrictions, and setting up of home associations." "Our perpetual restrictions," Nichols continued, referring to his innovative use of deed restrictions that automatically renewed themselves before they were set to expire, "were the first in the country and have been copied many, many times, all to the advantage of the home owner."[5]

In Chapter 2, we saw how racial identity stories (stories about racial categories, stories about which persons and which traits and behaviors fit those categories, and stories about the natural and the proper relationship between "the black and white races") were institutionalized and objectified in the early twentieth-century American city. The present chapter explores a parallel process of the institutionalization and objectification of an identity story: in this case, a story, in circulation during that same period, about the identity of the American public. This story was a story about who "we Americans" are. It was a story about what we need and what we deserve and value. It was a story about "the public good": what it is that serves the good of Americans as a whole, and how Americans ought to use their collective power and collective resources to promote that good.

I begin with the struggles faced by J. C. Nichols and other so-called community builders because of the key role these men played in constructing and circulating this narrative.[6] In the interwar years, Nichols and other leaders of the newly professionalized real estate industry began to press for state support for private, profit-driven development. They

---

[5] Ibid.

[6] *Community builders* designates those who designed, financed, assembled, developed, and then sold entire suburban communities, built from the ground up on the rural fringes of the twentieth-century city. See Marc Weiss, *The Rise of the Community Builders: The American Real Estate Industry and Urban Land Planning* (Washington, DC: Beard Books, 1987).

did so in significant part, I want to argue, by constructing and circulating a narrative linking home ownership to the American public good. Although relatively early on community builders won state support in the form of land use control (comprehensive zoning and municipal planning), through the decade of the 1920s they were almost entirely unsuccessful in their efforts to win state financial support. This failure was due in no small part to the fact that the story they told was not (to recall the argument in Chapter 1) a *good story*. America was not, in the early twentieth century, a nation of home owners. It was not a political society the members of which all would benefit from public support for private housing development. To the contrary, such support would benefit some (real estate developers and home owners) at the expense of others (tax-paying renters). It disproportionately would benefit big builders and home owners whose property values were high.

But, as I underscore in what follows, a story need not be a good story for it to be influential. When the stock market crash of 1929 and the recession that ensued aligned the immediate goals of public officials (job creation and the stabilization of the housing market) with the aims housing industry elites had pursued since war's end, Herbert Hoover, Franklin Delano Roosevelt, and other major state actors joined together with community builders to institutionalize in New Deal housing policies, and ultimately to objectify in the suburban built environment, the NAREB-promulgated narrative of a home-owning American public.

1. Own Your Own Home!

J. C. Nichols began purchasing land for what would become his famous Country Club District, near Kansas City, Missouri, in the spring of 1905.[7] By the late 1920s, he had assembled six thousand acres, and he had built six thousand homes, along with four golf courses, in a total of thirty-three separate subdivisions in the Country Club District. In many ways, the development borrowed from and extended Olmsted and Vaux's design for Riverside, Illinois. Eschewing the urban "grid iron" pattern (as did Riverside), its structures and its landscapes played

[7] See the discussions of Nichols's development in William Worley, *J. C. Nichols and the Shaping of Kansas City: Innovation in Planned Residential Communities* (Columbia: University of Missouri Press, 1990); Gwendolyn Wright, *Building the Dream: A Social History of Housing in America* (Cambridge, MA: MIT Press, 1981), chapter 11; and Kenneth Jackson, *Crabgrass Frontier: The Suburbanization of the United States* (New York: Oxford University Press, 1985), chapter 10, on which this paragraph draws.

upon and complemented the rural terrain. The Country Club District (like Riverside) included public spaces, such as public walks and parks. It included schools and churches and retail spaces as well. Its fabulously successful Country Club Plaza, with easy automobile access and ample parking, is often cited as the first car-oriented suburban shopping center.[8] Just as in Riverside, in the Country Club District, residential lots, houses, and setbacks from the street were large. Nichols set minimum construction costs for houses, in addition, and, pushing planned exclusivity to a new level, he specified a dizzying array of deed restrictions, including racial restrictions prohibiting home ownership or occupation by blacks and by members of other minoritized groups. By the mid-1920s, the Country Club District, marketed with the now-notorious slogan "3000 Acres Restricted," was the most exclusive residential community in the United States. The extensive restrictions, the developers stated unabashedly, were the key to its success. They were, to quote a brochure advertising the Country Club District in 1924, its "most valuable asset."[9]

But that asset, as Nichols underscored in his memoir, was an asset vulnerable to threat. Among the lessons he and his colleagues had learned from their survey of early twentieth-century suburbs were, first, that deed restrictions expire, and second, that "good residential communities" can be "seriously damaged by encroachment around the edges."[10] The solution to the first problem, Nichols proposed, was the self-perpetuating restriction (cited in the introduction to this chapter). At the time of his survey, deed restrictions nearing their date of expiration could be renewed only with a positive vote from the majority of the property owners in an exclusive community. "This involved a tremendous amount of work," Nichols explained. "[M]any of the owners had died and their heirs scattered far and wide … [F]requently the heirs were minors involving guardianship problems … so … it was an almost impossible task to get a majority of the signatures."[11] His innovation was to shift the burden toward those

---

[8] Kenneth Jackson, for instance, writes, "The multiple-store shopping center with free, off-street parking represented the ultimate retail adaptation to the requirements of automobility. Although the *Guinness Book of World Records* lists the Roland Park Shopping Center (1896) as the world's first shopping center, the first of the modern variety was Country Club Plaza in Kansas City. It was the effort of a single entrepreneur, Jesse Clyde Nichols, who put together a concentration of retail stores, and used leasing policy to determine the composition of stores in the concentration. By doing that, Nichols created the idea of the planned regional shopping center." Jackson, *Crabgrass Frontier*, 258.

[9] J. C. Nichols Investment Company, "Country Club District: 3000 Acres Restricted," April 1, 1924, p. 16. Copy on file with author.

[10] Nichols, "Memoir," 21.

[11] Ibid.

who would *alter* the status quo. Nichols wrote deed restrictions such that they would automatically be renewed unless, five years prior to their expiration, a majority of property owners agreed to suspend them. "Of course, this was just as difficult to do as it had been to get them extended at the end of a specified time," he explained, with unconcealed delight, "and so the result is perpetual restrictions, and neighborhoods that would remain fine places to live, and retain their residential character and value through generations!"[12]

The second problem Nichols and his colleagues had discovered, however – the problem of "encroachment around the edges" – posed a seemingly insuperable challenge for the community builder. Developers could attempt to buy the land that was adjacent to their developments, of course. But often owners would not sell, and, at any rate, there were limits to what any individual, or any corporation, could afford. Developers could attempt to convince the owners of adjoining developments to adopt covenants that were identical to, or at least very similar to, those they had put in place. Alternatively, they could situate their developments near natural barriers, if such barriers existed (near rivers, for instance), or near man-made barriers (such as roadways or railway tracks). But more often than not, developers could not control what happened on the other side of their property lines.

That, J. C. Nichols reasoned, is where land use restrictions, in the form of zoning and municipal planning, come in. Nichols began building for the Country Club District just a few years after the city of New York had enacted the nation's very first comprehensive zoning resolution. In his view, public land use regulation, working hand in hand with private deed restrictions, was key to preserving the "character and value" of upscale residential developments. "Our municipality," Nichols exhorted an early twentieth-century Kansas City audience, "should give protection to the home builders. I am not saying that the city should not have all the room necessary for the expansion of industrial activities. But everyone should realize and every city plan commission know that every step should be studied out in advance and in certain sections of your city you should offer security of value and permanent neighborhood."[13] Such planning, Nichols argued, was nothing if not rational, economical, and efficient.

---

[12] Ibid.

[13] Jesse Clyde Nichols, "City Planning," *Planning for Permanence*, Western Historical Manuscript Collection – Kansas City, 2007, 3. http://www.umkc.edu/whmckc/publications/JCN/JCNPDF/JCN087.pdf (accessed January 1, 2013).

"Few people realize," he explained, "the terrific economic waste ... of rapid changes in the character of residential neighborhoods in American cities": waste that could be eliminated if "stability, permanence [and] orderly progress [were] conceived and aided by city planning officials and by developers using deed restrictions."[14]

I quote Nichols's statement, not because it is unique or out of the ordinary, but to the contrary because it is in important ways representative of the types of political claims large-scale developers began to press around this time. Substantively, the two categories of state assistance early community builders wanted were, first, land use control through zoning and planning (as illustrated by the Nichols quote cited earlier) and second, financial support in the form of low-interest loans, tax exemptions for mortgage investments, and the like. Rhetorically, the way they pressed these claims was by equating, on one hand, the use of collective power and resources to promote private, profit-driven development, and on the other, values (such as "stability, permanence, and orderly progress") the pursuit of which, they asserted, promotes, *not* the good of community builders exclusively, not even the good of the wealthy, white, home-owning elite, but rather the good of all.

It is easy to see why community builders would *want* the power and resources of the state behind their endeavors. Between the time when Childs built Riverside and the time when Nichols built the Country Club District, it had become apparent to real estate entrepreneurs that, if the game they were playing was a game of developing land to sell at a profit, a winning strategy was to exercise relatively broad control over land use patterns, and to do so in a way that enabled the commodification and the marketing and sale of exclusivity.

The game's risks and pitfalls had become apparent as well. Securing investment capital to assemble large tracts and to fund improvements to undeveloped land; finding buyers with access to adequate down payments and with the ability to obtain and pay off mortgages; controlling future development to ensure "security of value and permanent neighborhood" – these tasks posed profound challenges for even the most savvy developers. But if collective power (the authority to zone, or the power to develop and implement municipal land use plans) and collective

---

[14] Jesse Clyde Nichols, "Developer's View of Deed Restrictions," *Planning for Permanence*, Western Historical Manuscript Collection – Kansas City, 2007, 10. http://www.umkc.edu/whmckc/publications/JCN/JCNPDF/JCN087.pdf (accessed July 15, 2010).

resources (tax dollars, or what amounts to the same, tax exemptions) could be mobilized to help amass capital and to assemble and develop land; if the state would subsidize improvements to undeveloped land and help potential buyers secure and pay off mortgages; if it would help create and preserve the exclusivity of "high-class subdivisions," then financial failures of the sort Childs had faced and Nichols had documented would be that much less common.

The trick was to *legitimize* state support for private development in a capitalist democracy. In a democratic political society, government is viewed as legitimate when it promotes, not the good of the powerful and the privileged, but the good of all, or, as the familiar phrase would have it, "the public good." In a capitalist democracy, where state interference in markets is inherently suspect, such support is viewed as legitimate if and only if understood to promote some pressing public good. Hence, if an Emery Childs or a J. C. Nichols wanted to make the case for such support, he would have had to argue that using collective power and resources to build and maintain exclusive residential communities serves, not the good of some at the expense of others, but the good of all.

Emery Childs expressed no such political ambition. He advanced no such normative claim. But in the interwar years, when J. C. Nichols and other leaders of the newly professionalized real estate industry began to organize and to lobby for state support for private development, they tried to make the case that such support would serve the public good. It was a hard case to make. The dominant, nearly uncontested view in the early twentieth-century United States was that the state should stay out of the private market in housing, or at least that it should intervene only in a regulatory capacity: by defining minimum construction standards for private builders, for example, or by setting minimum maintenance standards for private landlords.[15]

As far as coercive control over land use was concerned, the average builder (who, after all, built, not "communities," but just three or four houses per year) would not have viewed state intervention to promote

---

[15] Indeed, the American state had stayed out of the housing market entirely until the war years, when the United States Housing Corporation (USHC) and the Emergency Fleet Corporation (EFC) had built emergency housing for workers in industries regarded as essential to the nation's defense. Both programs had been small in scale, and both had been temporary. After the war, all of the state-constructed units had been sold to private buyers. This limited involvement was understood as a stop-gap measure justified only by the extraordinary circumstance of a shortage in housing for workers viewed as crucial to the war effort. See Baxandall and Ewen, *Picture Windows*, chapter 4 and Radford, *Modern Housing for America*, chapters 1–2.

exclusivity in "good residential communities" as serving his interests. For him, zoning and planning would be an unwelcome intrusion on his freedom to manipulate land use as necessary to generate short-term profit.

Nor would the average American homeowner, let alone the average tenant, view restrictions of the sort Nichols advocated as serving his interests. To the contrary, the average American was among the people whose "encroachment" such restrictions would prevent. If successful, Nichols would block, not only all African Americans' but also most whites' access to the amenities in the Country Club District: to its schools, to its public walks and parks, and to its elaborately landscaped residential streets. If the state employed collective resources to support the construction of communities like the Country Club District, if it used collective power to promote exclusivity there, it would serve the good of those who built and bought large, expensive private homes on big lots with big setbacks, and it would do so at the expense of everyone else.

Hence when Nichols and other community builders began to press claims for state support for private, profit-driven development, they supplemented their arguments with a story. This story was an *identity story* in the sense in which I have used that term throughout this book: a story about who "we Americans" are: about what we value, what we want and deserve, and what it is that serves our good. In its structure and logic it worked much as other identity narratives do. It selected, that is, from an almost infinite set of possibilities, a subset of beliefs, traits, and dispositions, which it interpreted in particular ways and attached to particular persons. Home ownership, according to this narrative – specifically, the private ownership of a detached, single-family, suburban house – is the "dream" not of some, but of all Americans.[16] It is not simply a good that many Americans happen to like: a relatively widely shared consumer preference. Instead, it is an important part of the American national identity: a long-standing tradition that reaches back to the Jeffersonian ideal of propertied citizenship. Home ownership is an important source of well-being for the families that comprise the American people. It is an important source of civic vitality for the American nation as a whole. Home ownership is patriotic. Home

---

[16] See LeeAnn Lands, "Be a Patriot, Buy a Home: Re-Imagining Home Owners and Home Ownership in Early 20th Century Atlanta," *Journal of Social History* 41, 4 (summer 2008): 943–65 and Paul Luken and Suzanne Vaughan, "' ... be a Genuine Homemaker in Your Own Home': Gender and Familial Relations in State Housing Practices, 1917–1922," *Social Forces* 83, 4 (June 2005): 1603–25, on which this paragraph draws.

ownership promotes civic virtue. Home ownership fosters healthy (traditional, nuclear) families and encourages (Christian) moral rectitude. It thus contributes to the well-being of the American polity and to the good of the American public.

According to Richard T. Ely, writing in 1926, "a home owner is almost invariably a good citizen."[17] Contributors to the *National Real Estate Journal* agreed: "[O]wn your own home," urged one, "and protect it with your life, and you will be a good citizen and patriot."[18] Another declared: "The home is the cornerstone in the foundation of the nation … I can not imagine a great nation if all its people are renters."[19] For realtor Paul Murphy, "Even though one profess to be a saint, leave to enlist for the trenches in France, or praise the Star Spangled banner all the year round, if he does not provide for his own household by building a home, which is the unit of society and Government, he robs his patriotism of practicability and his religion of reality."[20] Murphy continued: "[T]he man, who … buys a home … [and] secures for it a happy wife and raises therein patriotic well-educated American children, and sends them out to high moral ideals, to be a blessing to the community, has done the most patriotic and religious thing possible and incidently [*sic*] the most opportune thing for the betterment of human conditions."[21]

The latter quote comes from Murphy's address to the Interstate Realty Convention in 1917, the same year the National Association of Real Estate Boards launched "Own-Your-Own-Home": the interwar advertising and public relations campaign that served as a key forum for promulgating this narrative of Americans as a home-owning people. Two years later, the U.S. Department of Labor joined NAREB and the other business and civic groups that supported Own-Your-Own-Home, establishing an Own-Your-Own-Home Section in its Division of Public Works

[17] Ely goes on to assert: "In fact, the social importance attached to home ownership is more than an assumption: it is an axiom." Richard Ely, "The City Housing Corporation and 'Sunnyside,'" *Journal of Land and Public Utility* 2, 2 (April 1926): 172–85, here 181.

[18] Edward Haag, "Reasons for 'National Home Day,'" *National Real Estate Journal* 18 (December 1918): 164.

[19] S. W. Straus, "Home Owning Patriotic Thrift," *National Real Estate Journal* 18 (December 1918): 164.

[20] Paul C. Murphy, Address before the Interstate Realty Convention, Aberdeen and Hoquiam, August 9–11, 1917. National Archives and Records Administration, "Own Your Own Home" Section; Subject File; Entry PI 140 105; Box 462; Records of the U.S. Housing Corporation, Record Group 3, p. 1.

[21] Ibid.

and Construction Development.[22] Murphy was one of several industry leaders to move to Washington, DC during this period, in his case to head one of the Department of Labor units.[23] "It is as much a patriotic duty to build [a home] now as it was to render service and to make sacrifices in all possible ways during the war," read one of the pamphlets Murphy authored for distribution by the department.[24] Other materials distributed through the Own-Your-Own-Home campaign worked to establish a normative distinction in the popular consciousness between an owned "home" and a (merely) rented "house." Specifically, they linked a *home* to healthy family life, the appropriate performance of traditional gender roles, virtuous republican citizenship, and the realization of the American Dream.[25]

The Own-Your-Own-Home campaign was not, however, limited to activities in the nation's capital. Throughout the United States, local branches of this program constructed demonstration houses, which they made available for members of the public to tour. They plastered storefronts with posters touting Own-Your-Own-Home campaign slogans. They produced special "home ownership" issues for local newspapers, and they enlisted civic leaders, returning war heroes, and even local ministers to spread the home ownership gospel.[26] In Rochester, New York, a twenty-five-by-fifteen-foot electric sign bore the campaign's message, as did literature that was distributed in pay envelopes by the town's major employers, Eastman Kodak and Bausch & Lomb.[27] In Portland, Oregon, where the chairman of the local Own-Your-Own-Home campaign was also the mayor, the public opening ceremony for a model home featured a wedding at which a minister preached to the newlyweds and assembled guests the virtues of private home ownership.[28]

---

[22] Other groups heavily involved in Own-Your-Own-Home include the United States League of Building and Loan Associations and the National Federation of Construction Industries.

[23] Luken and Vaughn, "Genuine Homemaker in Your Own Home," 1607.

[24] Hornstein, *Nation of Realtors*, 120–1.

[25] For instance, one slogan from the Own-Your-Own-Home Campaign Handbook urged, "Own a Home for Your Children's Sake," while another warned, "Don't Promise a Home to Your Sweetheart and then Ask Her to Live in a Rented House." "Make Her Dreams Come True by Owning Your Home," said a third. See Hornstein, *Nation of Realtors*, 120–7.

[26] See Janet Hutchinson, "Building for Babbitt: The State and the Suburban Home Ideal," *Journal of Policy History* 9, 2 (1997): 184–210.

[27] Ibid., 188.

[28] Ibid.

Sociologists Paul Luken and Suzanne Vaughan, analyzing news-paper advertisements published throughout the United States as part of the Own-Your-Own-Home campaign, find that, without exception, the images used were images of white, male/female (and hence presumably heterosexual) couples, who were depicted either as having purchased or as being on the brink of purchasing detached, single-family houses in suburban settings.[29] The appropriate performance of (white) female gender roles, these advertisements underscored, requires a privately owned, single-family house. For instance, in an endorsement solicited for the campaign, actress Margaret Illington was quoted by the U.S. Department of Labor as asserting:

> A woman's simplest duty ... is to preserve the family interests by keeping her Home clean, wholesome and comfortable, and caring for the children properly. Yet, if their dwelling is a rented one, she cannot fulfill these fundamentally simple responsibilities in a way which will do her justice.[30]

Likewise, masculinity is best performed by providing one's wife and children with a privately owned home, campaign literature stressed. An advertisement by Philadelphia's Own-Your-Own-Home Committee, for example, explained that home ownership "places you among the bigger men of your community" and emphasized the duty of a husband and father to provide for his family by purchasing a house:

> Your family looks up to you to give them a home of their own. They know that there is more happiness and comfort in a home of one's own. Let your children grow up in a real "home" atmosphere. Give your wife an opportunity to show you that she can be a business woman and a loving wife and mother at the same time ... Own your own Home![31]

The campaign literature asserted a strong link, as well, between the private ownership of a detached, single-family house and the traits and

---

[29] Luken and Vaughan sum up their findings this way: "All the images depict a particular type of family: the nuclear family comprised of a husband, wife, and related children. None of the illustrations depicts unattached people dreaming or thinking of buying a home nor alternative housing structures such as multi-household cooperatives." Luken and Vaughan, "Genuine Homemaker in Your Own Home," 1611.

[30] Illington continued: "The Own Your Own Home Movement will give women an insight into what actual ownership of a home can mean, by giving women the opportunity to really supervise, as owners, those details in home operation and management which naturally belong to them, but which are constantly being overlooked or slighted in rented dwellings and apartments." Quoted in Luken and Vaughan, "Genuine Homemaker in Your Own Home," 1611–12.

[31] Quoted in ibid., 1614.

characteristics of the good American citizen. Homeowners are better men. They are also more civic-minded and (to quote an Own-Your-Own-Home advertisement) *"real* Americans."[32]

The Own-Your-Own-Home campaign was not the only vehicle for the construction and circulation of the early twentieth-century identity story of Americans as a home-owning people. Another important example, starting in the early 1920s, was the "Better Homes in America" (BHA) campaign, the stated mission of which was to "educate the American people to higher standards of home life" and to teach them the "inestimable values [that] lie in the true home."[33] Better Homes in America was the brainchild of Marie Meloney, editor of the *Delineator,* a mass circulation women's magazine. Meloney asked for and received endorsements from President Warren Harding, Secretary of Commerce Herbert Hoover, and the governors of twenty-eight American states. When Meloney established a National Advisory Council for BHA, Vice President Calvin Coolidge agreed to serve as its honorary head, and Herbert Hoover as its chair. In 1924, the organization incorporated as a national educational foundation and set up offices one block from the White House.[34]

Among Better Homes in America's endeavors was the production and distribution of guidebooks explaining how to become a homeowner and how to furnish and manage a home. Its most important initiative, however, was the construction, through local Better Homes Committees throughout the United States, of tens of thousands of demonstration houses. Owning private "homes," participants in this campaign underscored, promotes the happiness and well-being of *all* Americans. According to Caroline Bartlett Crane, for example, who chaired the Better Homes Committee in Kalamazoo, Michigan, home ownership was *not* the exclusive preserve of the middle class, let alone of the well-to-do. Instead, it was for *everyone,* or more precisely (to borrow Crane's language), "Everyman."

In 1925, Crane published a book about the Kalamazoo demonstration house, which she titled *Everyman's House.* "We must never rest satisfied," she wrote, "with any scheme of things which assumes that there is any class or cross-section of our people who 'of course' cannot hope to be

---

[32] The ad reads, "The Man Who Owns His Home – is a better Worker, Husband, Father, Citizen, and a *real* American." Quoted in Hornstein, *Nation of Realtors,* 127.

[33] Better Homes in America, *Guidebook of Better Homes in America: How to Organize the 1924 Campaign,* publication no. 1 (Washington, 1924), quoted in Hornstein, *Nation of Realtors,* 128.

[34] See Janet Hutchinson, "The Cure for Domestic Neglect: Better Homes in America, 1922–1935," *Perspectives in Vernacular Architecture* 2 (1986): 168–78.

'home-owners.'" "[T]he Everymans," she claimed, "mean about 90 percent of all of us."[35]

2. Power, Politics, and Crisis

In fact, not 90 percent, but closer to 45 percent of Americans were homeowners when Crane published *Everyman's House*.[36] As late as 1940, only 43.6 percent of Americans owned their homes, and that year the corresponding figure for black Americans was a mere 22.8 percent.[37] But of course Crane's aim – and more generally, the aim of participants in the Own-Your-Own-Home and Better Homes in America campaigns – was less to explain or describe the practice of home ownership in the United States than to construct and circulate a story that would prompt (white) Americans to identify as homeowners.

Hence those who told and retold this narrative (community builders and other industry elites, local civic leaders, and the state and national political officials who promoted the Own-Your-Own-Home and the Better Homes in America campaigns) ascribed to the American Dream of home ownership a universal status. They even (anachronistically) read that "dream" into the nation's collective past. In 1922, for instance, Secretary of Commerce Herbert Hoover declared: "[I]t is mainly through the hope of enjoying the ownership of a home that the latent energy of any citizenry is called forth. This universal yearning for better homes and the larger security, independence, and freedom that they imply, was the aspiration that carried our pioneers westward."[38] If the explicitly racial identity narrative in circulation during the early decades of the century was a story about what separates "us" from "them," this racialized story of the American public was a story about what binds "us" together.

---

[35] Caroline Bartlett Crane, *Everyman's House* (New York: Doubleday, 1925), 47–8.

[36] According to what was at that time the most recent census of housing, conducted in 1920, the American home ownership rate was 45.6 percent. Kenneth Snowden, "Housing Units, by Occupancy and Ownership: 1890–1997," Table Dc653–669 in *Historical Statistics of the United States, Earliest Times to the Present: Millennial Edition*, ed. Susan Carter, Scott Sigmund Gartner, Michael Haines, Alan Olmstead, Richard Sutch, and Gavin Wright (New York: Cambridge University Press, 2006).

[37] Ibid.

[38] "Hoover Declares Time Ripe to Push Home Building Revival," *Building Supply News*, September 26, 1922, 458. But, as historians of the nineteenth-century United States have shown, home ownership was not an "American Dream" from the time of the founding. See Margaret Garb, *City of American Dreams: A History of Home Ownership and Housing Reform in Chicago, 1871–1919* (Chicago, IL: University of Chicago Press, 2005).

Why "racialized"? Because this narrative assumed, very often without explicitly citing, the racial narrative. It assumed, that is, a normatively significant divide between "the black and white races"; a causal link between black racial identity and unfitness for home ownership; and both the desirability and the legitimacy of racial residential segregation. In Chapter 5, I make the case that, for my racially privileged respondents, white racial identity functions as the (invisible) norm against which racial difference is defined. Stories about "the American public" or "the American Dream" present "American" as if that identity were wholly devoid of racial particularity. But if whiteness is "the unmarked marker of others' differences," if "white" is invisible (for whites), if "white" (to recall Patrick Webber's claim, cited in Chapter 3) "doesn't matter," then when whites say *nothing* about race, they almost always mean *white*.[39]

The absence of race talk in an identity narrative, in other words, can be as significant as its presence. To my knowledge, the narrative promulgated through Own-Your-Own-Home and Better Homes in America *never once addressed* the dramatically disproportionately low rates of home ownership among black Americans, let alone the practice, widespread at that time, of racially restricting home ownership in high-status residential neighborhoods. American blacks were the "absent presence" in both campaigns. Only by assuming the explicitly racial narrative that was the subject of Chapter 2 could narrators of the story of Americans as a home-owning people exclude blacks from "the public" whose good they claimed home ownership promotes.

At the same time, those narrators papered over nontrivial differences within the (white) American "we." Recall J. C. Nichols and his "3000 Acres Restricted." The Country Club District's deed restrictions included racial restrictions, to be sure. But as noted earlier, they were not limited to racial restrictions. Instead, they worked to exclude anyone who could not afford to purchase large, expensive houses sited on large, expensive lots. Still, Nichols's claim was that deed and zoning restrictions served the good of *all*. In 1924, at a meeting of NAREB's Division of Home Builders and Subdividers, he went so far as to assert: "In our subdivision, whether we are dealing with a man [who] has only a thousand dollars or fifteen hundred dollars, or even if it is only a one- or two-room house, we

---

[39] "[U]nmarked marker of others' differences" is from Ruth Frankenberg, *White Women, Race Matters: The Social Construction of Whiteness* (Minneapolis: University of Minnesota Press, 1993), 198.

are going to give him the God-given rights of protection that his family deserves."[40]

As Nichols's biographer, William Worley, points out, this claim was disingenuous. There *were no* one- or two-room houses in the Country Club District, and there were certainly no houses that could be purchased for fifteen hundred dollars.[41] Indeed, it was the purpose of J. C. Nichols's self-perpetuating restrictions to ensure there never would be. Nichols never once included restrictions in the deeds of houses of the sort he described in this 1924 speech. Nor, after 1905, when he began work on the Country Club District, did he even build such houses.[42]

Still, as argued in section one, gestures toward "God-given rights" for *all* (that is, all *whites*) – rights to "protection," and more basically rights to the private ownership of a detached, single-family suburban "home" – were necessary to advance the *political* claim that Nichols and other community builders wanted to advance: the claim that the state should assist private developers with land use control (that state actors should engage in both municipal planning and comprehensive zoning to preserve "character and value"), and that the state should grant developers financial support, whether directly (for instance, through low-interest loans) or indirectly (for example, through tax exemptions aimed at stimulating the mortgage market).

As far as the first set of claims was concerned, efforts to win state support for land use control began in earnest in the second decade of the century. As early as 1914, zoning advocates began strategizing about making the case for zoning as a means to secure public "safety or comfort or order or health."[43] This particular framing was important for constitutional reasons. As Martha Lees explains:

According to constitutional doctrine, states could regulate property pursuant to the police power – that is, for the purpose of preserving the public health, safety, welfare, and morals – but were subject to the strictures of the Fourteenth

---

[40] J. C. Nichols, "Home Building and Subdividing Department," *National Real Estate Journal*, August 27, 1923, 28. Cited in Worley, *J. C. Nichols and the Shaping of Kansas City*, 138.

[41] Worley, *J. C. Nichols and the Shaping of Kansas City*, 138.

[42] Ibid.

[43] The quote is from municipal reformer Alfred Bettman, who urged an audience at the National Conference on City Planning (NCCP) to frame its case as motivated by concerns about the public welfare. Quoted in David Freund, *Colored Property: State Policy and White Racial Politics in Suburban America* (Chicago, IL: University of Chicago Press, 2007), 60.

Amendment, which forbade states to deprive any person of life, liberty, or property without due process of law. Thus, the constitutional problem was to determine whether zoning was within the police power or whether it was a deprivation of property without due process.[44]

Through the decade of the 1910s, zoning proponents adopted the strategy of arguing that zoning promoted public health, safety, welfare, and morals, and they won a series of legal victories in state and federal courts. In California, for example, *Ex parte Quong Wo* characterized a zoning ordinance to exclude a Chinese laundry as protecting "the public health, morals, safety, and comfort," and *Matter of Montgomery* affirmed a city's right to prohibit the operation of a lumber yard in a residential area on the grounds that "in a residence district such a place may be a menace to the safety of the property in its neighborhood for various reasons, among which may be mentioned the inflammable nature of the materials kept there."[45]

An important limit to the municipal power to zone was decided by the U.S. Supreme Court, however, in the 1917 case *Buchanan v. Warley*.[46] Although this case was discussed in Chapter 2, a more detailed consideration is now in order.

At issue in *Buchanan* was a 1914 ordinance from Louisville, Kentucky, which prohibited "colored persons" from occupying houses in blocks where the majority of houses were occupied by whites, and forbade whites to occupy houses in majority-black blocks. Charles Buchanan, a white seller, sold a property to William Warley, a black buyer. The two, political collaborators with the shared aim of challenging the Louisville ordinance, stipulated in their contract that the buyer would not be obligated to accept the deed or to pay for the property if he were not legally permitted to occupy it. As planned, Warley refused to close on the deal. Buchanan asserted that he was required to, on the grounds that the zoning ordinance was unconstitutional. He then brought suit against the city. The Court of Appeals of Kentucky upheld the ordinance.

But in 1917 the U.S. Supreme Court reversed the judgment of the Kentucky Court of Appeals, ruling that the Louisville ordinance violated

---

[44] Martha Lees, "Preserving Property Values? Preserving Proper Homes? Preserving Privilege? The Pre-*Euclid* Debate over Zoning for Exclusively Private Residential Areas, 1916–1926," *University of Pittsburgh Law Review* 56 (1994–5): 367–439, here 373.

[45] *Ex parte Quong Wo*, 161 Cal. 220, 230 118 P. 714 (1911); *Matter of Montgomery*, 163 Cal. 457, 460, 125 P. 1070, 1071 (1912). For a discussion of these and similar cases, see Freund, *Colored Property*, 66–70.

[46] *Buchanan v. Warley* 245 U.S. 60 (1917).

the Fourteenth Amendment by abridging the privileges and immunities of U.S. citizens to acquire and enjoy property, by unjustly taking property without due process of law, and by denying citizens equal protection of the law.[47] As contemporary legal scholars have emphasized, Justice Day's opinion in *Buchanan* focused principally, not on racial segregation, but on threats to property rights.[48] Indeed, the Court had recently upheld the legislation of racial segregation, both in railroad accommodations and in education.[49] But "[e]quality with regard to property rights ... was at the core of the Fourteenth Amendment, in a way that equality with regard to education ... and transportation ... was not."[50] According to Justice Day, property "is more than the mere thing which a person owns. It ... includes the right to acquire, use, and dispose of it ... Property consists of the free use, enjoyment, and disposal of a person's acquisitions without control or diminution save by the law of the land."[51] The zoning ordinance at issue, Day's claim was, violated property rights because it interfered with owners' freedom to use and to dispose of their land as they saw fit.

In the decade that followed this ruling, there took place, both inside and outside of American courts, a wide-ranging debate about the legitimacy of zoning. Opponents toed the line from *Buchanan*: zoning was an illegitimate use of state power, one that interfered with the property rights of individual citizens. Advocates, by contrast, attempted to make the case that zoning was a legitimate exercise of the state's police power, one that promoted the good of the public.

The latter group won a major political victory in 1921, when Secretary of Commerce Herbert Hoover appointed a Zoning Advisory Committee, which he staffed, not only with prominent architects and planners, but also with housing industry leaders and other business elites.[52] In 1924, this committee published *A Standard Zoning Enabling Act*, which subsequently was adopted by state legislatures across the nation.[53]

---

[47] Ibid.

[48] See, for instance, Michael Klarman, "Race and the Court in the Progressive Era," *Vanderbilt Law Review* 51 (1998): 881–952. For a critique of this view, see James Ely, "Reflections on *Buchanan v. Warley*, Property Rights, and Race," *Vanderbilt Law Review* 51 (1998): 953–73.

[49] *Plessy v. Ferguson* 163 U.S. 537 (1896); *Berea College v. Kentucky* 211 U.S. 45 (1911).

[50] Klarman, "Race and the Court in the Progressive Era," 937.

[51] *Buchanan v. Warley* 245 U.S. 60, 74 (1917).

[52] NAREB President Irving Hiett served on the committee, for example, as did Morris Knowles and John Ihlder of the U.S. Chamber of Commerce. Hornstein, *Nation of Realtors*, 141.

[53] By 1925, nineteen states had adopted the enabling act in whole or in part. Herbert Hoover, "Foreword," *Standard State Zoning Enabling Act, Revised Edition* (Washington, DC: Government Printing Office, 1926).

But even at the time of the publication of this act, the constitutionality of zoning remained in question. Two years later, the U.S. Supreme Court would settle the matter once and for all in its landmark *Village of Euclid v. Ambler Realty* opinion.[54] Again, this case – which marked a striking departure from the logic of *Buchanan* – is worth pausing to consider.

In 1922, the village of Euclid, located just outside Cleveland, had adopted a comprehensive zoning ordinance modeled on the ordinance passed in 1916 in New York. It divided the village into districts and regulated within each district, not only building and lot characteristics (such as height and size), but also uses. U-1 districts, for example, were "restricted to single-family dwellings, public parks, water towers and reservoirs, suburban and interurban electric railway stations and rights of way, and farming, non-commercial greenhouse nurseries and truck gardening."[55] U-2 districts, in addition to these uses, also permitted two-family dwellings, and U-3 districts allowed "apartment houses, hotels, churches, schools, public libraries, museums, private clubs, community center buildings, hospitals, sanitariums, public playgrounds and recreation buildings, a city hall and courthouse."[56]

The Ambler Realty Company brought suit against the village, claiming that the value of land that it held in what were now restricted zones was diminished as a result of the ordinance: an ordinance that, the company alleged, violated its property rights and constituted unjust takings. The U.S. District Court for the Northern District of Ohio agreed. It ruled the ordinance unconstitutional. Judge Westenhaver, in his (blatantly racist) opinion, cited *Buchanan*. If ever police power should be exercised to promote the public welfare through zoning, Westenhaver argued, it was to enforce specifically *racial* zoning. In his words:

[M]ore and stronger reasons exist, having real and substantial relation to the public peace, supporting [the Louisville racial zoning ordinance] than can be urged under any aspect of the police power to support the [Euclid, Ohio] ordinance ... The blighting of property values and the congesting of the population, whenever the colored or certain foreign races invade a residential section, are so well known as to be within the judicial cognizance.[57]

---

[54] *Village of Euclid et al. v. Ambler Realty Company* 272 US 365, 380 (1926).
[55] Ibid.
[56] Ibid. Three additional districts were increasingly inclusive of various types of business and industry and other uses the village deemed inappropriate in residential areas, such as, in the most inclusive district, sewage disposal and garbage incineration plants.
[57] *Ambler Realty Co. v. Village of Euclid*, 297 F. 307, 312–13 (N.D. Ohio 1924).

In short, if the claim to exercise police power at stake in *Buchanan* was illegitimate, then certainly the claim to exercise police power in *Euclid* was, as well.

The village appealed, and *Euclid* went to the U.S. Supreme Court, where lawyers for the Ambler Realty Company made the case that the law in question violated the Fourteenth Amendment. "Restrictions upon limited areas have always been established, when desired, by mutual contracts," they argued, "and such restrictions have been upheld so long as they were reasonable, in view of the changing growth and development of the country."[58] But, they continued:

> It has … only recently been suggested that use restrictions, which formerly lay in contract, may be imposed or abrogated by municipal regulation and that the fleeting legislative judgment and will of a municipal counsel can select which, out of a variety of admittedly innocent uses, it will permit the owners of land to enjoy … That our cities should be made beautiful and orderly is, of course, in the highest degree desirable, but it is even more important that our people should remain free. Their freedom depends upon the preservation of their constitutional immunities and privileges against the desire of others to control them."[59]

Was zoning an illegitimate imposition by the state that violated citizens' constitutional immunities and privileges? Was it a fundamental threat to individual property rights? Or, alternatively, was zoning a legitimate use of the police power of the state: a practice that served the good of the public as a whole by protecting the "health, safety, welfare, and morality" of all?

Writing for a divided Court, Justice Sutherland honed in on what he claimed was the crux of the matter. It was not controversial, by 1926, for the state to regulate building heights or lot sizes. Nor was it controversial to prohibit in residential areas "offensive or dangerous industries."[60] The real issue was the exclusion from single-family residential areas of retail establishments, especially of multifamily housing. On this matter, it is worth quoting Justice Sutherland at length:

> With particular reference to apartment houses, it is pointed out that the development of detached house sections is greatly retarded by the coming of apartment houses, which has sometimes resulted in destroying the entire section for private house purposes; that in such sections very often the apartment house is a mere

---

[58] Argument for Appellee at 376, *Village of Euclid v. Ambler Realty Co.* 272 U.S. 365 (1926) (No 31).

[59] Argument for Appellee at 376, 379, *Village of Euclid v. Ambler Realty Co.* 272 U.S. 365 (1926) (No 31).

[60] *Village of Euclid v. Ambler Realty Co.* 272 U.S. 365, 388 (1926).

parasite, constructed in order to take advantage of the open spaces and attractive surroundings created by the residential character of the district. Moreover, the coming of one apartment house is followed by others, interfering by their height and bulk with the free circulation of air and monopolizing the rays of sun which otherwise would fall upon the smaller homes, and bringing, as their necessary accompaniments, the disturbing noises incident to increased traffic and business, and the occupation, by means of moving and parked automobiles, of larger portions of the streets, thus detracting from their safety and depriving children of the privilege of quiet and open spaces for play, enjoyed by those in more favored localities, – until, finally, the residential character of the neighborhood and its desirability as a place of detached residences are utterly destroyed. Under these circumstances, apartment houses, which in a different environment would not only be entirely unobjectionable but highly desirable, come very near to being nuisances.[61]

In short, zoning to exclude multifamily housing from "more favored" localities is a legitimate use of the police power of the state, because "parasite"-like, such housing deprives residents of single-family detached homes of "the privilege of quiet and open spaces," and of safety and the health benefits of sun and freely circulating air. Apartments "come very near to being" in the category of traditional nuisances, like stockyards or slaughterhouses, when they are sited in residential districts that house detached, single-family homes.

The Supreme Court reversed the lower court's decree. It upheld Euclid's zoning ordinance, settling the question of the constitutionality of what today is called "Euclidean zoning." It thus legitimized the first of the two types of state support to which community builders like J. C. Nichols laid claim. In 1921, the year before Euclid adopted its zoning ordinance, only 48 American municipalities had zoning laws on the books.[62] By the close of the decade, in 1930, a full 800 did.[63]

Does this legal success suggest that early community builders and other actors who helped circulate the home ownership story had persuaded

---

[61] *Village of Euclid v. Ambler Realty Co.* 272 U.S. 365, 394–5 (1926).
[62] Freund, *Colored Property*, 88.
[63] Ibid. Comprehensive municipal planning followed a similar path. In 1928, Hoover's advisory committee (now renamed the Advisory Committee on City Planning and Zoning) published *A Standard City Planning Enabling Act*, which, like the 1924 document, many states made law. See Theodora Hubbard and Henry Hubbard, *Our Cities To-day and To-morrow: A Survey of Planning and Zoning Progress in the United States* (Cambridge, MA: Harvard University Press, 1929), especially pp. 20–1. Its basis, according to Marc Weiss, was a statement of planning principles drafted by the Home Builders and Subdividers Division of NAREB, the principal professional organization of large-scale developers like Nichols. Weiss, *Rise of the Community Builders*, chapter 5. See also Hornstein, *Nation of Realtors*, chapter 5.

Supreme Court justices and other influential Americans that it was a "good story"? It is not entirely inconceivable. In several of the pre-*Euclid* cases that upheld zoning ordinances across the country, state supreme court opinions came very close to citing the NAREB-promulgated home ownership narrative verbatim. In 1925, for example, in *Miller v. Board of Public Works*, the California state supreme court opined that the "justification for residential zoning may, in the last analysis, be rested upon the protection of the civic and social values of the American home."[64] The opinion continued:

The establishment of such districts is for the general welfare because it tends to promote and perpetuate the American home. It is axiomatic that the welfare, and indeed the very existence of a nation depend upon the character and caliber of its citizenry. The character and quality of manhood and womanhood are in a large measure the result of home environment. The home and its intrinsic influences are the very foundation of good citizenship, and any factor contributing to the establishment of homes and the fostering of home life doubtless tends to the enhancement not only of community life but the life of the nation as a whole.[65]

If one takes this and similar rhetoric at face value, it may seem like early twentieth-century Americans were increasingly persuaded by the home ownership narrative. At the same time, however, it seems quite likely that at least some zoning advocates (from city planners, to attorneys representing municipalities like Euclid, to pro-zoning judges) were less than fully sincere. After all, they *had to* argue that zoning promotes the public good if they wanted success in their effort to legitimize it. The U.S. constitution constrained them to argue along those lines.

What is more, arguments like Justice Sutherland's, which condoned excluding apartment buildings and two-family dwellings from single-family residential neighborhoods on the grounds that multifamily housing interfered with health, quiet, and safety, were internally inconsistent. If the aim of zoning was to promote the health, safety, welfare, and morals of *all*, then that aim could not be realized by an ordinance that deprived people who lived in multifamily housing of the "privilege[s] ... enjoyed by those in more favored localities."

Of course, when it comes to the intentions and the internal motivations of political actors, it is never possible to know for sure. But it seems quite plausible that, for reasons independent of the home ownership narrative

---

[64]   *Miller v. Board of Public Works*, 195 Cal. 477, 480, 234 P. 381 (1925).
[65]   *Miller v. Board of Public Works*, 195 Cal. 477, 492–3, 234 P. 381 (1925).

itself, early zoning advocates wanted that narrative institutionalized in American law and objectified in American urban and suburban space. It seems quite plausible that they *used* that narrative, even if they did not understand it to be a "good story," to justify its institutionalization and objectification.

Most likely, different motives drove different actors. Most community builders likely wanted their story institutionalized and objectified to bolster their profits. Certainly attorneys who represented clients like the Village of Euclid wanted it institutionalized and objectified because such an outcome was, for them, the definition of professional success. In addition, the 1917 *Buchanan* decision would have given racially privileged actors who, for whatever reason, wanted to segregate and to exclude along racial lines a different (or, in some cases, a supplementary) set of motivations. As Martha Lees underscores, "it is hard to imagine that [the] passage [of formally race-neutral zoning ordinances] was not influenced to some degree by the same racial fear and hatred that spawned their patently racist counterparts."[66] Lees cites Minnesota State Supreme Court Justice Dibell's claim that it was apartment *dwellers*, more so than apartments, that struck zoning advocates as nuisance-like: "Back of all the suggestion of aesthetic considerations," Dibell wrote, "is the disinclination of the exclusive district to have in its midst those who dwell in apartments." He continued:

It matters not how mentally fit, or how morally correct, or how decorous in conduct they are, they are unwelcome ... It is the same feeling which often finds expression in the making of distinctions based on race or nationality or upon natural or artificial social status.[67]

Lees cites, as well, the assertion of Frank Williams, a lawyer and city planner whose studies of zoning strongly influenced New York's 1916 ordinance, that:

[o]ften the growth or change of districts inhabited by members of a race considered inferior, like the Chinese or negroes, or the desire of some of its members for betterment, brings them into contact with other people in the same block ... this invasion of the inferior produces more or less discomfort or disorder, and has a distinct tendency to lower property values.[68]

[66] Lees, "Preserving Property Values?" 411.
[67] *Twin City II*, 176 N.W. at 163–4 (Brown, C. J. and Dibell, J. dissenting on rehearing), cited in Lees, "Preserving Property Values?" 411.
[68] Frank B. Williams, *The Law of City Planning and Zoning* (New York: MacMillan, 1922), 200, cited in Lees, "Preserving Property Values?" 412.

In a similar vein, Richard Chused, analyzing the very passage from Justice Sutherland's opinion cited earlier, notes that "[i]t was ... possible, without ever mentioning race, immigration, or tenement houses, to call upon other code words that had the same impact."[69]

In Chapters 2 and 3, I sketched a path by which an identity narrative might be institutionalized and objectified. If many people, I argued, or at least a large enough number of sufficiently influential people, think that a particular identity story is a *good* story, then that story might be built into institutions. It might be built, that is, into rules and laws and other collective norms that incentivize people to perform their identities "according to script." An identity narrative might be built into material forms as well: into objects or spaces that shape a kind of practical sense, which social actors incorporate as relatively enduring and embodied dispositions. If so, my claim was, then a significant shift at the level of discourse – even a shift that effects a change in dominant perceptions of how good the original story is – might *not* effect substantial identitarian change. Why not? Because institutionalized and objectified identity narratives encourage the production of ordinary stories: narratives of everyday lived experience that are *framed by* constructed identities.

This path can be expressed schematically as follows:

(discursive shift)

E(G)S, I/O ➜ OS

An extraordinary story (with the parenthetical "G" signaling an extraordinary, good story) is institutionalized and objectified *because* it is perceived as a good story. The result is ordinary stories: everyday stories in which the extraordinary story functions as a narrative frame, and does so even in the event of a significant shift at the level of discourse.

In the remainder of this chapter and the chapter that follows, I want to sketch a second path by which an identity narrative might be institutionalized and objectified. This second path can also be represented schematically:

E(B)S, I/O ➜ OS
↘
(discursive shift)

---

[69] Richard Chused, "*Euclid*'s Historical Imagery," *Case Western Law Review* 51 (2001): 597–616, here 614.

Clearly, it is in many ways similar to the first. But one important difference is that the extraordinary story is not, at the time when it is institutionalized and objectified, a *good* story. (The parenthetical "B" signals that it is an extraordinary, bad story.) Maybe this is a story about "who we are" that departs from what many or most people think is true. Maybe it is one that departs from what most people think is legitimate and/or one that includes important and relatively salient incoherencies.

Still, some contingency opens up a space for, not so much a new (good) story, but a new set of institutionalizations and objectifications: changes effected by political actors who succeed *notwithstanding the fact* that the stories with which they justify their actions are not good stories. I suggested previously that community builders may have succeeded in winning state support for land use planning, not by persuading most Americans that their story was a good story, so much as by forming a coalition with actors who, perhaps for different reasons, wanted the same result.

In the remainder of this chapter, I want to make an even stronger case for this second path. The Great Depression, I want to suggest, was a critical juncture that made possible an even more complete institutionalization and objectification of the home ownership story than was feasible through the decade of the 1920s. The result of this second path, I suggest in Chapter 5, is similar to the result of the first: ordinary stories in which the extraordinary story, now institutionalized and objectified, works as a narrative frame. But (as I indicate in the second diagram, and hope to show in the pages that follow) there is one nontrivial difference: institutionalization and objectification can effect a shift at the level of discourse. In other words, they can help make what once was a *bad* story better.

Recall that J. C. Nichols and other early community builders wanted, not only state-enforced land use planning, but also state *financial* support for their housing projects. Efforts to win public resources for private, profit-driven development, unlike efforts to win support for city planning and zoning, were largely unsuccessful through the second decade of the twentieth century.

As early as 1919, Frederick Law Olmsted, writing in the *Monthly Labor Review*, suggested that the federal government might provide low-interest, publicly funded loans to private real estate developers "parallel to the operation of the Federal Farm Loan Act."[70] That same year, the

[70] Frederick Law Olmstead, "Lessons from Housing Developments of the United States Housing Corporation," *Monthly Labor Review* 8 (May 1919): 1253–62, here 1260. The

United States League of Building and Loans and the National Federation of Construction Industries, working together with the Department of Labor, drafted legislation that, had it passed, would have created a federally supported secondary mortgage market.[71] Just one year later, in 1920, realtors and mortgage bankers testifying at a congressional hearing argued that the federal government should grant tax exemptions for mortgage investments, in order to lure private investors back to the flagging market.[72]

But it was one thing to zone and to plan with a view to promoting "stability, permanence, and orderly progress." It was quite another to try to justify state financial subsidies for the housing industry. "We have all sorts of trouble here ... in trying to get enough money to run the Government," Congressman William Oldfield told J. Willison Smith of the Land Title and Trust Company of Philadelphia in 1920, when Smith testified before the Real Estate Mortgage Taxes Subcommittee of the House Ways and Means Committee about the alleged need for tax exemptions for interest on mortgage investments. "[O]f course your business is hurt ... but it seems that everybody's business is hurt."[73] The following year, Senator William Calder, writing for the Select Committee on Reconstruction and Production, described the extreme overcrowding, the "insanitary and dangerous quarters," and the high rates of infant mortality, tuberculosis, and other communicable diseases in American cities.[74] Nevertheless, he underscored that "following the American custom, private enterprise must be depended upon to meet the crisis ... The Government is an organization to govern, not to build houses or operate mines or run railroads or banks."[75]

Through the decade of the 1920s, then, community builders and other industry elites were successful in their efforts to circulate a narrative of Americans as a home-owning people, and they were successful in forging alliances to promote comprehensive zoning and municipal planning. But

Federal Farm Loan Act of 1916 established twelve regional Farm Loan Banks, which made low-interest loans to farmers.
[71] The proposed secondary mortgage market was modeled on the Farm Loan Bank System of 1916, created to help farmers access low-cost credit. Radford, *Modern Housing for America*, 47–8.
[72] Hornstein, *A Nation of Realtors*, 134.
[73] House Committee on Ways and Means, Hearings on Real Estate Mortgage Taxes (H.R. 8080 and H.R. 14062, 66th Congress, 3rd Session, Dec. 11, 1920, 69–70.
[74] Quoted in National Housing Association, *Housing Betterment* 10 (New York: National Housing Association, 1921), 52.
[75] Quoted in ibid., 53.

they were almost entirely unsuccessful in their efforts to use claims about the public good and/or stories of Americans as a home-owning people to win state financial subsidies for their business ventures.

Then came the stock market crash of October 1929, followed by the most pronounced and the most prolonged economic downturn in American history. Between 1929 and 1933, the real GDP in the United States fell by 25 percent, and the nominal GDP by 50 percent.[76] Stock prices fell a full 82 percent between 1929 and 1932, and by 1934, unemployment had reached a staggering 21.7 percent.[77] Between 1929 and 1933, nearly eleven thousand commercial banks in the United States failed: 43 percent of the total number of banks in the United States at that time.[78]

As credit dried up, and as consumer spending plummeted, firms collapsed in almost every sector of the economy. But the housing industry was especially hard hit. Between 1928 and 1933, residential construction in the United States fell a full 90 percent.[79] Meanwhile, foreclosure rates soared. In 1926, before the start of the recession, there were roughly sixty-eight thousand foreclosures across the nation. That number increased nearly fourfold by 1933 to over two hundred fifty-two thousand.[80]

---

[76] Bureau of Economic Analysis, "Table 1.1.5. Gross Domestic Product" and "Table 1.1.3. Real Gross Domestic Product," in National Income and Product Accounts Table, Bureau of Economic Analysis, May 27, 2010. http://www.bea.gov/national/nipaweb/TablePrint. asp?FirstYear=1929&LastYear=1933&Freq=Year&SelectedTable=3&ViewSeries=NO &Java=no&MaxValue=33.695&MaxChars=6&Request3Place=N&3Place=N&From View=YES&Legal=&Land= (accessed June 19, 2010).

[77] Bloomberg L. P., "Index price graph for Dow Jones Industrial Average 9/3/1929 to 7/8/1932," Bloomberg database (St. Louis: Washington University in Saint Louis Olin Business Library, 2010); Stanley Lebergott, "Series D 1–10 Labor Force and its components: 1900 to 1947" in *Historical Statistics of the United States, Colonial Times to 1970*, Bicentennial Edition, Part 1 (Washington, DC: U.S. Census Bureau, 1975), 126.

[78] Howard Bodenhorn, Table Cj251–264, "Commercial banks – number and assets: 1834–1980," in *Historical Statistics of the United States: Millennial Edition Online*, ed. Susan B. Carter, Scott Sigmund Gartner, Michael R. Haines, Alan L. Olmstead, Richard Sutch, and Gavin Wright, available at http://hsus.cambridge.org/HSUSWeb/toc/tableToc. do?id=Cj251–264 (accessed May 15, 2012).

[79] The value of new residential buildings in 1926 was $4,926,000,000. By 1933, that figure had dropped to $499,000,000. U.S. Business and Defense Services Administration, "Series N 1–29. Value of New Private and Public construction put in place: 1915 to 1970," in *Historical Statistics of the United States, Colonial Times to 1970*, Bicentennial Edition, Part 2, ed. U.S. Census Bureau (Washington, DC: U.S. Census Bureau, 1975), 618.

[80] Federal Home Loan Bank Administration, "Series H 113–127. Nonfarm housing credit – Estimated volume of home mortgage loans made and outstanding, and of foreclosures: 1925 to 1945" in U.S. Bureau of the Census, *Historical Statistics of the United States, 1789–1945* (Washington DC: U.S. Bureau of the Census, 1949), 174.

By then, with home values dramatically reduced, in some cities more than half of home mortgages were in default.[81]

As the crisis progressed, not only community builders and other leaders of the housing industry, but also elected officials, among them Herbert Hoover and Franklin Delano Roosevelt, converged on the view that American state actors should intervene to buoy up the market in housing. Housing was not only a crucial need for individuals and for families, their claim was; it was also a critically important source of employment.[82] Hence many public officials – including officials who, through the 1920s, had opposed intervention in the market – came to the view that the state should pump capital back into housing: that it should jump-start construction with a view to creating homes and jobs.

Of course, there is more than one way the American state could have used public funds to help create jobs, and along with jobs, homes. The state could have built and/or it could have subsidized the building of housing priced such that rents would be affordable for working people, including people with average and below-average incomes. This option was not only conceivable in the abstract; it was in fact the option pursued by many European nations in the interwar years. In the United States, it was the option favored by many progressive housing reformers.

---

[81] According to the U.S. Department of Commerce, which surveyed twenty-two cities throughout the United States, by 1934, 62 percent of mortgaged properties in Cleveland, Ohio; 59 percent in Birmingham, Alabama; and 53 percent in Indianapolis, Indiana were in default. The median figure was 38 percent (for Atlanta), and the lowest was 21 percent (Richmond, Virginia). U.S. Department of Commerce, "Owner-Occupied Residential Properties: Value, Debt, Ratio of Debt to Value, and Loan Delinquency, Jan. 1, 1934, by Value Groups," *Financial Survey of Urban Housing: Statistics on Financial Aspects of Urban Housing* (Washington, DC: Government Printing Office, 1937), 27, 75, 127, 186, 235, 291, 359, 424, 476, 540, 591, 654, 709, 759, 820, 883, 942, 1003, 1040, 1085, 1145, 1207.

[82] Although this claim was overstated at times, the housing industry was an important source of employment before 1929, and an important source of unemployment after the crash. In construction alone, from 1928 to 1933, the number of employed workers halved to eight hundred nine thousand. Construction workers constituted 5.4 percent of all employees in 1928, but just 3.4 percent in 1933. Bureau of Labor, "Table Ba840–848: Employees on Nonagricultural Payrolls, by Industry: 1919–1999" in *Historical Statistics of the United States Millennial Edition Online*, ed. Susan B. Carter, Scott Sigmund Gartner, Michael R. Haines, Alan L. Olmstead, Richard Sutch, and Gavin Wright (New York: Cambridge University Press, 2006). According to a special unemployment census conducted in 1930, a full 24 percent of building laborers were unemployed. That year, unemployed building laborers represented 18 percent of all unemployed laborers. Bureau of the Census, "Table 3: Unemployment Classes A and B, by Sex and Occupation for the United States: 1930" in *Fifteenth Census of the United States 1930, Unemployment Volume II*, (Washington, DC: U.S. Bureau of the Census, 1975), 15.

Edith Elmer Wood, for instance, made the case in her 1931 book, *Recent Trends in American Housing*, that the United States should follow the European example and subsidize housing costs for those whose needs the private market could not meet.[83] Three years later, Catherine Bauer argued that the United States should remove from the private, profit-driven market, not only housing development for the poor, but also housing for the working and the lower-middle classes. What was needed, in Bauer's words, was "the transition of housing from a speculative business, operated solely for a maximum of immediate private profit, to a long-time public investment undertaking, recognized as of essential public utility and planned and controlled as such."[84]

Support for public housing was one possible response to the crisis: a response supported by one narrative of who the public was and of what served its good. But of course the option favored by community builders like J. C. Nichols, and supported by the story industry elites had been telling since the inception of the National Association of Real Estate Boards, was different. They favored subsidizing private, profit-driven development, and subsidizing the purchase of the houses that private developers built.

On the face of it, it seems this option should have been at least as difficult to justify as the option favored by reformers like Bauer and Wood. Subsidizing profit-oriented development is a form of market intervention, no less than is subsidizing public housing. But this option would use public funds to aid the wealthy and the privileged. It is far from clear why tax dollars should be channeled to business elites, and/or to those consumers – still a minority in the 1930s – who can afford to purchase private homes.

But in December 1931, when Herbert Hoover (now president) convened his White House Conference on Home Building and Home Ownership, it was this option he pursued. By that time, housing starts were at their lowest level in over a decade. Housing prices were down 30 percent in just five years, and the foreclosure rate in the United States was nearing the quarter million mark. Hoover's conference, which took this crisis as its raison d'être, was widely attended, not only by elected officials and other civic leaders, but also by powerful players in the real estate industry, keen to win federal subsidies for private development.

[83] See Edith Elmer Wood, *Recent Trends in American Housing* (New York: Macmillan, 1931).
[84] Catherine Bauer, *Modern Housing* (Boston, MA: Houghton Mifflin Company, 1934), 224.

This audience must have been pleased by Hoover's opening address, in which the president explicitly cited the NAREB-promulgated narrative of what Americans want, desire, and value, imputing to "almost every individual" in the United States, including "millions" of renters, the aspiration to own private homes. "I am confident," Hoover told his audience, "that the sentiment for homeownership is so embedded in the American heart that millions of people who dwell in tenements, apartments, and rented rows of solid brick have the aspiration for wider opportunity in ownership of their own homes. To possess one's own home is the hope and ambition of almost every individual in our country, whether he lives in hotel, apartment, or tenement."[85]

Hoover cited and endorsed, in other words, not only the NAREB narrative, but also that narrative's claim to universalism. He cited and endorsed its normative distinction between, in his words, "homes and mere housing," as well as its association of home ownership with "the racial longing of the American people":

Those immortal ballads, "Home, Sweet Home," "My Old Kentucky Home," and "The Little Gray Home in the West," were not written about tenements or apartments. They are expressions of racial longing which find outlet in the living poetry and songs of our people.[86]

But if the "racial longing" of "our people" was compatible with racial restrictions in private covenants and with widespread, state-sanctioned racial segregation, then the (unnamed) race of "our people," it seems, was white.

Hoover endorsed, finally, the association of private home ownership with the good of the (white) American public, claiming, as had real estate entrepreneurs through the 1910s and 1920s, that home ownership strengthens families, promotes civic virtue, and fosters freedom and democracy:

This aspiration [for home ownership] penetrates the heart of our national well-being. It makes for happier married life, it makes for better children, it makes for confidence and security, it makes for courage to meet the battle of life, it makes for better citizenship. There can be no fear for a democracy or self-government or for liberty or freedom from homeowners no matter how humble they may be.[87]

---

[85] Herbert Hoover, "Address to the White House Conference on Home Building and Home Ownership," December 2, 1931, available at http://www.presidency.ucsb.edu/ws/index.php?pid=22927&st=home+ownership&st1= (accessed July 7, 2010).

[86] Ibid.

[87] Ibid.

3. "A Proper Concern of the Government"

The result of the president's Conference on Home Building and Home Ownership was a series of reports on a range of topics, from financing the purchase of private houses and reducing real estate taxes, to planning residential districts, to addressing the problems of "slums" and "Negro housing."[88] The recommendations issued in these reports strongly influenced the New Deal legislation that followed Hoover's conference, starting just seven months later with the creation of the Federal Home Loan Bank Board. What jumps out for the contemporary reader of these reports is not simply that they sketch many of the policy innovations that would be introduced under Roosevelt, but also that they *justify* the major shift in policy that they recommend – namely, the direct intervention of the U.S. federal state in the private housing market – using the narrative constructed and circulated during the Own-Your-Own-Home and the Better Homes in America campaigns.[89]

Consider the report of the Committee on Home Finance and Taxation, which recommended, among other changes, reducing taxes on real estate; encouraging large-scale community building as opposed to small-scale development; providing home buyers with long-term, amortized mortgage loans; and employing, not just zoning and city planning, but also restrictive covenants "to safeguard residential values and the security of residential investments against the harm resulting from inharmonious types of building and incompatible ownership occupancy."[90] In the introduction to this report, the editors approvingly quote Hoover's claim, made at the first meeting of the Planning Committee for the conference,

[88] There were eleven publications total, titled as follows: "Planning for Residential Districts," "Home Finance and Taxation," "Slums, Large-Scale Housing, and Decentralization," "Home Ownership, Income and Types of Dwellings," "House Design, Construction and Equipment," "Negro Housing," "Farm and Village Housing," "Housing and the Community – Home Repair and Remodeling," "Household Management and Kitchens," "Homemaking, Home Furnishing and Information Services," and "Housing Objective and Program." *General Index to the Final Reports of the President's Conference on Home Building and Home Ownership*, ed. John Gries and James Ford (Washington, DC: The President's Conference on Home Building and Home Ownership, 1933).

[89] An important exception is the volume on "Negro Housing," prepared by sociologist Charles Johnson, which considers in some detail the causes and consequences of racial residential segregation, racial discrimination in mortgage lending, the dual market for rental apartments, and white violence and intimidation. John Gries and James Ford, ed., *Negro Housing* (Washington, DC: National Capital Press, 1932).

[90] John Gries and James Ford, eds., *Home Finance and Taxation* (Washington, DC: National Capital Press, 1932), 46.

that "It should be possible in our country for anybody of sound character and industrious habits to provide himself with adequate housing *and
preferably to buy his own home*."[91] A few pages later, in the summary of
the report, the editors underscore, "[T]oo much cannot be said about the
value of stimulating home ownership *because of its effect upon good citizenship and the strengthening of family ties*."[92]

Similar language appears throughout. For example, the Home Finance
Committee introduces its recommendations for strengthening the secondary mortgage market as follows: "[I]t is strongly urged that the
respective communities and states undertake this opportunity for service
as a means of further developing good citizenship."[93] The report avers:
"Successful home ownership is worthy of every effort *because it leads
to an enriched family life*." It explicitly cites NAREB's campaign slogan,
asserting, "Every American family which so desires and is able financially
should OWN THEIR OWN HOME."[94]

Even those committee members who dissented from particular recommendations did so using the language of the narrative of a home-owning
American public. Harry Kissell, for example, a member of the Finance
Committee, dissented from the recommendation that people only purchase houses if they are able to make a down payment of 25 percent.
According to Kissell, this guideline would amount to "condemning the
great majority of our people to die in rented houses."[95]

Home Finance and Taxation was published in 1932, the year Franklin
Delano Roosevelt was elected president of the United States. By the
spring of 1933, when Roosevelt took office, half of home mortgages in
the United States were in default.[96] That was the year the HOLC was
established. The focus of the discussion of the HOLC in Chapter 2 was
that agency's role in institutionalizing what was at the time a very widely

---

[91] Ibid., ix, emphasis added.

[92] Ibid., 1–2, emphasis added.

[93] In other words, states and local communities should take steps to create and maintain
strong secondary mortgage markets, not just to stimulate the economy, but to foster civic
virtue through home ownership. Ibid., 10, emphasis added.

[94] Ibid., 15, italics added, caps in original.

[95] Ibid., 50.

[96] Gail Radford, "The Federal Government and Housing during the Great Depression,"
103–20 in *From Tenements to the Taylor Homes: In Search of an Urban Housing Policy
in Twentieth Century America*, ed. John Bauman, Roger Biles, and Kristin Szylvian
(University Park: Pennsylvania State University Press, 2000), 107.

endorsed narrative of race and investment risk.[97] The HOLC's principal activities, however, were helping financial institutions by purchasing defaulting mortgages, and helping homeowners by refinancing short-term balloon loans with low-interest, amortized loans. The HOLC enacted and proved practicable, in other words, one of the major recommendations of the Committee on Home Finance and Taxation: the long-term, fully self-amortizing home mortgage, with uniform payments spread across the life of the loan.

This was a significant change from the pre-Depression status quo. As Jeffrey Hornstein explains, for the average American, securing a mortgage in the 1910s and 1920s was at once "complicated and risky."[98] At that time, most mortgages were short-term loans, often no more than three to five years in duration. They typically covered no more than 50 percent of costs, and, because they were not amortized, came due in lump sum at the end of the term.[99] The HOLC, by extending the period of the loan to as much as twenty years, and by standardizing the self-amortizing mortgage, took an important step toward institutionalizing, not just the racial story that was dominant in the early years of the twentieth century, but also the narrative of (white) Americans as a home-owning people. Indeed, Roosevelt explicitly cited that narrative when he introduced the legislation that would create the HOLC. Supporting private homeowners and the financial institutions that provided their mortgage loans was "a proper concern of the government," he assured the U.S. Congress, since the "broad interests of the Nation" "require … special safeguards [to be] thrown around home ownership."[100]

The following year, the U.S. federal government took another major step in that direction when it passed the National Housing Act of 1934 "to encourage improvement in housing standards and conditions [and] to provide a system of mutual mortgage insurance."[101] The National Housing Act created the Federal Housing Administration (FHA), through which the American state began insuring home mortgages, significantly reducing investment risk for private lenders. At the same time, it solved

[97] See pp. 66–7 on the HOLC's racist neighborhood rating system and its Residential Security Maps, which graphically depicted those ratings.
[98] Hornstein, *Nation of Realtors*, 122.
[99] Ibid.
[100] Franklin D. Roosevelt, "A Message Asking for Legislation to Save Small Home Mortgages from Foreclosure," April 13, 1933 in John T. Woolley and Gerhard Peters, *The American Presidency Project* [online]. Santa Barbara, CA. http://www.presidency. ucsb.edu/ws/?pid=14618. (accessed July 15, 2010).
[101] National Housing Act, 48 Stat. 1246 (1934).

the problem of scarce capital for large builders by providing in those developments that met FHA standards "conditional commitments" to underwrite mortgages for would-be buyers.

The focus of the discussion of the FHA in Chapter 2 was the racist character of the agency's underwriting standards. In addition, those standards were, quite consciously, favorable to large-scale suburban development. The FHA was explicit in its objective of supporting builders who planned and developed on a community-wide scale.[102] It favored, in particular, suburban residential communities comprised of new, detached, single-family units. Because the FHA guaranteed in advance that it would insure mortgages for approved homes in developments that conformed to its standards, it made it possible for big builders to obtain up-front financing, and thus to avoid many of the financial difficulties early community builders like Emery Childs had encountered.

The impact was enormous. By making widely available high loan-to-value, long-term, self-amortizing mortgages, the FHA enabled a massive expansion in private home ownership. As David Freund notes, "[F]or most eligible borrowers, buying a new, FHA-eligible suburban house suddenly became the least expensive alternative, often cheaper than renting an apartment in the central city."[103] Fewer than 44 percent of American householders owned private homes in 1940.[104] By 1950, that figure had jumped to 55 percent, and by 1960, almost 62 percent of American householders were homeowners – an increase of more than 40 percent in just two decades.[105] Because the FHA strongly favored new construction over renovation, and because it favored detached, single-family houses and suburban locations, the majority of these new "homes" *looked like* the houses in "Own-Your-Own-Home" advertisements. According to

---

[102] According to Jeffrey Hornstein, "Drawn almost directly from recommendations of the Subdivision Layout Committee of Hoover's conference of 1931, the FHA's *Operative Builders Guide* stated flatly that the government sought to "encourage the type of builder who … assumes responsibility for [the production of homes,] from the plotting and development of the land to the disposal of the completed dwelling unit." Hornstein, *Nation of Realtors*, 150.

[103] Freund estimates that, on average, FHA monthly mortgage payments in the 1930s were $39.74, less than 20 percent of the average family income, or about $5 per month more than rental housing in Detroit. Freund, *Colored Property*, 134.

[104] United States Census Bureau, "Historical Census of Housing Tables," available at http://www.census.gov/hhes/www/housing/census/historic/owner.html (accessed July 11, 2012).

[105] Ibid.

Hornstein, between 1934 and 1953, almost 84 percent of new, privately owned nonfarm dwellings were single-family houses.[106]

Together, the HOLC, the FHA, and other New Deal housing programs represented a tremendous investment of public resources in private housing. By the end of its loan program in 1936, the HOLC had bought and refinanced $3.1 billion in delinquent home loans. At that time, it owned more than 20 percent of the mortgages in the United States. That same year, the FHA insured the loans for 16 percent of new housing starts, a number that rose to 26.7 percent in 1938 and to 33.4 percent in 1940. By 1942, the FHA insured one in four American home mortgages.

Two years later, this program was effectively expanded through the Servicemen's Readjustment Act of 1944 (the so-called GI Bill), which authorized the Veterans Administration to guarantee mortgage loans for returning war veterans through a program closely modeled on the FHA.[107] Meanwhile, the Federal National Mortgage Association (FNMA, or "Fannie Mae"), chartered in 1938, created a government-run secondary mortgage market. FNMA purchased government-backed mortgages originated by private lenders, further reducing the risk and increasing the profitability of home mortgage lending.

The effect of New Deal housing policies, it is worth underscoring, reached beyond the market for government-backed mortgages. Lenders of conventional mortgages closely followed FHA appraising and lending principles, which quickly became established as industry standards. What is more, the American state lent directly to originators of conventional mortgages (at that time, mostly S & Ls) through the Federal Home Loan Bank system, and it insured conventional mortgages through the Federal Savings and Loan Insurance Corporation (FSLIC). In short, the New Deal fundamentally restructured the market for private home mortgages.

State programs expanded home finance credit to an historically unprecedented level, and they directed the capital that they helped generate toward single-family residential development in racially exclusive suburbs.

Identity stories sometimes gain dominance, and sometimes they eventually are institutionalized and objectified, because many people (or at

---

[106] Hornstein, *Nation of Realtors*, 151.

[107] One significant difference, however, was that no down payment was required for a VA-backed loan. The VA guaranteed as much as 50 percent of a mortgage loan, and VA loans could be combined with conventional loans to cover the entirety of the purchase price of a house.

least, some very influential people) buy into them. They find them compelling, that is to say. They think they are *good* (credible, legitimate, and coherent) stories. And so they tell them, and they retell them, and they act in ways that shape institutions and material forms that embody those narratives. This was the case with the racial story that was the focus of Chapter 2: a story that was institutionalized and objectified at a point in history at which it was widely accepted, especially by whites, and crucially *before* it was subjected to the scientific and normative critiques that eventually delegitimized it.

Not so the story of Americans as a home-owning people whose good is served by public support for private housing development. This story gained dominance, and eventually was institutionalized and objectified, even though many, perhaps *most* people did not find it compelling.

The home ownership narrative was far from noncontroversial. Indeed, it was actively and publicly contested, starting in the 1910s, by thinkers and activists on the left, who told a counternarrative of "the American public" and "the public good." "We Americans" are ordinary people, according to this alternative story. "We Americans" are workers. What serves our good is separate and distinct from what serves the good of big business. We ought to use our collective resources and power, not to aid profit-driven private development, but instead to create a robust, publicly funded alternative to the private market in housing.

Earlier in this chapter, I cited important works by Edith Elmer Wood and Catherine Bauer, published in the early 1930s, in the wake of the crash. Even before the onset of the First World War, however, thinkers on the left had begun to articulate this counternarrative. In 1909, in *An Introduction to City Planning: Democracy's Challenge to the American City*, Benjamin Clark Marsh called for "a radical change in the attitude of citizens toward government and the functions of government."[108] The new "attitude" he envisioned was one that "boldly demands the interest and effort of the government to preserve the health, morals and efficiency of the citizens equal to the effort and the zeal which is now expended in the futile task of trying to make amends for the exploitations by private citizens and the wanton disregard of the rights of the many."[109] Marsh urged the use of planning and zoning, not to create oases of exclusivity, but instead to promote the well-being of laborers and other common

---

[108] Benjamin Clarke Marsh, *An Introduction to City Planning: Democracy's Challenge to the American City* (New York: Benjamin Clarke Marsh, 1909), 27.
[109] Ibid.

people. He advocated the use of public funds to purchase land within and beyond the boundaries of America's growing cities, with a view to reigning in speculative development. He proposed, as well, the municipal taxation of increases in land values, arguing that growth should benefit, not only the owners of capital, land, and other property, but also the workers and the ordinary residents of America's municipalities, who participated in and contributed to that growth.

Marsh was an early advocate of state intervention in housing aimed at meeting the needs of those the private market failed. But he was hardly the only thinker in the United States to take this stance.[110] Just like housing industry elites, however, reformers found no real opening to try to institutionalize their narrative until after 1929.

What must have looked like a major victory came in June 1933 with the passage of the National Industrial Recovery Act (NIRA), Title II of which established the Public Works Administration (PWA) and appropriated federal funds for clearing slums and building housing. Between 1933 and 1937, the PWA gave grants to limited dividend and nonprofit housing corporations. It was under one such grant that the famous Carl Mackey houses in Philadelphia were built.[111] The PWA also directly constructed some twenty-two thousand housing units in fifty-nine different communities. As Mark Gelfand underscores, these numbers were small relative to need.[112] Still, from a design perspective, much PWA housing

[110] Lewis Mumford, for example, writing for *The Nation*, made the case that "The weakness of the city-planning movement up to the present has been due to its constriction within the present tangle of private property interests," and that "[h]ousing reform ... has only standardized the tenement." "It is fatuous," Mumford continued, "to suppose that private interests will correct this condition, for it is for the benefit of private interests that it exists." Lewis Mumford, "Attacking the Housing Problem on Three Fronts," *The Nation* 109, 2827 (September 6, 1919): 332–3, here 333. Staking out the most radical position during the interwar years was the American Federation of Labor (AFL), which advocated direct housing development by the state. See Radford, *Modern Housing for America*, chapter 2. Arguments along the lines advanced by March, Mumford, and others informed some early housing experiments at the level of individual states, and also some legislative proposals at the federal level. The latter included bills that, had they passed, would have authorized low-interest loans for noncommercial housing development. See the discussion in Edith Elmer Wood, *The Housing of the Unskilled Wage Earner: America's Next Promise* (New York: MacMillan, 1919), 209–28.

[111] The first grant, in fact. See Radford, *Modern Housing*, chapter 5 on the history of this project, which, although it did not fulfill its founders' political aims (they hoped it would serve as a model to be emulated by nonprofit developers across the United States), was, by all accounts, a tremendous success from a design perspective, and highly desirable for residents.

[112] Gelfand estimates that there were six million substandard urban dwellings in the United States at the time. Gelfand, *A Nation of Cities*, 60.

was a real success. What is more, although in 1936, income limits were set for residents of government-owned PWA units, none of the housing built by limited-dividend and nonprofit corporations was means tested. In other words, middle-income residents, including white-collar workers, were permitted to – and did – live in PWA housing.

Unsurprisingly, the real estate lobby objected. PWA projects, lobbyists claimed, threatened the private market. They were a step down "the road to socialism."[113] "GOVERNMENT HOUSING IS *NOT FREE*," declared one billboard prototype distributed as part of the anti-PWA campaign of the mid-1930s. "All government revenue comes from you, the tax payer," it adumbrated. "Because of large deficits, Federal income taxes have been raised again and again to pay for various subsidized programs." "Can you honestly afford to pay a portion of your neighbor's rent through increased taxes and still pay for your own housing expenses?" it asked, rhetorically. "Can your community afford to give a special group a FREE RIDE?"[114]

The irony, of course, is that this critique came from groups (prominent among them NAREB, the National Association of Home Builders, and the Mortgage Bankers Association) that *at the very same time* were pressing for the use of public funds to subsidize private, profit-driven development.

Through the mid-1930s, the progressive coalition worked to make permanent what it had accomplished through the PWA (which was a temporary agency). In the years leading up to the passage of the Wagner-Steagall Act of 1937, Catherine Bauer and other reformers worked closely with Robert Wagner to draft legislation and to press for its passage. But NAREB, along with the U.S. League of Building and Loans, the National Retail Lumber Dealers Association, and the Housing Division of the U.S. Chamber of Commerce, mobilized in opposition to the reformers' vision and pushed through significant changes to the bill. The United States Housing Act of 1937, which created the United States Housing Authority (USHA) to replace the PWA, represented an important setback for the progressives.

Starting in 1937, the U.S. federal government would not site, build, or manage a single subsidized rental housing unit. Instead, it limited its role to funding local housing authorities. As noted in Chapter 2, given prevailing patterns of race- and class-based metropolitan segregation, this change meant public housing would be for central cities and other disadvantaged communities only. Exclusive suburbs could simply decline to apply for federal subsidies, and thereby keep public housing out.

[113] Quoted in Wright, *Building the Dream*, 222.
[114] Reprinted in ibid., 221.

Under the 1937 Act, what is more, publicly funded housing was stringently means tested. To be eligible, tenants had to fall at least 20 percent below the income bracket that could afford the least expensive private housing in their area.[115] Maximum construction costs were set at very low levels, as well, which meant public housing would not only *be* housing for the poor, it would also *look like* housing for the poor.[116]

In short, 1937 marked the start of what Gail Radford has identified as a two-tiered federal housing policy in the United States: one that generously subsidizes the producers and consumers of market-rate housing while spending very little to provide poor-quality subsidized rental housing, and very little of it, for the poor.[117] By the start of the Second World War, USHA had supported the construction of fewer than one hundred thousand units of affordable housing.[118] After the war, although the National Housing Act of 1949 would set a goal of producing eight hundred ten thousand public housing units in six years (that is, an average of one hundred thirty-five thousand per year), on average there would be fewer than twenty-six thousand starts annually through the 1950s.[119] By 1964, only three hundred seventy thousand units had been completed: half the goal set for 1955.[120] By the 1980s, just 3 *percent* of American housing units would be owned by nonprofit or government agencies, compared with 23 percent in France, 30 percent in the United Kingdom, and 43 percent in the Netherlands.[121]

The progressives' counternarrative of the American public, and of what serves the public good, was not institutionalized. It was not objectified in the American urban built environment. The community builders' was. And, although the latter story did not prevail *because* it was a better story, when it did prevail, it *became* a better story. In 1950, for the first time in history, more than half of Americans "own[ed their] own homes." When the postwar state subsidized the development of, not just

[115] Ibid., 228.
[116] According to Gail Radford, "Redhook and Queensbridge, the first two complexes built in New York City under the new legislation, cost approximately one-half as much per room as the two projects built in the city by the PWA." Radford quotes Lewis Mumford, who described these developments as "unnecessarily barracklike and monotonous" and notes that USHA cut costs through measures such as leaving doors off closets, failing to separate kitchens from living rooms, and building elevators that did not stop on every floor. Radford, "The Federal Government and Housing during the Great Depression," 113.
[117] Radford, *Modern Housing for America.*
[118] Gelfand, *A Nation of Cities*, 122.
[119] Radford, *Modern Housing for America*, 200.
[120] Freund, *Colored Property*, 186.
[121] Radford, *Modern Housing for America*, 200.

"high-class subdivisions," but also modest, Levittown-style tract housing, it helped, if not the illusory "American public," at least millions of white, middle-class American citizens.

But all home ownership is not equivalent. It is one thing to live in Kansas City's Country Club District: to reap the benefits of state-supported exclusivity, and of tax subsidies that rise as home prices rise, in a wealthy community that delivers to its residents top-notch public services. It is quite another to live in a mass-produced tract house in the equivalent of a Levittown.

Working Americans who moved in the second half of the twentieth century to what Dolores Hayden has described as "thousands of almost identical 800-square-foot houses, with a living room, kitchen, two bedrooms, one bath and a driveway"[122] took modest tax deductions for their mortgage interest and reaped modest profits when and if their home values rose. They got a fraction of the subsidy and the profit reaped by developers like J. C. Nichols, or for that matter, by William and Alfred Levitt. They got a fraction of the subsidy and the profit reaped by their wealthy fellow citizens in exclusive developments like the Country Club District. At the same time, they lost the opportunity to ally themselves with the majority of "nonwhite" Americans and to push for a genuinely redistributive alternative to the profit-driven market.

Herbert Gans, in his classic 1967 *The Levittowners*, reported that the majority of the random sample of residents he interviewed liked living in Levittown "very much."[123] Many of Gans's female respondents stressed, in their interviews, their pleasure with the privacy afforded by their detached, single-family "homes." Many male respondents expressed feelings of pride in private home ownership.[124]

But these attitudes and preferences were more the *product* than the mere subject of the story of Americans as a home-owning people. Crucially, they were the product of the institutions and the spaces that story helped shape: institutions that incentivized suburban home ownership (while foreclosing other possibilities) and spaces that objectified the narrative of white Americans as a home-owning people.

---

[122] Hayden, *Building Suburbia*, 134.
[123] None disliked living in Levittown, and only a few were ambivalent. Herbert Gans, *The Levittowners: Ways of Life and Politics in a New Suburban Community* (New York: Columbia University Press, 1967), 271.
[124] Ibid, 277–8.

5

White Fences

In the spring of 1986, Leslie Wexner, the billionaire founder of The Limited, Inc., together with his business partner, developer John (Jack) Kessler, began to purchase property in New Albany, Ohio. A small, rural village northeast of Columbus, New Albany's population at that time was just over 400 people, most of them elderly, and most of them poor. No levy had been passed in the village since 1932, and the municipal budget was $80,000. Wexner and Kessler made their early land purchases anonymously, through third-party buyers like the Smith and Hale law firm. They then began to buy openly, through the New Albany Company (NACO), a development firm owned by Wexner and chaired by Kessler. Through the 1990s, NACO assembled large plots of land in New Albany and transformed the rural village into what relatively quickly became an upscale, Georgian-themed suburban enclave. NACO bordered its development with white-plank fences: an iconic symbol of rural America that, by 1990 in New Albany, Ohio, was also a status symbol, dividing those who could afford to buy in Wexner's new development from those who could not. The latter included most of New Albany's longtime residents, who eventually were enticed (by high-priced offers for their homes and farms) and/or constrained (by dramatically increasing property taxes) to leave.[1]

---

[1] This paragraph draws on my extensive reading of the *Columbus Dispatch*, the *Gahanna News*, the *Columbus Monthly*, and other local publications from 1986 through 2004. See especially Mary Yost, "New Albany? A Boom Town?" *Columbus Dispatch*, November 1, 1987, 1A; Ray Crumbley, "New Albany Fears Urban Overgrowth," *Columbus Dispatch*, April 6, 1996, 3D; Steve Wright, "Fast-growing New Albany May Acquire More Land," *Columbus Dispatch*, August 3, 1996, 4C; and Jeff Ortega and Ray Crumbley, "Suburbs with Room Have Grown, Study Shows," *Columbus Dispatch*, November 1, 1998, 1D.

Changes in New Albany were dramatic, and they were quick. By 1990, the population had increased nearly 300 percent, to sixteen hundred twenty-one: the result of growing density, due to development, and the annexation to the village of formerly unincorporated land.[2] Ten years later, the population of Wexner's white-fence community was more than thirty-seven hundred.[3] By 2010, it was more than seventy-seven hundred: an increase of almost 2,000 percent in just a quarter century.[4] Per capita income by the time of the 2000 census was $62,000.[5] By 2010, it was about $72,000: almost three times the per capita income for the city of Columbus.[6] New Albany, Ohio was the wealthiest municipality in the Columbus metropolitan area.

Developing New Albany at the end of the twentieth century was a very different enterprise than developing Riverside, Illinois had been at the end of the nineteenth. For Emery Childs, recall, the costly improvements to the rural landscape – the streets and the walkways, the sewers, the water distribution system – were important factors contributing to the failure of his project. Leslie Wexner, by contrast, was able to leverage public resources to significantly reduce his expenditure level, and hence his risk. He sited his community just outside Columbus's I-270 outerbelt, the interstate highway that would provide New Albany residents easy access to other municipalities in the metropolitan area, and also to the Port Columbus International Airport. For infrastructural development – the thirteen new school buildings that would comprise New Albany's 200-plus-acre public school campus, the new public roads, and the new fire station Wexner planned for his development – NACO petitioned for the formation of a special tax assessment district empowered to collect real estate taxes earmarked for capital improvements within its boundaries. For water and sewer services, the Village of New Albany contracted with the City of Columbus, which financed the construction of both

[2] U.S. Census Bureau, 2010 Census Redistricting Data (Public Law 94–171), Summary File for Ohio, Tables P1 and H1. Generated using http://factfinder.census.gov (accessed May 26, 2011).

[3] U.S. Census Bureau, 2000 Census of Population and Housing, Summary Tape File 3 for New Albany, OH. Generated using http://factfinder.census.gov (accessed March 24, 2011).

[4] U.S. Census Bureau, "State and County QuickFacts," available at http://quickfacts.census.gov/qfd/states/39/3979002.html (accessed February 27, 2012).

[5] U.S. Census Bureau, 2000 Census of Population and Housing, Summary Tape File 3 for New Albany, OH. Generated using http://factfinder.census.gov (accessed March 24, 2011).

[6] U.S. Census Bureau, "State and County QuickFacts," available at http://quickfacts.census.gov/qfd/states/39/3979002.html (accessed February 27, 2012).

systems up front, hoping to recoup its investment later by collecting user fees. Wexner won an array of tax abatements and state subsidies, as well, to attract firms to the business campus he built near New Albany's northern boundary. For Easton, the mixed-used development he constructed just southwest of the village, he won tax increment financing.[7, 8]

Leslie Wexner, in short, did not face the hurdles Emery Childs had faced when it came to raising capital for improvements to the land he purchased. Nor did he face the same hurdles when it came to finding buyers who could obtain, and who could afford to pay off, the substantial mortgages that even most affluent people would need to buy property in his development. Since mid-century, the federal secondary mortgage market and the mortgage insurance programs created during the New Deal years had expanded significantly. By the time Wexner began buying and building in New Albany, not only FNMA (which, in 1970, had become a private corporation) but also the Government National Mortgage Association (GNMA, or "Ginnie Mae") and the Federal Home Loan Mortgage Corporation (FHLMC, or "Freddie Mac") were in the business of buying, packaging, and reselling mortgage loans originated by private lenders.[9]

Lenders, of course, are more willing to lend when the risk of doing so is low. Hence the overall effect of the federal secondary mortgage market and mortgage insurance programs was to increase dramatically the supply of housing credit. More funds were available to Wexner's buyers than had

---

[7] In tax increment financing (TIF) districts, developers pay taxes into funds that they then use to finance, and hence to subsidize, development. Much of Easton's infrastructure development (the construction of parking garages for mall customers, for instance) was funded this way. See Barbara Carmen, "Easton Tax Deals," *Columbus Dispatch*, July 23, 1996, B1.

[8] This paragraph draws on articles from local Columbus publications from 1986 through 2004, including Kathy Gray Foster, "'Wexley' Fight Could Test School Pact," *Columbus Dispatch*, November 5, 1987, 1B; Jonathan Riskand and Mary Stephens, "District Would Assess Property," June 7, 1992, 1B; and Ray Crumbley, "New Albany Tax Deal OK'd for Stalled Novus Project," *Columbus Dispatch*, March 12, 1997, 2B.

[9] GNMA, a government agency, purchased mostly FHA and VA loans. FNMA and FHLMC purchased conforming loans. Both originally government agencies, they were subsequently transformed into government-sponsored entities (GSEs), which, although privately owned, retained important government links, privileges, and subsidies. They were exempt from paying state and local income taxes, for instance, and from registering their securities with the Securities and Exchange Commission (SEC). In addition, the secretary of the treasury could invest up to $2.25 billion in the securities of each. FNMA and FHLMC remained private until 2008, when in the wake of the financial crisis, the Housing and Economic Recovery Act established the Federal Housing Finance Agency, which placed both in conservatorship. United States Congress, *Congressional Budget Office, Fannie Mae, Freddie Mac, and the Federal Role in the Secondary Mortgage Market* (Washington, DC: Government Printing Office, 2010).

been available to Childs's, and those funds were available on better terms. What is more, the preferential treatment given to home ownership by the United States tax code translated into massive state subsidies for buyers, like Wexner's, who qualified for large mortgage loans.[10] By the close of the century, when Leslie Wexner's project was in full bloom, more than 70 percent of families earning over $100,000 annually (that is, families in the top 10 percent of the income distribution in the United States) filed tax returns claiming homeowner deductions, compared with less than 1 percent of families earning $20,000 or less (families in the bottom third of the income distribution).[11] The average value of the deduction taken by a family earning $200,000 or more (a family in the top 2 percent of the income distribution) was more than *seventy-five times* that taken by a family earning less than $10,000 (a family in the bottom 14 percent), and the mortgage interest tax subsidy for the top 10 percent alone exceeded the *total* of the federal housing subsidies administered by HUD.[12]

Wexner's enterprise differed, not only from Emery Childs's late nineteenth-century project, but also from J. C. Nichols's early twentieth-century development, since Wexner did not need to concern himself with what Nichols had called "encroachment around the edges." No builder would site an "incompatible use" near the Georgian-style mansions that comprised Wexner's New Albany, because the land he developed was annexed by an incorporated suburban municipality, which was legally empowered to engage in exclusionary zoning.

As Wexner began building, public officials rezoned rural New Albany for large, expensive, single-family houses on big lots with big setbacks.

---

[10] Homeowners can deduct mortgage interest payments and real estate taxes from their taxable income; defer paying capital gains tax on the profit they make when they sell their houses, as long as, within two years' time, they purchase new houses that are at least as expensive; and, at age fifty-five, take a one-time exemption from paying capital gains tax even if they do not purchase another house. To be sure, none of these rules was new in the late twentieth century. The mortgage interest deduction was initially introduced as part of the Revenue Act of 1864. Homeowners have been permitted to deduct the entirety of their interest payments since 1913, and they have been able to deduct property taxes on their houses since 1865. After World War II, however, with the dramatic rise in the rate of both income taxes and home ownership, the *effects* of these rules changed dramatically. See Irving Welfeld, "Tax Subsidies: Their Effect on the Rate of Homeownership," 225–35 in *Handbook of Housing and the Built Environment in the United States*, ed. Elizabeth Huttman and Willem van Vliet (New York: Greenwood Press, 1988).

[11] Peter Dreier, "Federal Housing Subsidies: Who Benefits and Why?" 105–38 in *A Right to Housing: Foundation for a New Social Agenda*, ed. Rachel Bratt, Michael Stone, and Chester Hartman (Philadelphia, PA: Temple University Press, 2006).

[12] In 2000, direct housing subsidies administered by HUD totaled $30.82 billion, while mortgage interest deductions for families making $100,000 and more totaled $35.8 billion. Ibid., 106, 108.

They did so not simply because Leslie Wexner exhorted them to (as J. C. Nichols had exhorted early twentieth-century Kansas City officials), but also and principally because it was in their *interest* to, and because they *could*. Over the course of the century, the state of Ohio had (as had all fifty American states) empowered suburban municipalities (like New Albany) to resist forcible annexation to urban centers (like Columbus). It had empowered them to annex adjacent unincorporated properties (like the properties in unincorporated Plain Township purchased by Wexner's firm), just so long as the majority of the owners of those properties (in this case, the majority being a single owner: NACO) found it in their interest to be annexed. The state had empowered municipalities, in addition, to raise and to make decisions about how to spend local property taxes; to enter into contracts with other municipalities; to set both funding and admissions policies for local public schools; and to decline to participate in programs aimed at desegregating racially segregated schools, if desegregation efforts crossed district boundaries.[13]

By the end of the twentieth century, then, Leslie Wexner could leverage, not only public resources, but also important public powers, to support and subsidize his profit-oriented development for the wealthy and the racially privileged. He could do so in large part because of the efforts of J. C. Nichols and other early housing industry elites, who had constructed, and then worked to institutionalize and objectify, a narrative of Americans as a home-owning people. I argued in the last chapter that this NAREB-promulgated narrative was a "bad story," one that through the early decades of the century was widely regarded as a bad story. Through the 1920s, most Americans, including most public officials, did not think state support for private, profit-oriented development served "the good of all." Nor did most Americans regard as legitimate the use of state power and tax dollars to aid the construction of what Nichols called "high-class subdivisions."

But in a sense, I suggested, NAREB's story came true when it was institutionalized. More Americans became homeowners, and public

[13] In 1905, when J. C. Nichols started building the Country Club District, courts and legislatures throughout the United States supported the forcible annexation of surrounding land by central cities. Over the course of the century, they reversed their position and increasingly enabled municipal incorporation and legal defense against annexation. See Richard Briffault, "Our Localism: Part II – Localism and Legal Theory," *Columbia Law Review* 90 (March 1990): 346–454. On the local politics of desegregation in Columbus, Ohio, see Gregory Jacobs, *Getting around Brown: Desegregation, Development, and the Columbus Public Schools* (Columbus: Ohio State University Press, 1998).

support for private development in fact helped more Americans. Still, even at the close of the twentieth century, I now want to argue, even as Leslie Wexner was building his upscale development in New Albany, Ohio, most Americans regarded as illegitimate the use of state power and collective resources to construct and maintain exclusive residential communities for the wealthy and the privileged. Or at least most *would*, I argue in the first section of this chapter, if state support for projects like Wexner's were part of their ordinary stories.

In the second and third sections, I return to Leslie Wexner's New Albany, arguing that, by the final decades of the twentieth century, NAREB's narrative of Americans as a home-owning people functioned, not as the subject of, but as a frame to ordinary stories.

First, however, allow me to introduce a thought experiment.

1. Exit

Imagine a group of families, all near the top of the income distribution in an American city – let's make it Columbus, Ohio – who decide they want to exit the city's troubled public school system. Imagine further that, because of past and ongoing racial discrimination, members of this income group are more than 95 percent white, and less than 2 percent black. Now imagine that several enterprising parents within the ranks of the group work to establish a private academy – call it Exit Academy – funded entirely by tuition dollars paid by the families of students who attend. Twenty percent of the best-off students in Columbus public schools, almost all of whom are white and very few of whom are black, immediately leave the system and enroll in Exit Academy. The district, which the year before had served a student body 74 percent of which the state classified as "economically disadvantaged" now serves students 92 percent of whom fall in this category.[14] What is more, although the district was 63 percent black and 29 percent white before Exit Academy opened its

---

[14] The 74 percent figure is from the Columbus Public Schools' "2005–2006 School Year Report Card," available at http://www.ode.state.oh.us/reportcardfiles/2005–2006/DIST/043802.pdf (accessed March 1, 2011). "Economically disadvantaged" students are those who receive public assistance, or whose guardians do, or who receive free or reduced-price lunches. To be eligible to receive free or reduced-price lunches, students' families' incomes must be at or below 130 percent (free) or 180 percent (reduced-price) of the federal poverty level. See the Glossary of Terms provided by the Ohio State Department of Education, at http://www.ode.state.oh.us/GD/Templates/Pages/ODE/ODEDetail.aspx?page=3&TopicRelationID=115&Content=15440 (accessed March 1, 2011).

doors, immediately after, its racial composition shifts to 87 percent black and just 2 percent white.[15]

No doubt, this scenario will be troubling to many readers. The establishment of Exit Academy increases racial and economic segregation in Columbus's schools. It isolates African American students and the "economically disadvantaged," concentrating them in institutions that now will struggle even more than they did before with social problems associated with concentrated poverty. It isolates the privileged, as well, depriving the best-off of in-school interaction with their peers from middle- and lower-income families, and largely depriving them of interaction with African Americans.

Some readers might find fault with the choices made by individual Exit Academy parents, perhaps especially the choices made by those who took the lead in founding the school. A more ethical response to Columbus public schools' difficulties (these readers might think) would have been to remain in the district, working to improve it by exercising "voice."[16] Still, many, perhaps most, will regard the political decision to legally permit exit from the Columbus public school system as a legitimate decision. At least since the landmark *Society of Sisters v. Pierce* ruling in 1925, it has been widely accepted in this country that such an option is needed to limit the state's power over compulsory schooling.[17] The American state can, and it should, mandate that children be educated up to a certain age and/or a certain level of competence, most agree. It should regulate curricular and other academic standards, and it should require basic civic education. But the state should not have monopoly power over the provision of compulsory schooling, since such unchecked power would threaten the rights of religious and other minorities, indeed of all parents and all families with counter-majoritarian educational values.[18] "The child is not the mere creature of the state," Justice McReynolds wrote for the unanimous Court in the *Pierce* opinion. "[T]hose who nurture him

[15] The 63 percent and 29 percent figures are from the Columbus Public Schools' "2005–2006 School Year Report Card," available at http://www.ode.state.oh.us/reportcard-files/2005–2006/ DIST/043802.pdf (accessed March 1, 2011).

[16] See Albert Hirschman, *Exit, Voice, and Loyalty: Responses to Decline in Firms, Organizations, and States* (Cambridge, MA: Cambridge University Press, 1970).

[17] 268 U.S. 510 (1925), at 535.

[18] The Oregon ordinance at the center of the *Pierce* case, as David Tyack has shown, had strong roots in anti-Catholic Nativism, in the racial and ethnic hatred of groups like the Ku Klux Klan, and in the early twentieth-century movement for "100 percent Americanism." See Tyack, "The Perils of Pluralism: The Background of the Pierce Case," *American Historical Review* **74**, 1 (October 1968): 74–98.

and direct his destiny have the right, coupled with the high duty, to recognize and prepare him for additional obligations."[19]

Imagine now that, not long into their venture, the founders of Exit Academy realize that, to remain solvent, they will need to charge a tuition so high that even the vast majority of their potential clients – even most families near the top of Columbus's income distribution – will be unable to pay. The parents lobby legislators for the State of Ohio, who promptly pass an ordinance granting tuition subsidies to students attending elite private schools. The legislature sizes these subsidies such that they place tuition at Exit Academy within the reach of Columbus's best-off residents, but fall short of making the school affordable for the general public. Now imagine that the state provides the academy with additional forms of support: publicly subsidized educational equipment, perhaps, such as classroom computers. Imagine that the Columbus Public School District subsidizes the private school as well, for example, by transferring to it the title to a building the district owns. Meanwhile, support for educational bond issues in Columbus drops sharply, as the city's wealthiest voters, no longer patrons of the public school system, begin, on a regular basis, to oppose proposed levies.

This second scenario is separated from the first by a qualitative difference. In the first case, the state permits privileged families to pool their resources to create a private alternative that fulfills a function the state continues to fill on a public basis. To be sure, this first "Exit" has adverse effects on schoolchildren left behind in the public system. For many readers, such effects will be worrisome, given the importance attached in the contemporary United States to primary and secondary schooling as means to enabling children to function as competent adults in the workplace and the social and political world.[20] Even still, many readers are likely to remain convinced, and reasonably so, that to legally prohibit (the first) Exit would be to grant excessive power to the state.

---

[19] 268 U.S. 510 (1925), at 535.

[20] Chief Justice Warren, writing for the majority in *Brown v. the Board of Education*, made this point forcefully: "Today, education is perhaps the most important function of state and local governments," Warren wrote. "Compulsory school attendance laws and the great expenditures for education both demonstrate our recognition of the importance of education to our democratic society." He elaborated, "It is required in the performance of our most basic public responsibilities, even service in the armed forces. It is the very foundation of good citizenship. Today it is a principal instrument in awakening the child to cultural values, in preparing him for later professional training, and in helping him to adjust normally to his environment. In these days, it is doubtful that any child may reasonably be expected to succeed in life if he is denied the opportunity of an education." *Brown et al. v. Board of Education of Topeka et al.* 347 U.S. 483, at 493.

But the second Exit is different. This is not a case of individual families pooling their surplus funds – funds above and beyond those used to support the public system – and employing those funds to finance a private alternative. Instead, it is a case of privileged people using the power of the state to capture collective resources and to divert those resources from a public to a nonpublic system. Examining post-*Pierce* jurisprudence on state support for private schooling, or reading the policy debates that surround the issue of educational vouchers, one would be hard-pressed to find any argument offering support for a case like this. In the legal community, debates about the legitimacy and the constitutionality of state support for private schooling center principally on trade-offs between maintaining church-state separation and protecting religious freedom. On both sides of those debates, even to the far right of the ideological spectrum, participants converge on the principle that state support for private schooling must serve some public purpose.[21] Of course, not everyone emphasizes the goal of reducing inequality. Some stress the importance of promoting pluralism, while others emphasize protecting religious freedom or parental choice.[22] But many underscore the importance of reducing inequality of educational opportunity, and no one – no federal judge, no state judge, no participant in scholarly debates on the constitutionality of state support for private schooling – suggests public subsidies should support private education with a view to perpetuating or augmenting advantages enjoyed by the racially privileged and economically well-off.

A case in point is the highly publicized *Zelman v. Simmons-Harris* ruling, which school voucher proponents hailed as a major victory.[23] Chief Justice Rehnquist, writing for the majority, made a point of noting in his opinion that the Cleveland voucher program under consideration, a program that gave priority for tuition subsidies to students from low-income families, served the public purpose of aiding poor children in a failing district.[24] Justice Thomas, in a separate concurring opinion, developed this point further and highlighted the racial dimension of the Cleveland case. Quoting Frederick Douglass and citing *Brown v. the*

---

[21] That a private educational institution must serve some "valid secular purpose" is the first of the three criteria for eligibility for state funding enumerated in *Lemon v. Kurtzman*, 403 U.S. 602 (1971).
[22] See Michael Stick, "Educational Vouchers: A Constitutional Analysis," *Columbia Journal of Law and Social Problems* 28, 3 (Spring 1995): 423–74.
[23] 536 U.S. 639 (2002).
[24] Ibid.

Board of Education, Thomas underscored both the disproportionate impact that failing public schools have on African Americans and the widespread support for school choice among black parents. He argued:

> The failure to provide education to poor urban children perpetuates a vicious
> cycle of poverty, dependence, criminality, and alienation that continues for the
> remainder of their lives. If society cannot end racial discrimination, at least it can
> arm minorities with the education to defend themselves from some of discrimina-
> tion's effects.[25]

One need not accept Thomas's premises about a "poor urban" culture
of poverty to acknowledge how far his position is from one that would
urge state support for Exit Academy. A similar pattern obtains in policy
debates on the merits (and demerits) of vouchers. Like the jurisprudential
debates, these do not focus exclusively, or even principally, on questions
of equality.[26] Still, participants devote considerable attention to the relation between, on the one hand, vouchers, and on the other, (in)equality
in access to educational opportunity. Vouchers exacerbate educational
inequalities, some critics suggest, because they draw the very best students
away from poor schools, worsening conditions for those left behind.[27]
Disadvantaged parents, others argue, are less able than the privileged to
take advantage of private school tuition subsidies.[28]

Proponents of voucher plans challenge these and related claims
about the inegalitarian effects of school vouchers. But they do so within
a broader context of principled agreement about both the value of

[25] Ibid., Thomas, concurring.
[26] Efficiency, pluralism, and choice are, arguably, the concerns most central to this de-
bate. See Joseph Viteritti, *Choosing Equality: School Choice, the Constitution, and Civil
Society* (Washington, DC: Brookings Institution, 1999), especially chapter 4; Viteritti,
"Reading *Zelman*: The Triumph of Pluralism, and its Effects on Liberty, Equality, and
Choice," *Southern California Law Review* 76, 5 (2003): 1105–87; and James Dwyer,
Vouchers within Reason: A Child-Centered Approach to Education Reform (Ithaca, NY:
Cornell University Press, 2002), especially chapter 3.
[27] Bruce Fuller, Richard Elmore, and Gary Orfield, *Who Chooses? Who Loses? Culture,
Institutions, and the Unequal Effects of School Choice* (New York: Teachers College
Press, 1996); Eric Hanushek, "Will Quality of Peers Doom Those Left in the Public
Schools?" 121–46 in *Choice with Equity,* ed. Paul Hill (Stanford, CA: Hoover Institution
Press, 2002); and Dan Goldhaber, Kacey Guin, Jeffrey Henig, Frederick Hess, and Janet
Weiss, "How School Choice Affects Students Who Do Not Choose," 101–29 in *Getting
Choice Right: Ensuring Equity and Efficiency in Education Policy,* ed. Julian R. Betts and
Tom Loveless (Washington, DC: Brookings Institution, 2005).
[28] Because of differential access to information, for example, or to transportation. See
Viteritti, *Choosing Equality,* chapter 1; Viteritti, "Reading *Zelman,*" 1179; and Brian
Gill, *Rhetoric versus Reality: What We Know and What We Need to Know about
Vouchers and Charter Schools* (Santa Monica, CA: Rand Education, 2007), chapter 5.

educational equality and the proper relation of school voucher programs to that value.[29] Thus proponents suggest one virtue of state-subsidized choice plans is that they reduce status quo inequalities by decoupling parents' ability to choose which schools their children attend from socio-economic and racial status.[30]

I do not mean to suggest that *no one* would advance a principled argument for state support for Exit Academy. But one would have to look far to the right of a William Rehnquist or a Clarence Thomas to find someone who would. By contrast, in the American political mainstream, there is relatively widespread support for what I want to suggest is the equivalent: state-subsidized exit to elite suburbs, like New Albany, Ohio, and to elite suburban public schools, like the New Albany schools Leslie Wexner helped rebuild. Of course, exclusive suburbs and their school systems are (by definition) priced such that only the best-off benefit from these subsidies. And, because of past and present racial discrimination, they are disproportionately white.

"Wait just one minute," I imagine a skeptic objecting. "There are significant differences between private academies and suburban public schools." Indeed there are. Perhaps the most obvious is that in the hypothetical Exit Academy, parents pay private school tuition, which the state subsidizes with various forms of direct and indirect support. By contrast, parents of students in elite suburban public schools, like New Albany High School, do not make regular tuition payments to the district. They make mortgage payments to the bank and property tax payments to the local municipality instead.

But the latter funds are used, just as tuition funds would be used at Exit, to pay teachers' salaries and to cover other school expenses, such as building and equipment costs. They are used to cover such expenses

---

[29] For Kenneth Godwin and Frank Kemerer, for instance, "Achieving greater equality of educational opportunity requires a radical expansion of school choice." See Godwin and Kemerer, *School Choice Tradeoffs: Liberty, Equity, and Diversity* (Austin: University of Texas, 2002), 5–6. See also Viteritti, *Choosing Equality*, chapter 8 and Terry Moe, *Schools, Vouchers, and the American Public* (Washington, DC: Brookings Institution, 2001), especially chapter 1.

[30] Joseph Viteritti, for example, defending Cleveland's school voucher program, argues, "What is especially troubling about the prevailing arrangement in American education is that it makes choice a function of income, violating both liberty and equality. The point of voucher programs, like the one implemented in Cleveland, is to allow disadvantaged families to enjoy a level of religious and educational freedom that resembles that enjoyed by their more privileged neighbors." Viteritti, "Reading *Zelman*," 1169.

at schools that are no more open to nonresidents than an Exit Academy would be to non-matriculants. Wordnet defines *tuition* as "a fee paid for instruction."[31] The way parents pay for instruction in New Albany's top-ranked public schools – the *tuition* they pay, one might say, if willing to stretch that term beyond colloquial usage – is massively subsidized by the state, for example through the special tax assessment district cited at the start of this chapter, and through the income tax deductions on home mortgage interest.

The source of financing, then, seems inadequate to make Exit Academy and New Albany High disanalogous in the relevant ways. A modification to the thought experiment should confirm. Imagine that school officials establish a public "Exit High" as part of the Columbus public school district; assign to Exit only students from the top of the income distribution (more than 95 percent of whom are white and less than 2 percent of whom are black); and then allocate district resources such that educational funds go disproportionately to Exit. Not only would most readers likely object to such a scheme; it would, in fact, be unconstitutional.[32] That New Albany High is financed by tax dollars while Exit Academy is financed by tuition dollars cannot account for the difference in perceived legitimacy.

At least two additional differences are worth considering: one centered on the value many Americans assign to parental choice in education, and the other on the value of local control over schools. Let's consider each in turn.

"New Albany, Ohio is part of a larger system of multiple local governments," my skeptical interlocutor might point out. "Each offers a distinct package of public services and tax expenditure levels, from which citizens are able to choose 'with their feet.' In the Exit Academy hypothetical, those left behind have *no choice* but to suffer an underfunded and ineffective

---

[31] http://wordnet.princeton.edu/perl/webwn?s=tuition (accessed January 1, 2013).

[32] Indeed, in 1977 Federal District Court Judge Robert Duncan ruled in *Penick v. Columbus Board of Education* that, through actions (such as school siting decisions and the definition of school attendance zones) and inactions (the failure to act to alter the predictably segregating effects of these decisions) the board reproduced and reinforced unconstitutional racial segregation in Columbus. In Duncan's words, "Viewed in the context of segregative optional attendance zones, segregative faculty and administrative hiring and assignments, and the other such actions and decisions of the Columbus Board of Education in recent and remote history, it is fair and reasonable to draw an inference of segregative intent from the Board's actions and omissions." *Gary L. Penick et al. v. Columbus Board of Education et al.* 429 F. Supp. 229 [1977], 97. For a helpful discussion of the *Penick* case, see Jacobs, *Getting around Brown*, chapter 1.

educational system: one made worse off by private school parents who, after exiting, continue to use their votes to oppose levies. In the system of municipal governance of which New Albany is part, by contrast, people are free to move from community to community in pursuit of the package of services and taxes that best meets their needs. No one need accept a school system or a rate of public school funding – indeed, no one need accept *any* package of public service and public service expenditure – that is radically different from the package they desire."

An argument along these lines first was sketched by Charles Tiebout in his seminal 1956 article, "A Pure Theory of Local Expenditures."[33] Tiebout's theory has been developed, tested, and refined in the decades since.[34] One need not delve far into this literature, however, to see the very basic problems with using it to draw principled distinctions between Exit Academy and New Albany High. The model defines the differential ability to pay for schooling (or for security, or for any other public service) as a difference in "preference," implying, implausibly, that those who lack income and wealth (including those who lack income and wealth because of racial discrimination in employment and housing) prefer not to live in safe neighborhoods or to send their children to effective schools. It relies, what is more, on the baldly counterfactual assumption that people are free to move wherever they choose: an assumption that, if fanciful today, was nothing short of incredible in 1956. And it is entirely undiscriminating with respect to the substance of people's expressed preferences. My preference for Pringles may be morally equivalent to your preference for Doritos, but if I regard my desire to transmit to my child unearned class-based and racial privileges as equivalent to your desire to ensure that your child receives a sound education, I have (to paraphrase Jon Elster) confused the logic of the market with the logic of the forum.[35]

---

[33] Charles Tiebout, "A Pure Theory of Local Expenditures," *Journal of Political Economy* 64, 5 (October 1956): 416–24.

[34] See, for instance, Susan Rose-Ackerman, "Market Models of Local Government: Exit, Voting, and the Land Market," *Journal of Urban Economics* 6, 3 (July 1979): 319–37; David Lowery and William Lyons, "The Impact of Jurisdictional Boundaries: An Individual-Level Test of the Tiebout Model," *Journal of Politics* 51, 1 (February 1989): 73–97; Dennis Epple and Holger Sieg, "Estimating Equilibrium Models of Local Jurisdictions," *Journal of Political Economy* 107, 4 (August 1999): 645–81; and Dennis Epple, Thomas Romer, and Holger Sieg, "Interjurisdictional Sorting and Majority Rule: An Empirical Analysis," *Econometrica* 69, 6 (November 2001): 1437–65.

[35] Jon Elster, "The Market and the Forum: Three Varieties of Political Theory," 3–34 in *Deliberative Democracy: Essays on Reason and Politics*, ed. James Bohman and William Rehg (Cambridge, MA: MIT Press, 1997).

Self-regarding preferences, although often appropriate determinants of individual consumer choices, are, by themselves, inappropriate for deciding collective norms: norms that affect, not a sovereign and solitary consumer, but a network of people connected through relations of interdependence and mutual vulnerability.

Again, an adjustment to our thought experiment should confirm the intuition. Imagine that the state of Ohio grants subsidies, not only to elite private academies like Exit, but to a wide range of private schools that charge a wide range of tuitions. Imagine further that, in every case, the quality of education mirrors the cost. State subsidies are priced, let us stipulate, such that only those near the top of the income distribution (more than 95 percent of whom are white and less than 2 percent of whom are black) can afford to send their children to the very best private schools, while those near the bottom (the majority of whom are African American) can "choose" only among schools with exceedingly limited resources and exceptionally low levels of performance. Most readers, it seems safe to say, would regard as illegitimate the state's role in promoting an educational scheme such as this one. Freedom to choose, when strongly constrained by the ability to pay, cannot account for the difference in perceived legitimacy between Exit Academy and New Albany High.

What, then, of a third difference: the difference in the structure of governance in the public compared with the private system? "In a public school district," my interlocutor might suggest, "citizens can come together, and they can deliberate about educational ends and policies. They can elect school board members to represent their interests, and they can hold those officials to account. They can vote to approve or to reject educational levies. State support, because it helps make such local self-governance possible, is defensible on *democratic* grounds. No similar argument can be made in favor of state support for Exit Academy, since educational decisions in that institution are made by publicly unaccountable elites. In fact, much of what is troubling about the hypothetical is that, by subsidizing Exit Academy, the state enables the economically and racially privileged within Columbus to act in ways that affect the majority of Columbus's citizens, and to do so without attending to their claims, their interests, or their good."

This third distinction, like the first two, provides weak grounds for a principled defense of state support for New Albany public schools, since it remains silent about who must be included in and who legitimately can be excluded from New Albany's (internally democratic) decision processes. As Robert Dahl has argued, no plausible democratic theory can be indifferent about the definition of the *demos*, since indifference on this matter renders democracy indistinguishable from other forms of government, such as oligarchy.[36]

Perhaps the strongest defense of my interlocutor's position is one grounded in the democratic principle of subsidiarity: a principle that recommends granting as much political authority as possible to lower-level jurisdictions, such as member states in the European Union, with a view to maximizing political participation and the democratic responsiveness of government. Local governance of New Albany public schools, my interlocutor might suggest, maximizes collective political autonomy in a way that metropolitan-wide or higher levels of governance would not. It does so for at least two analytically distinct sets of reasons. First, local participation best enables the development of citizens' democratic skills and capacities, as well as their sense of political efficacy, both of which are crucial for democratic politics. Second, local decision making best protects people against domination by central state authorities and best enables them to effectively help shape collective norms.[37]

From a democratic standpoint, these are important considerations, other things equal. But in the case at hand, other things are not equal. The relevant political association – New Albany, Ohio – is an association born of racial and class-based distinction, one carved from a larger political association with which it remains deeply interdependent. Collective actions taken in New Albany significantly affect the interests of those on the other side of its jurisdictional boundaries. Laws and other collective norms enacted in New Albany (think of exclusionary zoning laws or public school attendance policies) subject, not only its residents, but also would-be residents who these norms ensure *cannot* live in New Albany. In such a case, the all-things-equal preference for locating political authority at lower-level jurisdictions must be overridden by one of two more fundamental democratic principles: what democratic theorists call the "all affected" principle or what they call the "all subjected principle."

---

[36] Robert Dahl, *Democracy and Its Critics* (New Haven, CT: Yale University Press, 1989), 119–22. For a recent discussion of the problem of the definition of the *demos* and an argument that its boundaries should coincide with those of the nation-state, see Sarah Song, "The Boundary Problem in Democratic Theory: Why the Demos Should be Bounded by the State," *International Theory* 4,1 (2012): 39–68.

[37] See Andreas Føllesdal, "Survey Article: Subsidiarity," *Journal of Political Philosophy* 6, 2 (1998): 190–218. Føllesdal also discusses forms of justification that aren't specifically democratic, for example, those based exclusively on claims about efficiency and those rooted in religious doctrine.

The former dictates that all persons affected by a political decision should have the right to participate in the processes of making it.[38] The latter defines the *demos* to include, not all *affected by*, but all *subjected to* collective norms. Notwithstanding important differences between the two, for practical purposes, in the New Albany case, the "all affected" and "all subjected" principles overlap. As Arash Abizadeh underscores, one important means of political subjection is the constraint of options.[39] If Community X passes a zoning ordinance that prohibits multifamily housing, it subjects those who cannot afford single-family houses to its decision, by removing their option to live in Community X, even as it significantly affects their basic interests.

The "all affected" and "all subjected" principles draw attention to relations of power that *cross* jurisdictional boundaries. The boundaries people draw when they create public school districts, or when they construct exclusive suburban municipalities or other forms of local government, *fail to distinguish* those who are affected by and/or subjected to decisions taken locally from those who are not. This distinction is crucial from a democratic standpoint, as one final modification to my thought experiment will show.

Imagine that the Columbus Public School District establishes Exit High, and creates admissions policies that define as eligible to attend only students from the very top of the income distribution (more than 95 percent of whom are white and less than 2 percent of whom are black). Instead of *directly* channeling resources to Exit, however, the district allows the parents of Exit students to vote to allocate their tax dollars to the school and to divert those funds away from the schools that serve middle- and lower-income students. Columbus Public School parents whose children are ineligible to attend Exit High (the majority of the parents in the

[38] Robert Dahl's early formulation of this principle reads, "Everyone who is affected by the decisions of a government should have the right to participate in that government." See Dahl, *After the Revolution?: Authority in a Good Society* (New Haven, CT: Yale University Press, 1970), 49. His later "Principle of Equal Consideration of Interests" emphasizes that equal weight should be given to the interests of all affected by a collective decision. Dahl, *Democracy and Its Critics* 85–6. For a critical discussion of various interpretations of the principle, see Robert Goodin, "Enfranchising All Affected Interests, and Its Alternatives," *Philosophy and Public Affairs* 35, 1 (2007): 40–68. For a defense of the all affected principle against territory- and membership-centered definitions of the democratic *demos*, see Clarissa Hayward, "The Dark Side of Citizenship: Membership, Territory, and the (Anti-)Democratic Polity," *Issues in Legal Scholarship* 9, 1 (2011), Article 1, on which this discussion draws.

[39] Arash Abizadeh, "Democratic Theory and Border Coercion: No Right to Unilaterally Control Your Own Borders," *Political Theory* 36, 1 (February 2008): 37–65.

district) object to this funding scheme, which has predictably devastating consequences for the schools to which their children are assigned. But the district defends its move on democratic grounds. Exit High, officials argue, is internally democratic, even if highly exclusionary.

Again, it seems safe to say that few would be persuaded by this argument. Just so long as students and parents from Exit and the other Columbus public schools stand to one another in relations of power – and for that matter, just so long as students and parents from Columbus public schools and New Albany public schools stand to one another in relations of power – there is no nontautological democratic defense of the exit option.

2. "Nice" Places

The difference between Exit Academy and New Albany High School cannot be reduced, then, to funding, or to the value many Americans accord school choice, or to the value they accord local democratic control. What *is* the difference? Why would most Americans see state support for the Exit of the thought experiment as illegitimate, even as they endorse, or at the very least accept and tolerate, state-subsidized exit to enclaves like Leslie Wexner's New Albany?

Recall the argument from Chapter 3 that ordinary life stories do not take collective identity stories as their subjects, but instead rely on them as frames that sort the events that comprise "what happened" from mere background. We saw in Chapter 4 how the collective identity story J. C. Nichols helped construct in the early decades of the past century was institutionalized in New Deal housing policies and in legal norms such as zoning laws and laws governing the incorporation of suburban municipalities. We saw, in addition, how that story was objectified in the built form of what Nichols called "good residential communities."

I now want to suggest that, by the later decades of the century, NAREB's narrative of Americans as a home-owning people – a people whose good is served by state support for private, profit-driven development – functioned as a frame to many ordinary stories. When prospective home buyers considered moving to Wexner's New Albany, they did not tell themselves, "I plan to take advantage of public subsidies for private housing for the privileged, which I endorse as legitimate," but instead, "It's in my interest to move here," and "I like this place."

Listen to Joanne DiMarco, who moved to New Albany from New Jersey when her husband got a high-paying job near Columbus. DiMarco recalls that she and her husband decided they would choose their children's school first, and only after that select the neighborhood in which they would buy their new house:

We decided, we were coming to the Midwest, you know, we're coming to the middle of nowhere. We're going to find the very, very best school, and that's where our kids are going to go. And that's where we'll live. So we weren't going to pick a place to live, and then see if the schools are good. And I wasn't going to end up living in hell, if my kids weren't going to be better off in an excellent school.

By the end of the twentieth century, it was in the DiMarcos' interest to choose a place, like New Albany, Ohio, where their children would attend "an excellent school." It was in their interest because the institutionalization of the early twentieth-century narrative of Americans as a home-owning people ensured that it was. This interest was a *state-constructed interest*, no less so than was the mid-century interest in buying in neighborhoods where the FHA insured loans. And, much like that mid-century (white) interest, it was wholly independent of the DiMarcos' acceptance of the story that initially helped justify state support for private, profit-driven development.

If the institutionalization of that early twentieth-century narrative constructed an interest in moving to an enclave like New Albany, its *objectification* – its materialization, that is to say, in the form of "good residential communities" – helped obscure the political actions and the collective choices that create and maintain such places. Consider once more DiMarco's account of her move. After narrowing their options to the "good-school communities" in suburban Columbus, DiMarco recalls, she and her husband considered the features that, in their view, make some places, but not others, "nice." They considered architectural style and planning, for instance. ("You know [New Albany] is lovely," DiMarco tells me. "And the planning of the community is, it's brilliant … you know, they're doing everything right.") They considered proximity to other "nice" (and not-nice) places, rejecting Bexley, for one (the suburb Calvin Moore identified as across the railroad tracks from Columbus's East Side), in DiMarco's words, "because it was surrounded by areas that weren't nice."

In these recollections and perceptions, Joanne DiMarco is fairly typical of the "new" New Albany residents I interviewed (that is, those who moved after Wexner redeveloped the area in the late 1980s and 1990s), almost all of whom cited as their reasons for choosing New Albany (above and beyond considerations of interest, such as their estimates of

the quality of the local schools or the soundness of the real estate investment), a preference for qualities, such as "niceness" or "newness," which
they said they appreciate and value. Gene Cooke, for example, a forty-
three-year-old businessman, stressed "the beauty of the area. Just that
whole Georgian look is very appealing." Patrick Webber recalled that he
and his wife "chose New Albany because we liked the newness. And we
liked the school system and community and all that," adding, "It's beautiful, you know." Jack O'Donnell, a retiree, explained his choice by noting
that "everything [in New Albany] is new and so pretty and nice."

Karl Marx famously argued that, in capitalist societies, people fetishize
commodities. They make fetishes of them, that is to say, much as people
in "the mist-enveloped regions of the religious world" make fetishes of
charms and other man-made objects, which they invest with supernatural powers.[40] For Robinson Crusoe on his island, Marx wrote, there is
nothing mysterious about the fact that the value of the goods he produces
(the tools and the furniture he makes, the fish and the game he hunts) is
a function of the labor he puts into their production. Nor, in the Middle
Ages, were the power relations that structured value production mysterious to the serf, who was forcibly compelled to labor for his lord. Yet,
under capitalism, value appears as if it were a property of *things*. The
commodity form, Marx's claim is, conceals both value's human origin
and the power relationships among those who work to produce it.[41]

As Henri Lefebvre has suggested, the objectification of place works
analogously.[42] It obscures the human processes of choice and action that
produce some, rather than other possible places, while at the same time
making *what people do to other people through physical space* appear as
if it were an innate attribute of – a quality that emanates from within – a
particular place.

Imagine that Joanne DiMarco were to take her family's assets and invest them in a backyard pool, neglecting to repair the foundation of her
house. If she were to do this, it would be no less obvious to her why her
pool was "nice," but her house was "not nice," than it was obvious to
Robinson Crusoe why he caught only those beasts he hunted.

Now recall whites in the pre-civil-rights-era United States, who
barred blacks from particular schools and particular jobs. For those who

---

[40] Karl Marx, *Capital*, Vol. 1, 294–442 in *The Marx-Engels Reader, Second Edition*, ed.
Robert Tucker (New York: W. W. Norton, 1978), 321.
[41] Ibid., 319–29.
[42] Henri Lefebvre, *The Production of Space*, transl. Donald Nicholson-Smith (Oxford:
Blackwell, 1991), especially chapter 2.

behaved this way, and for those they affected, it was no less obvious that their actions constituted an exercise of power by whites over blacks than it was obvious to medieval lords and serfs that the former dominated the latter.

But when Joanne DiMarco moves to a "lovely" place in a "good-school community," when Jack O'Donnell chooses to move to a place that is "new and so pretty and nice," each sees that place (as Marx might put it) through a mist that disguises both its social origin and its political structure. "Things lie," writes Lefebvre (citing Marx).[43] And space is "the absolute Thing."[44]

When she relocated her family, Joanne DiMarco looked for an excellent school for her children, and a place to live that was "nice" and not too near other places that "weren't nice." She constructs these particular happenings as events when she tells her life story, because these are the elements of her lived experience that, in the moment, were variable and struck her as novel. She constructs these particular happenings as events because, as she looks back, these are the elements she posits as causally significant and reportable. The institutionalized and objectified form of the early twentieth-century NAREB-promulgated identity narrative, by contrast (the federal tax laws that disproportionately subsidize the wealthy, the state and state-sponsored agencies that comprise the U.S. secondary mortgage market, the TIF districts that enable developers to channel public funds toward projects that serve and benefit the privileged) is a nonevent in Joanne DiMarco's ordinary story.

It may be instructive to contrast DiMarco's inattention to the politics of place-making with the views of those who lived in and near New Albany when Leslie Wexner first entered the scene. Observers of NACO's involvement in the New Albany of the late 1980s and early 1990s – journalists, for instance, local officials who commented on the development in the press and in other public fora, and most of the longtime New Albany residents I interviewed, when they looked back and recalled the early Wexner years – *did* narrativize, and often in overtly critical ways, NACO's use of public resources and public power for the benefit of the wealthy and the privileged.

Much of this critique was directed at Leslie Wexner himself and at his closest associates. In 2000, for example, Columbus City School Board

---

[43] Ibid., 81.
[44] Ibid., 83.

member Bill Moss filed a federal school discrimination lawsuit alleging that, through the late 1980s, Wexner, Kessler, and the Smith and Hale law firm had used campaign donations and other gifts to influence Columbus City Council members' decision to grant water and sewer service contracts to New Albany without demanding annexation.[45] Similarly, Plain Township trustee Harry Reeb criticized NACO's capture of public funds to promote its private ends and the good of its privileged clients. Reeb's focus, in particular, was the tax abatements New Albany granted to attract firms to Wexner's business campus. "Unless the village and school district stop the tax abatements," he declared, "I won't vote for any new tax." "The growth is too rapid," he claimed, adding, "These multi-billion dollar companies coming in here should pay their fair share of taxes."[46]

The longtime residents of New Albany and Plain Township whom I interviewed expressed similar views. Although some accepted (some grudgingly) the NACO-led development, many criticized the company's use of public resources and public powers to advance private ends. NACO dominates collective decisions about taxation, many emphasized. It drives the development process, others complained. NACO captures public monies – "from the state: *your* tax dollars, *your* gas dollars," longtime township resident William Adler underscored – and directs them to advantage its wealthy buyers and to protect its investment.

Steven Mullins emphasized NACO's role in driving the tremendous increase in property taxes in New Albany: taxes used to fund new school construction and other investments he said he and most long-term residents viewed as unnecessary. He accused the New Albany Company of, in his words, "dominat[ing]" the village. The company imposed its vision on this place, he told me, like a sculptor building with clay. In Mullins's words:

What the New Albany Company has done – besides stealing the name New Albany for their business venture – is they have totally taken over and dominated an area of land. And, you know, took the raw dirt, turned it into clay, took the clay, and made it into their city.

[45] Wexner and Kessler were two among many plaintiffs named in *Moss v. Columbus Board of Education*, which Moss filed in U.S. District Court. The case was dismissed in 2002. See Robert Ruth, Ruth Sternberg, and Bill Bush, "Moss Files Discrimination Suit," *Columbus Dispatch*, August 2, 2000, 1B; Robert Ruth, "Bias Suit Revisits '87 Dispute over Nightclub," *Columbus Dispatch*, December 12, 2000, 2C; and Kevin Mayhood, "Bias Suit against District Dismissed," *Columbus Dispatch*, August 21, 2002, 2C.

[46] Quoted in Ray Crumbley, "Third Vote on Fire Levy Coming in Plain Township: Residents Defeated Requests for More Tax Money in November and May," *Columbus Dispatch*, October 3, 1999, 6D.

What leaps out from these comments and others like them is an unambiguous, and unambiguously critical, focus on the New Albany Company's capture of collective power and collective resources. It is less than surprising that Leslie Wexner and the New Albany Company of the late 1980s and 1990s would attract criticism along these lines. They not only violated what the Exit thought experiment suggests are fairly widely endorsed principles of political legitimacy, but did so through a series of highly reportable or tellable actions. A prominent firm, and within that firm an easily identifiable group of agents – including the man the *Columbus Monthly* had named the "most powerful person in the city" – took positive actions that were novel and that had immediately significant effects.[47] Wexner and NACO altered political jurisdictional boundaries (for example, through their multiple successful petitions for annexation), while effectively blocking efforts by others to do so. They created entirely new jurisdictions, such as the special tax assessment district, and through these profoundly influenced both how and where collective resources were spent. They built, and they rebuilt, public institutions and public spaces, subjecting the Village of New Albany, over the course of just a single decade, to what Margaret Farrar (in a very different context) has called an "extreme, [sub]urban make-over."[48] All the while, Wexner and NACO erected miles upon miles of white painted fence, with which they boldly marked off the enclave they had built.

People tend to view space as an empty container, a "passive receptacle."[49] The power relations that we institutionalize and objectify in physical space typically appear to be "where events happen": not causally significant forces, which shape and drive life narratives, but instead just background to the action of the stories of our lives. New Albany, Ohio, for a brief period near the close of the twentieth century, was an exception. People focused attention on how action shapes action through space: through decisions about land use and local development, for instance, through decisions about the spatial distribution of people and problems and resources, through the creation and recreation of territorially based political jurisdictions.

[47] Between 1976 and 2010, the magazine published seven rankings of the most powerful men in Columbus. Four of those seven times, including each time the list was published in the 1990s and 2000s, Wexner ranked first. "Three Decades of Power in Columbus," *Columbus Monthly*, August 12, 2010, available at http://columbusmonthly.com/articles/2010/08/12/power/doc4a29243394a38277273669.txt (accessed May 16, 2011).
[48] Margaret Farrar, *Building the Body Politic: Power and Urban Space in Washington, D.C.* (Champaign: University of Illinois Press, 2008), 89.
[49] The language here is Lefebvre's. See *The Production of Space*, 90.

Place-making became an event. For those whom it immediately and directly affected, it became part of the story they wove from their lived experience. "When NACO took the actions it took," they told themselves (and others), "when Leslie Wexner exercised political power to 'dominate' this place and its inhabitants, those actions caused me to lose my farm. They caused me to move away from (or, at the very least, to see transformed before my eyes) this village, this community, this place that, for years and years, I had thought of as home."

Stories of this sort make possible – indeed, they serve as necessary preconditions for – the kinds of popular challenge to place-making practices that emerged in New Albany near the close of the century. But such stories are rare.

In New Albany, the demographic shifts sketched at the start of this chapter (the arrival en masse of the Joanne DiMarcos, the Patrick Webbers, the Jack O'Donnells, and the other new home buyers to whom longtime residents referred as "white-fence people") produced by century's end a local population largely content with the package of taxes and services the New Albany Company attached to the village. Leslie Wexner's New Albany, with its Georgian-themed residential developments and its top-notch public schools, became the backdrop against which "white-fence people" lived their lives. It became, not something people do to other people through physical space, but (merely) the setting within which the events that comprise a life narrative play out.

3. White-Fence People

Calvin Moore, recall, characterizes the places he has lived as "black places," and the schools he has attended as "black schools." If New Albany, Ohio represents the institutionalization and the objectification of a narrative of Americans as a home-owning (white) public – a narrative that works hand in hand with the racial narrative institutionalized and objectified in Columbus, Ohio, and in older, Northern and Midwestern cities more generally – then is New Albany a "white place"?

It depends on whom you ask. In Chapter 3, I noted a pronounced racial pattern in the responses to the "Who am I?" portion of the semi-structured interviews I conducted for this book. All thirteen respondents who self-identified as "black" invoked a racial identity during the course of the interviews, while not a single one of the seventeen white respondents did the same. When I prompted several white respondents, asking specifically whether they might use the category "white" to complete the statement "My name is [Name], and I am _____," none agreed that this was an answer that (s)he would or should give. In the words of one, "I wouldn't describe myself as white ... I mean, it doesn't matter."[50]

Perhaps it is unsurprising, then, that when discussing New Albany, Ohio, none of these seventeen white respondents mentioned white racial identity, let alone white privilege. None characterized New Albany as a "white place," notwithstanding the fact that nearly 88 percent of its residents are classified by the U.S. Census Bureau as "white" (more than 40 percent above the 61.5 percent "white" figure in adjacent Columbus), while only 3 percent (a little more than 10 percent above the corresponding figure for Columbus) are classified as "black."[51] In New Albany, as elsewhere, these interviews imply, race simply "doesn't matter."

The two black New Albany respondents I was able to interview, however, suggest a different answer.[52] Walter Barrett is an African American orthopedic surgeon. I excerpted his life history briefly in Chapter 3. Barrett, recall, marks as a turning point in his life his transfer from an urban public to a private school, where, he says, he observed the lifestyles of the affluent and became motivated to pursue a professional career. He did just that, and in the early 1990s, by then a successful medical professional, he moved to New Albany with his wife, Tricia, and their preschool-aged sons.

Several years after the family's move, Barrett began writing a semi-autobiographical novel in the evenings after work. He completed it shortly before our interview. "My book," he tells me when we meet, "is really about being in a place where you're not expected to be." It is about:

a black surgeon, [who] has a family ... and lives in a nice neighborhood. And he grew up kind of wanting to be like Lance Armstrong, with his bike ... So what

---

[50] This pattern is one that others have noticed. Lani Guinier and Gerald Torres, for instance, argue that many whites, unlike most African Americans, assume race is and/or should be, in Guinier and Torres's words "like a vapor ... nonconstraining ... evanescent." They illustrate with the story of (white) Harvard law school students who, when asked to display visually their ideal of "race," hold up blank sheets of (white) paper. One student "accompanie[s] her image with a verbal explanation that in her view 'race is silly.'" Lani Guinier and Gerald Torres, *The Miner's Canary: Enlisting Race, Resisting Power, Transforming Democracy* (Cambridge, MA: Harvard University Press, 2002), 90–1.

[51] All data are from the 2010 census. At that time, 28 percent of Columbus city residents were black. U.S. Census Bureau, "State and County QuickFacts," available at http://quickfacts.census.gov/qfd/states/39/3979002.html (accessed February 27, 2012).

[52] None of the New Albany residents who responded to my initial call for respondents was African American. I recruited Walter Barrett for the project through his wife, Tricia, who was an acquaintance (Tricia worked out at my gym). Tricia Barrett herself was the other black New Albany respondent.

happens is, his wife [is] going away for ... a weekend ... and there is a series of ... little robberies in the neighborhood. So, it's ... evening, and he is riding his bike home, and there has been a call, because of a robbery at his house ... and the police respond. You can see what's going to happen ... He is riding his bike. The cop ... sees that he is a black man, assumes that he is the robber, and shoots him.

"You can see what's going to happen." My interview with Walter Barrett took place years before the widely publicized and criticized arrest of Henry Louis Gates, Jr. at his own home in Cambridge, Massachusetts.[53] Yet, as Barrett suggests, it is not difficult to predict the conclusion of his novel once he begins to sketch its plot.

That plot was inspired, he tells me, by his own experience of repeatedly finding himself "in a place where [he was] not expected to be." He was where he was not expected to be, Barrett says, as the only black student in his class at the private school he attended as a child. He was where he was not expected to be as the only black player on the school's lacrosse team, and as the first black valedictorian in its 200-year history. After medical school, he was where he was not expected to be when, as the only black surgery resident in his program, he made rounds and people "assumed [he was] the food service guy."

In New Albany, Ohio, Walter Barrett tells me, he was where he was not expected to be when he and his family were the first black family to move to their development. He explains: "You're in your yard, doing some yard work, and someone would drive up, like ... a landscaping service ... And they're like, 'Who lives here?'" Barrett continues: "You know, so what happens, is when you move to New Albany, you are one black face. And [there are] hundreds of non-black people ... who don't expect to see you there."

Walter Barrett's wife, Tricia Barrett, in a separate interview, presents a similar view of New Albany as a place where race *does* matter. In the New Albany of the twenty-first century, she says, the racial beliefs whites hold and the racial assumptions that shape their actions are often "subtle." They are not necessarily conscious. Yet, speaking of her children's teachers in New Albany public schools (all of whom are white), she tells me:

[They] look at New Albany, and [they] don't expect much diversity there. [They] expect kids to be of a certain – I mean, you *can* have African American kids who are wealthy, but black kids stick out more ... they are more identifiable.

[53] Gates, a prominent Harvard professor, was arrested by Cambridge police in July 2009.

Tricia Barrett says feels she needs to warn her children that they may attract negative attention in school simply because of their race. "And I told my kids," she recalls, "'You know what? You're saying that you and Johnny were doing the same thing. But *they saw you.*'"

Whites in predominantly white places like New Albany, Ohio, the Barretts' claim is, typically behave in ways that suggest that they expect to see and to interact with other whites. But, as my interviews with white New Albany respondents suggest, at the same time, they typically fail to notice this expectation. Places that seem to the racially marked like "white places" appear to the racially privileged to be race neutral. They appear to be places where "race doesn't matter."

How do the racially privileged account for the racial demographics of the neighborhoods in which they live, and of the schools that their children attend, while maintaining the belief that "race doesn't matter"? One possible way they might do so is by using better stories than the "bad stories" that helped produce those patterns. At the turn of the twenty-first century, whites might reach for class reductivist stories, for instance: stories according to which, not race, but income and wealth alone, produce and reproduce differential access to important resources and opportunities.[54] Alternatively (or simultaneously), they might reach for "race-into-culture" stories, according to which deeply engrained and enduring social dispositions produce these patterns.[55] Such stories are "better" along the normative/ethical dimension. They play a legitimizing role within an ideological discourse that accepts those inequalities as fair that are presumed to be earned. They are better, as well, in that they purport to reject delegitimized racist stereotypes, even as they posit class and culture as mapping almost perfectly onto racial categories.

But such stories are still not good stories along the empirical dimension. Racial hierarchies, as the Barretts' experience attests, are *not* reducible to class-based hierarchies, and even with all the right culture (Walter and Tricia Barrett are both highly educated and accomplished professionals),

---

[54] For an influential, albeit qualified argument along these lines, see William Julius Wilson, *The Declining Significance of Race: Blacks and Changing American Institutions, Second Edition* (Chicago, IL: University of Chicago Press, 1980).

[55] I take this phrase from Walter Benn Michaels, who uses it to capture the early twentieth-century representation of "culture" as a biologically rooted inheritance that a person could, in principle, fail to perform correctly. Walter Benn Michaels, "Race into Culture: A Critical Genealogy of Cultural Identity," *Critical Inquiry* 18, 4 (Summer 1982): 665–85. See also Eduardo Bonilla-Silva's discussion of "cultural racism" in *Racism without Racists: Color-Blind Racism and the Persistence of Racial Inequality in the United States, Second Edition* (New York: Rowman and Littlefield, 2006), 39–43.

black people are still "unexpected" in white places. The widely publicized Gates incident is one illustration among many that specifically *racial* hierarchy remains (to recall the language from Chapter 1) a knowable fact about the world as it is.

The racially privileged might, in principle, reach for better stories, then. But very often they do not. Very often they *need* not, since the story of "who we Americans are" that was built into the institutional and material form of the postwar suburban enclave includes an implicit definition of *who we are not*. When institutionalized (for instance, in zoning laws that, although not explicitly racial, have predictable racial effects) and when objectified (in majority-white enclaves, like New Albany's "white-fence" communities), this narrative enables the racially privileged to write race out of their ordinary stories.

I could pull off the Jappy-ness a little bit. But, you know, I couldn't pull off the thinness or the tan. I could never really do it. So, it's like, I couldn't be blue enough in high school, I couldn't be tan enough in college ... I was, you know, kind of the border guy ... always kept beyond the border.

This interview excerpt, from Joanne DiMarco's life narrative, captures the way her experience of collective identities departs from Calvin Moore's and Steven Mullins's. DiMarco understands herself to be a person who craves, but yet never achieves, what she characterizes as the wholeness, the completeness of identity. She wants to surround herself, she tells me, with people who are like her and who accept her. She wants to surround herself with people with whom she has everything in common. She longs to feel at home among some group larger than her family and her circle of familiars. But she is, in her own words, a "border" person: someone who, through life, has moved from community to community, while always remaining on, or very near to, the outside.

DiMarco begins her life narrative impressionistically, describing her childhood in small-town Connecticut, where she says she perceived herself as different from her friends and her neighbors. "I guess I always felt and always knew," she tells me, "[that] I wouldn't stay in [Connecticut]":

I mean we spent a lot of time in New York City ... spent a lot of time in the city from a very young age. Like, I always got my hair cut in the city ... And we would go and see Broadway shows ... all the time. And my friends weren't like that.

DiMarco begins to construct the events that drive her narrative when she recalls leaving small-town life during her first year of high school to attend a private boarding school, which was "completely different from anything" she had known before. The other girls at boarding school, she says, were "blue, blue, blue, blue-bloods":

> They had come from day schools and private schools, and they were in the social register. And they … played girl's hockey and lacrosse from a young age. And they were, you know, perfect and beautiful … And, you know, they all had … last names for middle names…. None of them, not one of my friends, had an actual middle name that's, like, a name. So middle names were, like, Lincoln, and Moore, and Roche.

In retrospect, DiMarco tells me, she realizes she was happy at the boarding school. But she says she could not recognize her happiness at that time. She felt "depressed," and so she was glad when her parents, citing financial difficulties, took her out of the private school for her senior year.

They moved to Stamford, Connecticut, and enrolled her in a public high school, which DiMarco remembers as "half Jewish, half black." "Neither of which," she underscores, "I had much exposure to in my life":

> I mean, I grew up Jewish. I *was* Jewish. I went to the Sunday school for twelve years. I was bat mitzvah'd … all that stuff. But I never was around more than, you know, three, four Jewish girls.

At public school in Stamford, DiMarco tells me, she was "like an island." She "didn't understand how we call teachers by their last names, because we didn't do that at boarding school." She "didn't understand lockers, because there was no bedroom." She says she wore her (L.L.) "Bean Blutchers," which she characterizes as the most "absolutely preppy shoes in the world, even though, you know, no one in public school did." "And some people thought it was cool," she tells me. "Some people thought I was a freak. And I didn't really make friends."

DiMarco's college years brought more of the same. The person in charge of housing assignments at her university, she recalls, made what she characterizes as "a horrible mistake," by assigning dormitory rooms according to social security numbers. "Social security numbers are geographic," says DiMarco, "but some people don't realize that." "(So) black people were grouped, were put as roommates with people they had grown up next door to … And we [DiMarco and her friend, who had grown up near her] … ended up in the middle of the five towns of Long Island." "I don't know if you know much about Long Island, or the five towns," she comments. Then she explains: "It's like the center of all that is … heinous in New York, about … you know, Jewish-American Princesses." Because freshman year friendships are strongly determined by dormitory assignments, DiMarco says, and because she "could pull off the Jappy-ness a little bit" but "couldn't pull off the thinness or the tan," once again, she felt outside, "beyond the border."

After college, according to DiMarco, she continued to be an outsider: now vis-à-vis those whom she characterizes as "yuppies" at the job she got in New York City after she graduated. DiMarco was successful at her work, she recalls – more than successful: a "superstar." But at the age of twenty-three, she decided she wanted to get married. Two years later, she decided she wanted to have a baby. "So, this is unheard of," she tells me:

You know who has babies at [the company where I worked]? Secretaries. And people who are forty-two or forty-three. And senior or executive vice presidents, right? And, all the male staffers: all their *wives* have babies. But for the women, you don't. *You just don't.*

Having her first baby while on staff, DiMarco says, may have been "slightly accepted." But when she decided to have a second baby soon after the first, it was "a disaster." She and her family moved to New Jersey, and she began to commute to work. Her supervisor at the time, she says, tried to be supportive. But the supervisor's way of being supportive was to ensure that DiMarco continued to advance through the ranks at the same pace at which she had advanced before the birth of her children. The pace of the work, combined with the long commute to the city, proved too stressful, so DiMarco left her job and began to freelance from home.

Around this time, DiMarco recalls, she and her family moved locally to a New Jersey neighborhood that she characterizes as "very upscale." DiMarco recalls that she and her husband had expected this move to make them happy, but that, to their surprise, they found they had little in common with their new neighbors. In particular, the neighbors, whom she describes as "blue-collar people," did not share the DiMarcos's views about the importance of education.

We thought, we'll move them [the children] to this place with a lot more money. We'll have more in common with them [the neighbors]. But they were just, you know, really, really successful blue-collar people, instead of – and I mean, not that I have anything against blue-collar people, but we didn't have anything in common. Nothing. You know, they didn't value the same things. I sent my kids to private school, and my friends were like, [imitating a whining voice] "Why do you do that? The schools here are really good!" [Laughs]. And I was like, "No they're not, they're awful! Don't you read anything, you know? They're like, right at the bottom in the state." And I can't tolerate or be friends with anybody who doesn't value educating their children.

Perhaps the most striking feature of this excerpt from Joanne DiMarco's life narrative is the contrast between, on one hand, the narrator's near-unequivocal social identification of "other" people ("blue-collar people," for instance, and "blue-bloods"), and on the other, her strong sense that the identities socially ascribed to her never quite fit. "I grew up Jewish," DiMarco tells me. "I *was* Jewish." (Just like I *was* a middle-class girl in Connecticut, and later I *was* a professional woman in New York.) I *was* this identity in the narrow sense that it accurately describes how I was socially categorized. But the fit between, on one hand, this identity category (and the other categories DiMarco names as naming her), and on the other, my personal identity – who I am as a unique individual – never was a good fit. The particular expectations attached to the identities ascribed to DiMarco, that is to say, did not match her personal values, her capacities and dispositions, her aspirations. Hence, even as she tells me of her longing for identities that "fit," she seems to evince a real pride in those choices she makes that are counter-normative vis-à-vis her identities (her unconventional reproductive choices, for example, or her unconventional footwear).

Other people, by contrast, DiMarco suggests, very often do fit their identities. What is more, other people fit those *places* to which their identities correspond. Joanne DiMarco, not unlike Calvin Moore, conceives particular identities as tied to particular places: territorialized. And DiMarco, again not unlike Moore, imagines most (other) people as well suited to their places. Thus blue-bloods ("perfect and beautiful") can live at boarding schools without becoming depressed, while "blue-collar people" can be content with what are objectively "awful" schools. The traits that link each set of individuals to one another at the same time link them to these particular places.

DiMarco applies this logic, as does Moore, to identities that conventionally are racialized. Public schools in Stamford, Connecticut, she describes as "half black, half Jewish." She applies it, as well, to class-based identities, which, as her characterization of her "really, really successful blue-collar" neighbors implies, are, for her (relatively enduring) worldviews and value orientations, and not merely (more or less mutable) positions in relation to the means of production or to material goods and opportunities. If I am not "blue-blood" by birth, DiMarco's logic suggests, (if I do not have a blue-blood name, if I was not raised "from a young age playing" blue-blood sports) then, although I may make myself physically present in a blue-blood place (the boarding school, in DiMarco's case), I never really will belong.

It is this distance between other people's apparently easy accommodation to their (place-based) identities and DiMarco's own "border" status that, in her narrative, drives her frequent moves from place to place. *My family and I were not like our neighbors (who really were all the things people from Connecticut are supposed to be), and that is why we went to New York on the weekends, and why, as soon as I was able, I left more permanently for boarding school. But I was not like the blue-bloods (blue was not in my blood), and that is why I was happy when my parents took me out of the academy.*

Yet Joanne DiMarco, as she moves from place to place, does not consciously seek out places that match her ascribed identities. That is not, at least, a motive she names in the story she tells. She does not move to the "upscale" New Jersey neighborhood, for instance, because she perceives it as a "Jewish place," or a "white place," or even an upper middle-class American place, but rather because she hopes it will be peopled by others who "value educating their children." She moves to the upscale New Jersey neighborhood for the same reason she eventually moves to New Albany, Ohio: because she hopes it will serve her interests, satisfy her preferences, and accord with her (reflexively endorsed) values.

Other people can have identities that fit neatly, if not seamlessly. Other people can belong to places tied to those identities. I, by contrast, am rootless, restless: a "border" person. I have no identity that (really) fits and no place to which I (really) belong. So I move from place to place, choosing from among them those that best meet my individual needs and the needs of my family.

Steven Mullins cites a (canonical) narrative of American national identity, and he weaves that narrative into the story he tells about his lived experience. "Americans do (or they think or they value) x," the logic of Mullins's narrative is. "I am an American. Therefore I do (or I think or I value) x." For Calvin Moore, by contrast, collective identity narratives serve as frames to the narrative of personal identity. They rarely enter the story explicitly, but they nonetheless play an important role in helping shape it, by sorting events from nonevents. Joanne DiMarco's life narrative illustrates a third way collective identity stories can work in personal life stories. DiMarco explicitly cites collective identity narratives: stories about women, for instance; stories about "yuppies"; stories about "Jewish American Princesses." She acknowledges that some of these narratives are stories about identities that are socially ascribed to her. Yet, unlike Mullins, and also unlike Moore, she repudiates those identity stories.

"I am an *X*," her logic suggests. ("I am Jewish, I am a woman, I am a professional.") "These identities are an important part of how other people see me, and, at least on some level, I recognize myself as fitting these identity categories. Still, the stories associated with these categories are not quite right as stories about me. They do not quite capture what it is that makes me who I am. They do not account for how I act, or what I value, or where I place my loyalties. They do not capture much of what is significant about me and my lived experience."

The 2 x 2 table below illustrates these three ways people use collective identity stories. The rows track whether narrators endorse identities that are socially ascribed to them, while the columns track whether, in telling their own life stories, they cite those identities. The top-left cell represents narrators like Steven Mullins: a patriot in his case, but more generally, narrators who thematize and endorse collective identity stories, which they then weave into the stories they tell of their own lives. The bottom-left cell is occupied by narrators like Calvin Moore: in his case, a racialized subject (and a gendered subject) but more generally, narrators who frame their life narratives with taken-for-granted stories of collective identity, which they rarely, if ever, thematize. Narrators like Joanne DiMarco occupy the top-right cell. This cell is for "border" people, who cite (at least some of) their ascribed identities in the stories they tell about their lives, but only, or mostly, in order to refuse them.

	Endorses socially ascribed identity	Does not endorse socially ascribed identity
Cites socially ascribed identity	Steven Mullins / patriot	Joanne DiMarco / "border" person
Does not cite socially ascribed identity	Calvin Moore / racialized subject	

But Joanne DiMarco simultaneously occupies the bottom-right cell, since she frames her life narrative with an identity – white racial identity – that she refuses, without citing. Notice that when DiMarco makes explicit reference to racial identities, those are, without exception, the identities of the racially marked. Public high school in Stamford, Connecticut was "half Jewish, half black," for example, and in university housing, "black people were grouped, were put as roommates with people they had grown up next door to." DiMarco thematizes her Jewish identity. She thematizes black racial identity. But she never makes direct and explicit reference to her own (white) racial identity. In this, she conforms to a pattern that is uninterrupted, not only through her life narrative, but through more than fifty-two hours of interviews with all seventeen of the respondents who, when pressed, self-identify as "white."

White racial identity is nevertheless a frame in DiMarco's life narrative, since it serves as the norm against which racial difference is defined. As others have argued, for the racially privileged, the racially marked very often appear to "have" race in a way that is noticeable and significant, while whites seem not to.[56] Whiteness is at once "a location of structural advantage, of race privilege," "a 'standpoint,' a place from which white people look at [themselves], at others, and at society," and "a set of cultural practices that are usually unmarked and unnamed."[57]

Framing their life narratives with this repudiated identity encourages the racially privileged to write out of their stories the relation between the advantages they enjoy (for instance, as residents of enclaves like New Albany, Ohio) and the disadvantages on the other side of the (white) fence. If white (fence) people tend not to see "white," if whiteness is not part of the narrative they construct from their lived experience, then it is that much less likely they will be motivated to challenge, or to act with others to change white dominance.

I argued at the start of this chapter that the public support and the public subsidies available to Leslie Wexner in the late twentieth century distinguished his project in New Albany from the early suburban enclaves built by Emery Childs and J. C. Nichols. An important continuity, however, links these three developments: the role each played in perpetuating and helping reproduce racial hierarchy. To be sure, after passage of the Civil Rights Acts of the mid-1960s, many of the most heavy-handed mechanisms of racial exclusion and racial policing were no longer sanctioned by the American state.[58] Unlike J. C. Nichols, Leslie

---

[56] For an early and influential statement of this view, see Richard Dyer, "White," *Screen* **29**, 4 (Autumn 1988): 44–64. Dyer's essay was later expanded into book form and published as *White: Essays on Race and Culture* (London: Routledge, 1997). See also the essays collected in Ruth Frankenberg, ed., *Displacing Whiteness: Essays in Social and Culture Criticism* (Durham, NC: Duke University Press, 1997), especially Rebecca Aanerud, "Fictions of Whiteness: Speaking the Names of Whiteness in U.S. Literature," 35–59.

[57] Frankenberg, *White Women, Race Matters*, 1.

[58] The Fair Housing Act of 1968 marked a turning point. This law legally prohibited racial discrimination in housing sales and rentals. Specifically, it prohibited refusing to sell or to rent a home because of the race of the prospective buyer or renter, discriminating when setting terms and conditions for real estate sales and rentals, and discriminating when advertising properties for sale or for rent. The 1968 act explicitly prohibited blockbusting, as well, by prohibiting agents from making comments to homeowners about the race of people living in, or moving into, their neighborhood to induce them to sell their

Wexner could not legally exclude would-be buyers from New Albany along racial lines. NACO could not write racial covenants into the deeds of the houses it built and sold. Nor could the New Albany school district bar African American students from matriculating. Redlining, blockbusting, and racial steering were no longer state-sanctioned practices, and Leslie Wexner could not tout the racial exclusivity of his enclave (as had Nichols) with a banner advertising "3000 Acres Restricted."

Nevertheless, the role place played in reproducing racial hierarchy was not eliminated. Home owners in de facto "white places" had, by the second half of the century, accumulated tremendous wealth in the form of equity in properties purchased in racially discriminatory markets. The decade of the 1960s saw a dramatic appreciation in the value of privately owned houses in this country. Between 1970 and 1985 (that is, in the decade and a half between the passage of fair housing legislation and its amendment to encourage effective enforcement) median home prices in the United States grew by nearly 230 percent.[59] Housing prices grew more rapidly in the second half of the century than did consumer prices generally, and they grew considerably more rapidly in "white places" like New Albany than in "black places" like Columbus's East Side.[60] This rapid growth continued through the close of the century. Between 1985 and 2005 (that is, during the years after passage of fair housing legislation, when New Albany developed into the wealthiest suburb of Columbus, Ohio), the United States House Price Index rose more than 180 percent.[61]

properties. For an overview, see the discussion on the HUD website, available at http://portal.hud.gov/hudportal/HUD?src=/program_offices/fair_housing_Equal_opp/prog-desc/title8 (accessed May 17, 2011). Although in its practical effects, this law was notoriously weak, it did signal a public commitment to the principle of open housing. The Fair Housing Amendment Act of 1988 put (some) teeth to the principle by empowering HUD to initiate investigations of alleged discriminatory actions, subjecting violators of fair housing laws to nontrivial penalties, and enabling successful plaintiffs in fair housing suits to recover both their legal fees and substantial damages. See the discussion on the HUD website at http://portal.hud.gov/hudportal/HUD?src=/program_offices/fair_housing_Equal_opp/progdesc/title8 (accessed May 17, 2011).

[59] See the discussion in George Lipsitz, *The Possessive Investment in Whiteness: How White People Profit from Identity Politics* (Philadelphia, PA: Temple University Press, 2006). Lipsitz cites this 230 percent increase at p. 32.

[60] Ibid.

[61] The House Price Index is a broad measure of the movement of single-family house prices determined by analyzing price changes in repeat sales on the same properties. http://www.fhfa.gov/Default.aspx?Page=81. According to the U.S. Federal Housing Finance Agency, the HPI for the East North Central region (which includes Ohio) increased 182 percent between 1985 and 2005. The HPI for the U.S. as a whole increased 190 percent during that same period. http://www.fhfa.gov/Default.aspx?Page=87.

Meanwhile, the subprime mortgage crisis was brewing. Over the course of the 1990s, according to Richard Williams and his colleagues, subprime lending accounted for 23.3 percent of the increase in home ownership in the United States, but for a full 43.5 percent of the increase in home ownership among African Americans.[62] Hence, when the housing bubble burst in 2007, the burden was disproportionately borne in "black places" and by black borrowers. As Jacob Rugh and Douglas Massey have argued, "By concentrating underserved, financially unsophisticated, and needy minority group members who are accustomed to exploitation [by pay-day lenders, cash checking services, and the like] in certain well-defined neighborhoods, segregation made it easy for brokers to target them when marketing sub-prime loans."[63] Rugh and Massey show that blacks were more likely to receive subprime loans and more likely to receive loans with unfavorable terms (such as prepayment penalties, which can prevent borrowers from refinancing) than were whites who were similar along the relevant dimensions (credit profile, for example, down payment ratio, residential location, etc.).[64]

What is more, because municipalities like New Albany were legally empowered to engage in exclusionary zoning, to tax, and to spend tax their dollars on local schools and other public services that they make available to residents only, whites who accumulated wealth through discriminatory housing markets in the postwar decades (as well as their children, to whom they typically transmitted the wealth thus accumulated) were able to preserve the profits and the privileges reaped from racial apartheid. The legal boundaries that demarcate "white places" thus shifted from explicitly racially coded laws and the state sanction of overtly racially discriminatory actions, to the protection of local autonomy over taxation, public service provision, and land use and other collective decisions.[65]

For whites, this shift had the crucial ideological effect of rendering the reproduction of place-based racial hierarchy compatible with the explicit disavowal of a racist past. *Those people back then* (whites could

---

[62] Richard Williams, Reynold Nesiba, and Eileen Diaz McConnell, "The Changing Face of Inequality in Home Mortgage Lending," *Social Problems* 52, 2 (May, 2005): 181–208, here 193.

[63] Jacob Rugh and Douglas Massey, "Racial Segregation and the American Foreclosure Crisis," *American Sociological Review* 75, 5 (October 2010): 629–51, here 631.

[64] Ibid.

[65] See Clarissa Hayward and Todd Swanstrom, "Thick Injustice," 1–29 in *Justice and the American Metropolis* Clarissa Hayward and Todd Swanstrom, eds. (Minneapolis: University of Minnesota Press, 2011).

tell themselves), *the Southerners, the rednecks, the racists of the pre-civil-rights-movement years: they thought and did things we now know to have been ignorant and morally reprehensible. But their beliefs and their practices have nothing to do with us, except in the most abstract and genealogical of ways.*

Public support and subsidy for Leslie Wexner's New Albany is analogous to public support and subsidy for the hypothetical Exit Academy, in that it enables the wealthy, most of whom are white, to capture public resources and to exit the public system, effectively using collective power and resources to advance their private ends. When first introduced, public support and subsidy for private housing for the privileged was justified with an identity story of (white) Americans as a home-owning people whose good such state support serves. That narrative, I argued in Chapter 4, was then built into institutional forms, such as zoning laws and laws governing municipal incorporation, and into material forms, such as New Albany, Ohio's white-fence communities.

Institutionalization and objectification make all the difference. If Exit parents build new schools and petition the state to subsidize them (or for that matter, if Leslie Wexner builds new schools, new roads, and a new regional shopping mall, and petitions the state to subsidize them) those affected will likely narrate such actions as causally significant and tellable happenings: events that drive their life stories and shape those stories' outcomes.

Institutions and spaces, by contrast, are just background to ordinary stories. They are frames: frames, in this case, that enable the privileged to enjoy unearned advantages, even as they write those advantages out of the stories they tell about their lives.

Conclusion

Stories, Institutions, and Spaces

In *Bodies that Matter*, Judith Butler underscores that performativity cannot be reduced to a single moment, a single act.[1] It is never (to recall the example with which I opened this book) just one dance. Instead, it is a compulsory, reiterative practice: the forced citation, time and again, of dominant norms. When I perform my gender as I dance the Argentine tango, what I do is I cite (neither for the first time, nor for the last) social norms that I am *required* to cite. I am compelled to cite them if I am to be culturally intelligible: if, in Butler's terms, I am to achieve the status of a recognized subject in a social system governed by normative heterosexuality.

It is my performance, then – over and over again, on the dance floor and off – together with yours, and together with everybody else's, that produces and reproduces our shared sense of the fixity, the stability of gender. But crucially, for Butler, because identitarian norms rely on our performances for their reproduction, they never achieve complete and lasting stability. Instead, it is always possible that we will disrupt them. Every citation, every performance creates this possibility anew.

Butler advances this argument in part to distance herself from an overly voluntaristic view of identity performance. It is not the case, she writes, that people "[wake] in the morning, [peruse] the closet or some more open space for the gender of choice, [don] that gender for the day, and then [restore] the garment to its place at night."[2]

---

[1] Judith Butler, *Bodies that Matter: On the Discursive Limits of "Sex"* (New York: Routledge, 1993).
[2] Ibid., x.

Butler distances herself, as well, from an overly deterministic view. That I am compelled to cite gender norms does not mean that those norms determine my action. To the contrary, the fact that *I* perform my identity, means I retain some agency in this performance. It means that not only resistance (that is, not only preserving some space for my personal freedom by failing fully to comply), but also *change* is possible. People can, in Butler's terms, radically resignify identitarian and other hegemonic norms.

It is possible to read this argument in a way that weights very heavily the likelihood of identitarian change through such subversive performances. If my dance partner and I reject the male-lead / female-follow relation, I might imagine, we thus help subvert the gender norms that structure Argentine tango. Or (to cite an oft-cited example from Butler's work): if people parodically conform to gender norms through the performance of drag, they "[work] the weakness in the norm," encouraging change by exposing their audiences to failures in the heterosexual regime.[3]

It is possible to read the argument this way. But at the same time, Butler does acknowledge that to parody dominant norms is very often insufficient to displace them. Norms that are "twisted" and "queered," she writes, "are not, for that reason, necessarily subverted in the process."[4] "Neither power nor discourse are rendered anew at every moment; they are not as weightless as the utopics of radical resignification might imply."[5]

This latter claim resonates strongly with my own emphasis throughout this book, where my focus has been less the performance of identity than the institutionalization and objectification of the narratives and other forms of discourse through which identities are produced. My focus, in other words, has been the stickiness of identity. It has been stasis, and inertia. It has been the social *reproduction* of dominant understandings of "who we are."

My argument therefore raises the question: How can, and how do, people *change* the identities bad stories produce? With Butler, I want to underscore that neither resistance to dominant identitarian norms nor uncoordinated acts of subversion are sufficient.

---

[3] Ibid., 237. Butler first discussed the example of drag in *Gender Trouble*. She clarifies her position through an analysis of the film *Paris is Burning* in chapter 4 of *Bodies that Matter*.

[4] Butler, *Bodies that Matter*, 237.

[5] Ibid., 224.

Nor is telling better stories. Identitarian change, I want to suggest in this conclusion, requires telling stories that are *extraordinary* in the sense in which I used that term in Chapter 3: stories that take collective identity narratives as their subject matter, and then work to explain, to criticize, and/or to revise them. But change requires extraordinary stories of a very particular type. It requires stories that motivate both institutional redesign and the reconstruction of material forms.

1. Stories

On August 28, 1963, Martin Luther King, Jr. addressed a crowd of two hundred thousand from the steps of the Lincoln Memorial. "When the architects of our republic wrote the magnificent words of the Constitution and the Declaration of Independence," he told his audience, "They were signing a promissory note to which every American was to fall heir. This note was a promise that all men, yes, black men as well as white men, would be guaranteed the 'unalienable rights' of 'Life, Liberty, and the pursuit of Happiness.'"[6]

King's "I Have a Dream" speech was an exemplar of what I have called an extraordinary story. It took a collective identity narrative – a story about who "we Americans" are – as its subject matter, interpreted that narrative, and subjected it to what Michael Walzer calls "connected" social criticism.[7] The speech appealed to values and principles that King argued were constitutive of American national identity, while underscoring the divergence between those liberal and egalitarian norms and the gross rights violations and inequalities that had marked the African American experience to that point in history. King continued:

It is obvious today that America has defaulted on this promissory note insofar as her citizens of color are concerned. Instead of honoring this sacred obligation, America has given the Negro people a bad check, a check which has come back marked "insufficient funds."[8]

King's "I Have a Dream" speech was not exclusively critical, however. It also offered a new, aspirational vision of who "we Americans" are, or more precisely, of who we might become. King's famous "dream" of

---

[6] Martin Luther King, Jr., "I Have a Dream," available at http://www.americanrhetoric. com/speeches/mlkihaveadream.htm (accessed January 15, 2013).
[7] Michael Walzer, *Interpretation and Social Criticism* (Cambridge, MA: Harvard University Press, 1987).
[8] King, "I Have a Dream."

freedom and justice for all, which he characterized as "deeply rooted in the American dream," was a dream that Americans would one day live according to the principles that he emphasized they had professed since the time of the founding.[9]

There is a certain hagiography of Martin Luther King, Jr. according to which this "extraordinary story" – this identity narrative that offered an internal critique of American racial practices and also a new sense of who "we Americans" might become – was largely responsible for enacting the progressive changes of the mid- to late 1960s. King's story moved everyone (on this view), even many whites who were privileged by the pre-civil-rights status quo. King persuaded the majority to reject the old, bad story of who "we Americans" are, according to which racial hierarchy is legitimate and American freedoms are for the racially privileged only, and to adopt a new, better (because more inclusive and racially egalitarian) narrative. And so they did.

There are three main problems with this view. First, although King was a brilliant orator, he was far from the only person telling and retelling this (extraordinary) narrative of American identity in the postwar years. Local civil rights leaders in communities like Montgomery, Alabama, Little Rock, Arkansas, and Oxford, Mississippi; other national-level civil rights leaders like A. Philip Randolph and W.E.B. DuBois; and the student activists who founded SNCC (the Student Nonviolent Coordinating Committee) and who organized countless marches, boycotts, and sit-ins are examples of the many people who told and retold extraordinary stories about who "we Americans" are that at once criticized and called for the transformation of racial hierarchy. Indeed, such stories had been told since the start of the American republic. More than a century before King gave his "I Have a Dream" speech, Frederick Douglass delivered his famous "What to the Slave is the Fourth of July" oration, asking his audience, "What have I, or those I represent, to do with your national independence? Are the great principles of political freedom and of natural justice, embodied in that Declaration of Independence, extended to us?"[10]

Second, it was less the *story* told by King and by other civil rights leaders that induced progressive change than the way these political actors

---

[9] Ibid.
[10] Frederick Douglass, "What to the Slave is the Fourth of July?" available at http://www.americanrhetoric.com/speeches/frederickdouglassslaveto4thofjuly.htm (accessed January 14, 2013).

used that story to motivate collective action, to build coalitions, and to create electoral and other forms of political pressure. To be sure, there are instances in which storytelling is instrumental in persuading power wielders to implement change. Some legal victories can be read this way. But as Martin Luther King himself emphasized, "History is the long and tragic story of the fact that privileged groups seldom give up their privileges voluntarily."[11]

Third and finally, as I have argued throughout the pages of this book, new stories are rarely adequate to challenge and to change social practice. Recall the female tango dancer from the introduction, and imagine that she and her fellow dancers engage in a collective effort to articulate a "good" story to inform their dance. Imagine that the dancers take a break and sit down and deliberate together, for hours, perhaps for days, until at last they arrive at a narrative that accords with their deeply held ontological and normative beliefs. Or: imagine that a particularly brilliant orator articulates for the dancers a new identity story, which they all then reflectively endorse.

When the music starts up, how will the dancers dance? If they have neglected to translate their new story into institutional form (if they have not used it to redefine the standards that govern the practice of dancing the tango), and if they have neglected to translate it into material form (if they have not designed a new version of the Comme Il Faut), then the male dancers will lead, as before, and the female dancers will follow. Compare this approach with the approach adopted by the civil rights leaders and activists who eventually won passage of the Civil Rights Act of 1964, the Voting Rights Act of 1965, and the Fair Housing Act of 1968. These people constructed an "extraordinary story," to be sure. But that is not all they did. They also molded and circulated that narrative in a way that was targeted at institutionalizing it: at giving it form in grassroots and other civil rights organizations, and ultimately in political institutions, including statutory law.

These are the types of narratives that change identity. Rarely told in a single sitting or by a single narrator, they are typically constructed over time and through a process of trial and error: a process more iterative than consciously and simultaneously collaborative. Identity-transforming stories are extraordinary stories that translate into calls for institutional reform.

[11] Martin Luther King, Jr., "Letter from a Birmingham Jail," available at http://www.mlkonline.net/jail.html (accessed January 15, 2013).

2. Institutions

Postwar civil rights leaders and activists did not only tell stories, then. In addition, they worked toward institutionalizing the narratives they constructed. In particular, they used Cold War-era concerns about the foreign policy impact of racial strife in the United States to pressure American state officials to enact change.[12] In Birmingham in the spring of 1963, when civil rights leaders and activists staged demonstrations and collective acts of civil disobedience challenging Jim Crow, they knew full well that Public Safety Commissioner Eugene "Bull" Connor would use physical force to try to contain the protests. And they hoped (as was the case) that the resulting media coverage of the conflict – including, crucially, the extensive international coverage – would pressure the Kennedy administration to act.

It was that spring that Kennedy first called for landmark civil rights legislation in a televised address to the nation, marking a dramatic shift in his position on this issue. According to Mary Dudziak, who has carefully documented the strategic use civil rights reformers made of the U.S. government's Cold War foreign policy concerns, the Civil Rights Bill of 1964 was supported by a coalition of players that, although it no doubt included some who endorsed the bill for principled reasons, also included many who endorsed it for pragmatic reasons, especially from concern about the impact of racial strife on America's international image.[13]

I argued in Chapter 4 that, although one way to use an identity story to implement change is to persuade people that it is a "good" story, another is to forge alliances with political actors who, for disparate reasons, want that story institutionalized. Community builders benefited when Hoover, Franklin Delano Roosevelt, and others acted to jumpstart the economy in the wake of the Great Depression by directing public funds to the flagging market in private housing. Similarly, civil rights leaders benefited when Kennedy, Johnson, and others acted to repair the U.S. international image in the context of the Cold War. The result was the institutionalization of the extraordinary story told by King and by other leaders and by grassroots participants in the civil rights movement. The Civil Rights Act of 1964 prohibited racial segregation in public accommodations, racial discrimination in employment, and discrimination by federally funded

---

[12] See Mary Dudziak, *Cold War Civil Rights: Race and the Image of American Democracy* (Princeton, NJ: Princeton University Press, 2000), especially chapter 5.
[13] Ibid.

government agencies. The Voting Rights Act of 1965 banned discriminatory voting practices, enabling many black Americans to vote for the very first time. The Fair Housing Act of 1968 prohibited discrimination in the sale and the rental of housing, removing state sanction from the racist housing practices that were the focus of Chapter 2.

As Philip Klinkner and Rogers Smith have noted, at the time of the passage of these bills, "most white Americans supported [them] only with great reluctance and under great pressures."[14] But, much as the community builders' narrative of Americans as a home-owning people gained acceptance with institutionalization, so did the civil rights movement leaders' extraordinary story. By the turn of the century, most Americans accepted, at least in principle, the racial egalitarianism of the civil rights acts of the 1960s. Americans *became* what in 1963 they had not been: a people that does not sanction overt racial discrimination.

Nevertheless, as I have underscored in the pages of this book, overt discrimination is neither the only nor the principal mechanism for perpetuating racial hierarchy. The story I have told points to an additional set of institutions that racial egalitarians must target: the institutions of local governance that decentralize authority to politically autonomous municipalities, like New Albany, Ohio. Political fragmentation in the American metropolis, I have argued, coupled with the political autonomy that American states grant incorporated municipalities, enables the wealthy and the racially privileged to make decisions that affect the disadvantaged without engaging them politically. Fragmentation and local autonomy enable the privileged affect the disadvantaged in ways that appear entirely unbiased and race neutral.

Consider the decentralized political process through which most land use decisions are made. If residents of New Albany want to create local zoning laws that exclude all forms of housing but detached, single-family dwellings, if they want to zone for large lots sizes and large setbacks, and if they want to require expensive architectural features, such as those that follow Georgian stylistic conventions, they can do so without engaging the people who live on the other side of their municipality's white fences.

Yet those who live on the other side are not only subjected to, but also significantly affected by such decisions because of local control over taxation and public service provision. People who are kept out of New

14 Philip Klinkner with Rogers Smith, *The Unsteady March: The Rise and Decline of Racial Equality in America* (Chicago, IL: University of Chicago Press, 1999), 287.

Albany by exclusionary zoning laws are kept from New Albany's top-notch public schools (and from other locally provided public services, including those that meet very basic needs, such as needs for safety and security). They are excluded no less so than would be families formally excluded from the hypothetical Exit Academy. Local control over taxation, public service provision, and land use and other collective decisions enables the wealthy – including whites who accumulated wealth in the dual housing market of the pre-civil-rights-movement years – to preserve their wealth and to transmit it to future generations. Extraordinary stories in the post-civil-rights-movement era must target institutions such as these.

Of course, if Martin Luther King could not single-handedly effect change through storytelling, it would be beyond impudent to think that I might, in a book such as this. I will not attempt in these concluding pages to develop a detailed program for institutional reform or to recommend a political strategy for implementing change, let alone to end my story in a way that persuades the privileged to surrender their privilege. I will, however, sketch briefly what strike me as feasible avenues for reform, which policy-minded thinkers have proposed and debated, and which some political actors have, at least to a limited extent, begun to institutionalize.

To begin, many policy experts and political activists urge recentralizing authority over collective decisions to the metropolitan, or even to the regional level. Three sets of collective decision-making powers are key: the power to raise and to spend tax dollars, the power to regulate land use, and the power to set housing policy.

As far as the first is concerned, Minneapolis-St. Paul is the exemplar of a metropolitan region in the United States that has adopted a regional tax-base sharing program. All jurisdictions within the seven-county area that have the authority to tax must contribute 40 percent of funds from commercial and industrial tax base growth to a regional pool, which is then redistributed according to a formula that takes into account both population and tax capacity. According to Myron Orfield, who was instrumental in building the coalition that made tax-base sharing possible in Minneapolis-St. Paul, this system reduces not only fiscal inequity, but also inter-municipal competition for commercial and industrial development.[15]

---

[15] See Myron Orfield, *Metropolitics: A Regional Agenda for Community and Stability* (Washington, DC: Brookings Institute, 1997) and Orfield, *American Metropolitics: The New Suburban Reality* (Washington, DC: Brookings Institute, 2002).

As far as the second (land use regulation) is concerned, Portland, Oregon provides a case of a metropolitan-wide governing body, the Metro Council, that manages transportation and land use planning on a regional level. In 1973, the state of Oregon passed a Land-Use Planning Act, which required local governments to curb sprawl by creating flexible urban growth boundaries beyond which development would be prohibited. Metro is the agency that plans within these guidelines for the Portland metropolitan area. According to David Rusk, regional-level planning by the Metro Council, constrained by Portland's growth boundary, redirects market demand from the periphery of the metropolitan area toward the center.[16]

As far as the third (housing policy) is concerned, the local government in the United States that has had the best success at integrating affordable housing into middle- and upper-income neighborhoods is Montgomery County, Maryland. In 1973, Montgomery County passed the Moderately Priced Dwelling Unit Ordinance, which requires all new subdivisions to include a mix of housing for buyers at different income levels. It requires, as well, that moderate-priced units be integrated with market-rate housing, and that the county's public housing authority have first right of purchase for a third of all new units. According to Rusk, Montgomery County, Maryland – the nation's sixth richest county – "stands out for its integrated neighborhoods, integrated both by racial and ethnic group and ... by income class."[17]

In none of these three cases, however – indeed, in no local government in the contemporary United States – are the powers to raise and to spend taxes, to regulate land use, and to determine housing policy combined in a single governing body. Legal scholar Gerald Frug has proposed an institutional reform that would go beyond these existing models: the creation of a regional legislature comprised of elected representatives of all municipalities in a metropolitan area.[18] Inspired by institutional innovations in the European Union, Frug argues that regional legislatures should adopt qualified majority voting in order to balance concerns about the fair

[16] David Rusk, *Cities without Suburbs, Third Edition: A Census 2000 Update* (Washington, DC: Woodrow Wilson Center Press, 2003), 97–8; Rusk, *Inside Game/Outside Game: Winning Strategies for Saving Urban America* (Washington, DC: Brookings Institute, 1999), chapter 8.

[17] Rusk, *Inside Game/Outside Game*, 184.

[18] Gerald Frug, *City Making: Building Communities without Building Walls* (Princeton, NJ: Princeton University Press, 1999), chapter 4; Frug, "Beyond Regional Government," *Harvard Law Review* 115 (May 2002): 1764–836.

representation of all municipalities against worries about domination by one or a few large jurisdictions. He argues for party representation within the legislature, as well, to encourage inter-municipal alliance formation, and for project-based redistribution modeled on the European Union's structural funds, to encourage inter-municipal awareness of collective problems and to foster political support for redistribution.

How might such institutional change be implemented? Storytelling – but storytelling of a very particular sort – seems key. As Rusk, Orfield, Frug, and others have emphasized, the aim should be building coalitions, both at the grassroots level and in state legislatures: a goal that requires recognizing – and exploiting – the fact that there exists no political monolith called "the suburbs."[19] To the contrary, as Orfield stresses (reflecting on his experience helping forge a state-level coalition to promote institutional reform in Minneapolis-St. Paul), central cities, inner-ring suburbs, and what he calls "bedroom-developing" suburbs that lack the tax dollars to build schools and other infrastructure often have overlapping interests in regionalizing local governance.[20] Extraordinary stories, then, might challenge extant understandings of "who we are" at the local and metropolitan level and build a new identity based on a new sense of what we value and what serves our interest.

But centralizing political authority to the regional or metropolitan level is not the only viable form of institutional change. An alternative would be to leave much decision making at the local level, but to detach political rights, including rights to vote in local elections, from place of residence. Gerald Frug, in addition to making the case for regional legislatures, has argued for changing local voting rules to enable nonresidents who are subjected to and/or significantly affected by a municipality's decisions to vote in its elections. Frug proposes granting all residents of a metropolitan area a fixed number of votes and allowing them to choose the local elections in which to cast them.[21]

Under such a system, some voters might cast one or more votes in the election of the municipality in which they work, perhaps with the aim of changing tax policy there, or policing practices. Some might vote in the

[19] Action at the level of the state is important because, by United States law, municipalities and other local governments are creations of the states. The U.S. Constitution implicitly grants governing authority over local governments to state governments, which can merge existing local governments and create new ones.

[20] Orfield, *American Metropolitics*, chapter 2.

[21] Gerald Frug, "Decentering Decentralization," *University of Chicago Law Review* 60, 2 (Spring 1993): 253–338.

election of a municipality that borders the one in which they live, with the aim of influencing land use decisions that have cross-border effects. Still others might vote in the election of a municipality in which they would *like* to live, but where they cannot, because they cannot afford housing, with the aim of changing exclusionary zoning policies.[22]

Extraordinary stories might target such institutional change by criticizing and challenging collective identities rooted in place of residence. Frug sketches some of the experiences of city living on which such stories might draw:

The kinds of issues that cities are responsible for – providing local services, regulating land use, patrolling the streets, stimulating economic development – have immediate, direct effects on the everyday life of those now excluded from the franchise ... At the same time, the metropolitan nature of city life describes the daily experience of countless city residents; it is not unusual for them to cross local boundaries to work, go out, or shop on a daily basis.[23]

Extraordinary stories might target institutions at the federal level, as well. They might target federal public housing policies, for instance, the federal home ownership subsidies discussed in Chapter 5, and the regulatory systems that govern the mortgage industry. This list is not meant to be exhaustive. Instead, its point is to illustrate the larger claim that, for extraordinary stories to make a difference, they must do more than attempt to persuade or move their audiences. They must target laws, policies, and other institutions.

3. Spaces

At the same time, extraordinary stories must target material forms. Throughout this book, I have argued that when identity stories are not only institutionalized, but also objectified in material form, then people learn constructed identities corporeally. A story according to which women are graceful but passive is built into shoes that facilitate walking backwards while tilting the axis of the body forwards. A dancer puts them

---

[22] As Richard Briffault has argued, however, it is not clear that a voting system such as this one would challenge hierarchies of power and privilege. Affluent and racially privileged political actors might well form coalitions that strongly influence urban elections. Absent local experiments with such institutional reform, it is impossible to know what its effects would be. Briffault, "The Local Government Boundary Problem in Metropolitan Areas." *Stanford Law Review* 48 (May 1996): 1115–71.

[23] Gerald Frug, "Voting and Justice," in *Justice and the American Metropolis*, ed. Hayward and Swanstrom, 201–21, here 218.

on, and she learns to follow. Or: a story according to which members of "the black and white races" are differentially qualified for and deserving of home ownership is built into racialized urban and suburban space. A city dweller walks the streets and he learns his place. If corporeal learning reinforces the identitarian lessons that are taught through narratives and through institutional incentives, then changing identities requires telling extraordinary stories that target change in material forms.

Stories can shape material forms directly. An extraordinary story might inspire an individual architect or an individual city planner, for instance, to design a particular project differently than he or she otherwise would. But stories can also shape material forms *through institutions*, and in so doing, I want to suggest, they can produce relatively comprehensive and far-reaching change.

To return to an example from the previous section, regional tax-sharing of the sort recommended by many urbanists and institutionalized in Minneapolis-St. Paul, if widely adopted, would help alter the stratified place-structure of the contemporary American metropolis. In the contemporary metropolis, as I have argued, collective investment is concentrated in selected areas. These are, as a result, clean, safe, and well-maintained; they are, to recall Joanne DiMarco's language, "nice" places. Other urban areas, by contrast, are "not nice," because they are the sites of collective disinvestment. They are, quite predictably, unsafe, unsanitary, and physically deteriorated.

America's metropolitan areas are, as they ought to be, spatially diverse. Particular neighborhoods within particular cities (ought to) vary from one another, both to reflect and to accommodate people's differing affiliations and attachments, lifestyle preferences, desires, and needs. But as I emphasized in Chapter 5, no one prefers, and no one needs, a lack of physical security or an unsanitary living or working environment. Extraordinary stories should work through institutions (such as regional tax-sharing) to disrupt the spatial hierarchy that characterizes the American metropolis.

In addition, they should work through institutions, such as the housing laws in place in Montgomery County, Maryland, to target racial and class-based segregation. Iris Marion Young has argued compellingly for distinguishing *desegregation* from *integration*. Integration as an ideal, Young writes, "rejects the validity of people's desire to live and associate with others for whom they feel particular affinity."[24] "Especially when

---

[24] Iris Marion Young, *Inclusion and Democracy* (Oxford University Press, 2000), 216.

members of a cultural group experience discrimination, deprecating stereotypes, exclusion, and comparative disadvantage," she continues, "the neighborhood clustering of the group can serve as an important source of self-organization, self-esteem, relaxation, and resistance."[25]

Coerced segregation, however, which produces ghettos and enclaves like Columbus's East Side and New Albany, Ohio, *furthers* discrimination, exclusion, and comparative disadvantage. Hence the need for institutions such as laws requiring the construction of affordable housing units alongside market-rate housing: institutions that reshape urban and suburban space by desegregating along class-based and racial lines. Recall Walter Barrett's experience of living "in a place where [he was] not expected to be." Not only Barrett (a successful black professional) but also the low- and moderate-income men and women interviewed for this project, should "belong" – and they should *feel* like they belong – in flourishing communities like Montgomery County, Maryland or New Albany, Ohio.

Extraordinary stories should, what is more, target institutions (such as laws requiring developers to construct public spaces as part of all new projects) that encourage the creation of urban and suburban space that is open to all residents of a given metropolitan area. In political and social theory, there is a tendency to overburden the idea of public space. Some suggest that, by exposing people to unfamiliar and dissimilar others, public space changes political attitudes in progressive ways: that it promotes cognizance of interdependencies and mutual vulnerabilities, for example, or political openness to the needs and the claims of strangers.[26] The empirical evidence for such a view, however, is weak.[27]

[25] Ibid., 216–17.

[26] This view is, roughly, that adopted by Iris Young, who, elaborating what she calls a democratic ideal of city life, writes that "city dwelling situates one's own identity and activity in relation to a horizon of a vast variety of other activity, and the awareness that this unknown, unfamiliar activity affects the conditions of one's own." Iris Marion Young, *Justice and the Politics of Difference* (Princeton University Press, 1990), 237–8. In a similar vein, Susan Bickford claims that "literally bringing people together in a variety of ways through their daily experience makes a difference in how they think politically ... in terms of the awareness of different perspectives that must be taken into account in forming opinions." Bickford, "Constructing Inequality: City Spaces and the Architecture of Citizenship," *Political Theory* 28, 3: 355–76, here 370.

[27] Contact among strangers of the sort fostered by public space is unlikely to produce the effects Young and others hope it will. Instead, social psychological research on identity and social categorization suggests that, when people come into contact with others whom they experience as "strange," they socially distance themselves from those others and selectively ignore evidence that disconfirms the stereotypes they hold. See Judith Howard, "Social Psychology of Identities," *Annual Review of Sociology* 26

Still, public space is crucial for enabling collective political action. As Margaret Kohn has argued:

Access to public space is important, because public forums are used to communicate ideas to allies and adversaries through techniques such as street speaking, demonstrations, picketing, leafleting, and petitioning ... Although there are many other sources of political information, such as television advertisements and direct mail, these other forms of communication do not allow the citizen to answer back, ask a question, or take immediate action.[28]

One can appreciate the force of Kohn's point by considering the role that black churches and university campuses played as bases for organizing during the Civil Rights Movement, or, more recently, the role played by public space in the 2011 Arab Spring and Occupy movements.

Public space may have a political role to play, what is more, in shaping ordinary, day-to-day life. Consider the political function of *nonpublic* space of the sort typified by the "white-fence" communities of New Albany. Nonpublic space – space that bars those who lack the capital and/ or the social privilege required to gain access – shields the admitted from those defined as their "others." In New Albany, people drive to work, or to their children's schools, or to the shopping mall at Easton, and they do so in the privacy of their cars. Along the way, they need not interact with anyone, let alone with anyone from the "other" side of the white fence.

(2000): 367–93. Nor is there reason to assume that engagement with strangers of the sort public space promotes reduces cognitive, affective, or behavioral biases. Evidence from research on what social psychologists call "the contact hypothesis" suggests that encounters reduce such biases only under a highly constrained set of conditions, which include engagement in cooperative work aimed at achieving a shared goal, status equality, the disconfirmation of group stereotypes, the prevalence of egalitarian social norms, and the potential for becoming acquaintances. Gordon Allport was the first to articulate the contact hypothesis, in *The Nature of Prejudice* (Reading, MA: Addison-Wesley, 1954). For an overview of work on the contact hypothesis, see Thomas Pettigrew, "Intergroup Contact Theory," *Annual Review of Psychology* 49 (1998): 65–85. For a meta-analysis, see Thomas Pettigrew and Linda Tropp, "Does Intergroup Contact Reduce Prejudice? Recent Meta-Analytic Findings," 93–114 in *Reducing Prejudice and Discrimination*, ed. Stuart Oskam (Mahway, NJ: Earlbaum, 2000).

[28] Margaret Kohn, *Brave New Neighborhoods: The Privatization of Public Space* (New York: Routledge, 2004), 6. Indeed, in an empirical study using data from the Social Capital Community Benchmark Survey, Thad Williamson has shown a strong link between, on one hand, residence in older, densely populated, pedestrian-friendly urban neighborhoods, where public space abounds, and on the other, those forms of civic participation that require engagement with other people, such as joining political organizations, attending rallies and protests, and participating in boycotts. See Thad Williamson, *Sprawl, Justice, and Citizenship: The Civic Costs of the American Way of Life* (New York: Oxford, 2010), chapter 7.

When they return at the end of the day, those with whom they cohabit the place they call home pose them no psychic risk, no threat. They induce no sense of exposure or unease. New Albany, Ohio (and, more generally, the nonpublic forms of space that it exemplifies) fosters feelings of security through design that plays to what Richard Sennett characterizes as an adolescent instinct to cope with uncertainty by avoiding exposure to the unfamiliar.[29]

In Chapter 2, I argued that siting collective problems such that the privileged are compelled to confront them would, at the very least, force the recognition of those problems *as* collective problems. In a similar vein, public space, because it promotes unplanned encounters among strangers, disrupts the sense of security that Richard Sennett so powerfully criticizes.

Hence the political significance – the *open-ended* political significance – of public space. If I am unsettled by an encounter with a stranger whose views and perspective depart sharply from my own, will I recall that exchange when I construct my life narrative? If do recall it, will I judge it to be tellable, and will I narrate it? And if I do narrate it, *how* will I narrate it? It is impossible to predict. But I am certain not to narrate an encounter that does not happen. Although it is a mistake to assume that public space will produce progressive political attitudes, it is important to acknowledge that it can temper the depoliticization encouraged by ordinary stories told in nonpublic space.

In the previous chapter, I suggested that most contemporary Americans, at least at their most reflective, regard as illegitimate the use of state power and collective resources to compound the advantages of the wealthy and the racially privileged. If so, then stories that tap that ethical sensibility might motivate institutional change. I have argued throughout this book that contemporary Americans learn the common sense of race by acting and interacting in racialized space. Extraordinary stories should challenge that pedagogy. More concretely, they should target institutions that disrupt the spatial hierarchy that characterizes the contemporary metropolis, institutions that desegregate America's cities and its suburbs, and institutions that encourage the construction of spaces that are public in the sense of "open to all."

Such changes would make a real difference in the life story of a Steven Mullins, a Calvin Moore, or a Joanne DiMarco. In some cases, they would

[29] Richard Sennett, *The Uses of Disorder: Personal Identity and City Life* (New York: Alfred A. Knopf, 1970).

make an immediate and a very concrete difference. Calvin Moore, for example, and other men and women whose lives are strongly shaped by ghettoization and urban disinvestment, would be able to traverse freely the proverbial railroad tracks that, today, divide what Moore calls "high society" from what he calls "the hood." They would have more, and they would have better, choices of places to live, places to work, and places to raise and to educate their children. At the same time, Steven Mullins, Joanne DiMarco, and other privileged subjects who hold a normative commitment to racial equality would be constrained to confront the tension between that commitment and the racial practices in which they (often unconsciously) take part. Changing the institutions and the spaces that frame the ordinary stories of the racially privileged is a crucial step toward changing how Americans make and remake racial identity.

Appendix

Interview Respondents and Interview Schedule

I began the research that informs this book by conducting interviews with a total of thirty residents of what I think of as three distinct local communities: East Side Columbus and the "old" (i.e., prior to the Wexner development) and "new" (post-Wexner) New Albanies. I conducted these interviews between April and November 2003, a period when New Albany's relatively quick redevelopment was also relatively recent. This timing enabled me to interview people who had lived in rural New Albany before its transformation and also residents who had settled in the new suburb over the course of the 1990s and early 2000s. I chose Columbus's East Side as an additional research site because I wanted to focus on a single metropolitan area (the city of Columbus and New Albany are both part of metropolitan Columbus) while interviewing residents of a ghetto-ized section of an older American city.

With two exceptions (marked with asterisks in the table below), I recruited respondents by distributing flyers through community organizations: a locally important church that provided educational training and other social services in the East Side (I distributed flyers through the church's programs, including the GED program in which Calvin Moore was enrolled); the local historical society in "old" New Albany; and a particularly active local voluntary association in "new" New Albany.

In East Side Columbus, because I was white and a university professor in a predominantly African American community with relatively low levels of educational attainment, I also served as a volunteer tutor in the GED program for several months before beginning to conduct interviews. My goal was to become a familiar face around the institution and to establish rapport with potential respondents. I hoped not only to encourage people to volunteer, but also to put them at ease in discussing potentially sensitive and personal issues were they in fact to volunteer to be interviewed.

From the pool of volunteers who responded to my flyer, I selected respondents who were (1) residents of the areas on which my study was to focus, and (2) roughly demographically representative of those areas in terms of self-reported income, educational attainment, age, race, and gender. The exceptions were two African American respondents from New Albany, who are atypical in terms of race (although not in terms of income or educational attainment) and whom I recruited using my personal networks. I sought out these respondents for substantive reasons. As explained in Chapter 5, white racial identity and white privilege were not mentioned in any of the interviews I conducted with white New Albany respondents. This silence prompted me to want to interview African American New Albany residents to see whether, in their view, it was the case that, in New Albany, (as asserted by one of the white respondents) race "doesn't matter."

All respondents' names, as used in this book, are pseudonyms. Demographic data on the respondents follows:

Pseudonym	Age	Race	Gender	Household income	Education
East Side Columbus					
Jane Bowers	58	B	F	$32,000	High school
Eliza Brown	54	B	F	$38,000	Some college
John Carr	58	B	M	n/a	College +
Mae James	57	B	F	n/a	High school
Charlene Johnson-Lewis	27	B	F	$13,000	Grade 10
Erica Jones	52	B	F	n/a	n/a
Calvin Moore	35	B	M	< $15,000	Grade 10
Theo Richardson	45	B	M	$6,000–8,000	Grade 9
Judy Samuels	74	B	F	$22,000	High school
Anita Smith	43	B	F	$12,000	Some college
Alvin Thomas	44	B	M	$6,000–8,000	Some college
Old New Albany					
William Adler	72	W	M	$30,000	High school
Nate Ballard	59	W	M	$110,000	College +
Ray Carpenter	59	W	M	$90,000	College
Karen Collins	60	W	F	$75,000–80,000	Some college
Clint Ferrell	79	W	M	$80,000	College +
Donnie Friedland	46	W	F	$75,000	College

Chris Hays	42	W	M	$100,000	College +
Steven Mullins	32	W	M	$85,000	High school
Peggy Schenker	44	W	F	$100,000	College +
Dave Whiton	52	W	M	n/a	College
New New Albany					
Tricia Barrett*	45	B	F	$400,000	College
Walter Barrett*	43	B	M	$400,000	College+
Cynthia Byron	40	W	F	$500,000	College+
Gene Cooke	43	W	M	$140,000	College+
Joanne DiMarco	37	W	F	$800,000	College
Heidi Fischer	38	W	F	$300,000	College+
Jack O'Donnell	72	W	M	$300,000	College+
Heather Rubens	48	W	F	$150,000	College+
Patrick Webber	33	W	M	$275,000	College

* = Recruited through personal networks.

The total interview time for each respondent ranged in length from just under two hours to just over seven. In most cases, if I had spent more than three hours with a particular respondent without concluding both portions of the interview, we wrapped up our session with the completion of the life history narrative and then resumed a second time for the semi-structured interview. In all cases, I recorded the interviews and, with student research assistance, transcribed them.

I began each interview by briefly introducing myself and my project. Because I was concerned not to prime respondents to structure their life narratives around topics that were of particular interest to me (such as racial identity or identity more generally), I kept this introduction deliberatively vague, explaining that I was hoping to learn how people "think about themselves, how they think about their lives, and how they think about the communities they belong to." I explained that the interview had two parts: "an open-ended section in which you'll tell the story of your life, and a second, more structured section, in which I'll ask you a series of questions, and you'll also fill out several questionnaires." I stressed that the interviews were confidential and that respondents' names would not be used in any publications that resulted from the research. Then, as agreed with my institution's review board, I asked each respondent for written consent to participate.

I structured the interview sessions by beginning with the life narrative, rather than with the semi-structured interview, because I was concerned not to influence respondents to tell their life stories in ways that they thought would fit my research agenda. Thus my first question was simply an invitation to tell me "how you came to be who you are and where you are today." Only on completion of this first part of the interview did I follow up with the semi-structured interview, which focused on respondents' identities. In addition, because I was concerned not to prime respondents to talk about the particular identities on which my research focused, I began the semi-structured interview with the "Who am I?" questionnaire cited at various points in the text of this book ("My name is _____, and I am _____.") All follow-up questions were questions about the identities that respondents themselves had named when they completed this questionnaire.

The text of the interview schedule is reproduced below.

1. Life History Interview

During the first part of our conversation, which I expect will take much, maybe even all, of our first session, I'm not going to ask many questions. In fact, I'm only going to ask one, big question. Which is, I'm going to ask you to tell me the story of your life: how you came to be who and where you are today.

You should start with your family background and your early life. And end with today. And just tell me what happened in between.

I realize that's a *very* big question. And I expect it to take a long time to answer. So, take your time. And tell your story just however it makes sense to you to tell it.

[During this part of the interview, the interviewer prompts, as necessary, for clarification and to encourage a full account. Prompts will vary according to the content of the narrative.]

2. Semi-Structured Interview

I am going to start the second part of our interview with this questionnaire, which, as you can see, says, "My name is blank, and I am blank." Think carefully about how you could best complete that statement. What are the ten ways you can best describe the person you are? When you are ready, write your answers down. If you don't have ten answers, just list as many as you have.

[Respondent completes form. Ask with respect to respondent-generated answers:]

Would you say that being _____ makes you part of a group of people who are _____?

[If respondent identifies more than three as group traits:] You've identified [#] traits that are group traits. I want to ask you a detailed set of questions about just two or three of them. Which three of these traits describe the groups that are *most* important in defining who you are? Rank them from #1–the most important in defining who you are–to #3, the third most important.

[Ask with respect to up to three responses identified as group or communal traits:]

Suppose you were speaking to an intelligent child who didn't know what it meant to be _____. If that child asked you, "What does that mean, to be _____?" how would you explain?

What if the child asked you, "How can you tell if a person is _____?" how would you answer?

What if the child asked, "How does a person become _____?"

What is a real or a true _____?

What is the opposite of a real or a true _____?

Can you think of a time in your recent memory when you thought about yourself or you pictured yourself as _____?

How often would you say you think about yourself as _____?

What is the first time in your life that you can remember thinking about yourself as _____?

Thinking back over your life, are there other times that stand out in your memory when you recall thinking about yourself as _____?

Have there been times when *somebody else* thought about you mostly as _____?

Are there people who, when you think about *them*, you think about them mostly as _____?

Are there people who, when you think about them, you think about them mostly as *not* _____?

When the interviews were completed and transcribed, the result was approximately 1,000 single-spaced pages of life history and semi-structured interview data. After a first read, I began to analyze this data by searching for patterns. I then returned to the transcriptions, checking systematically whether and to what extent the patterns I initially had identified in fact obtained. For example, as I developed the thesis (eventually elaborated in Chapter 3) that certain types of events tend to comprise ordinary life stories, and that certain types of forces (such as the choices and the actions of human agents) tend to be posited as casually signifi-cant and tellable, I went back to each life history interview and identified the events that comprised the narrative, the forces narrated as driving those events, and the elements of each story that the narrator presented as "just background."

In the text that comprises this book, I made the decision to highlight a small number of interviews, rather than to spend equal amounts of time discussing smaller portions of most, or of all. Specifically, I gave Steven Mullins, Calvin Moore, and Joanne DiMarco center stage. I focused on these particular interviews because each captured one of the three prin-cipal ways that I found respondents used narratives of collective identity. As argued in Chapter 5, Mullins thematized a collective identity story (a story of who "we Americans" are), which he wove into the story of his life; Moore framed his life narrative with taken-for-granted stories of collective identity (including racial identity narratives), which he largely failed to thematize; and DiMarco cited collective identity narratives (for example, narratives of Jewish-American identity), even as she refused them.

When I recognized these particular uses of identity stories as theoret-ically significant, I decided to hone in on the individual interviews that best illustrated each of the three. Of course, since each of the thirty inter-views that I conducted was unique, this choice was not without cost. It meant passing over details that I might, in principle, have included: varia-tions that might have added nuance to the book.

Still, I believe there is a real benefit to allowing Mullins, Moore, and DiMarco to present relatively thick accounts of their lives and their self-understandings. I chose depth over breadth with the hope that careful attention to how these subjects narrate their lived experience would aid my interpretive project.

Index

Made in the USA
Middletown, DE
13 August 2020